GERRY CONLON

PROVED INNOCENT

PENGUIN BOOKS

PENGUIN BOOKS

Published by the Penguin Group
Penguin Books Ltd, 27 Wrights Lane, London W8 5TZ, England
Penguin Books USA Inc., 375 Hudson Street, New York, New York 10014, USA
Penguin Books Australia Ltd, Ringwood, Victoria, Australia
Penguin Books Canada Ltd, 10 Alcorn Avenue, Toronto, Ontario, Canada M4V 3B2
Penguin Books (NZ) Ltd, 182–190 Wairau Road, Auckland 10, New Zealand

Penguin Books Ltd, Registered Offices: Harmondsworth, Middlesex, England

First published by Hamish Hamilton 1990
Published in Penguin Books 1991
17 19 20 18

Penguin Film and TV Tie-in edition published 1993

Printed in England by Clays Ltd, St Ives plc

This book is dedicated to
my father and my family

Contents

Contents

My death is going to clear your name.
Then you clear mine –
Guiseppe Conlon, 18 January 1980

Acknowledgements

I owe a debt of gratitude to the following:

Gareth Peirce and family, Hugh and Kate Maguire, Cardinal Basil Hume and Cardinal O'Fiaich, Sister Sarah Clarke, Father Faul, Father Murray, Father McKinley, Lord Scarman, Lord Devlin, Lord Fitt, Philip Whitehead, Andrew Bennett, MP, Jeremy Corbyn, MP, Chris Mullin, MP, David Andrews, TD, Nial Andrews, EMP, The Rt Hon. Merlyn Rees, MP, Lord Jenkins of Hillhead, Pascoe Mooney, Bob Woofinden, Robert Kee, Ludovic Kennedy, Grant McKee, Ros Franey, Chris Jamieson, Bridget and David Loughran, Lily Hill, Errol and Theresa Smalley, Tom Barron, Diana St James, Kathleen Doody, Tony O'Neill, Paul O'Dwyer, Sandy Boyer, Kerry Lynnbohen, Michael Farrell, Nuala Kelly and the Irish Commission for Prisoners Overseas both in New York and in San Francisco, Philyis David, and Moya.

I would like to acknowledge the 'Birmingham Six' – Paddy Hill, John Walker, Gerry Hunter, Billy Power, Hughie Callaghan and Richard McIlkenny – and their campaigners. Let's hope you're all out soon, and I'll be continuing the campaign for your release and to clear your names.

Finally, I would like to thank David Pallister and Robin Blake, without whose help this book could not have been written.

Gerry Conlon's Years in Prison

The Years in Prison

    Winchester (on remand): 6 December to March 1975

1975 *Brixton* (on remand): March–October

    22 October: convicted of Guildford pub bombing

    Wandsworth: October 1975 to February 1976

1976 *Wakefield:* February 1976 to August 1977

    4 March: Maguire Seven found guilty of possession of nitro-glycerine

1977 *Canterbury:* August–September

    Brixton: September–October

    Strangeways: October–December

    Wormwood Scrubs: December 1977 to September 1979

1979 *Wandsworth:* September–October

    Winchester: October–December

    Wormwood Scrubs: December 1979 to April 1980

1980 *Parkhurst:* April 1980 to November 1981

    23 January 1980: Guiseppe Conlon dies

Gerry Conlon's Years in Prison

1981 *Long Lartin:* November 1981 to March 1988

1988 *Full Sutton:* March–April

    Durham: April–May

    Full Sutton: May–June

    Gartree: June 1988 to October 1989

1989   *Brixton:* 17–19 October (released)

Prologue

There we are, sitting mesmerized in the dock, each of us holding a carnation. The three of us men grew up Catholic boys in the poorest part of Belfast, the Lower Falls. The woman was a working-class girl from London. But that is all a long while ago. Our faces are pale and tense, the cheeks and the eye sockets a wee bit hollow. Our faces have no spare flesh.

The Lord Chief Justice of England is speaking. I get the idea he wants to avoid my eye, all our eyes. In the days to come I'm not going to recall much or anything of what he's saying, and yet I'm listening hard, waiting for one word.

The judge is telling the court that for all the reasons he has just given, he is forced to the conclusion that the verdicts handed out to these four people are now unsafe, and that it is therefore his duty to pronounce them –

At this moment, at this *exact* moment, I jump up and pull back my arm. With all the strength I can find, I toss my white carnation high above the well of the court. It curves up and over and down like a shooting star.

And by then he's said it – *QUASHED*.

I jerk up both my arms in the air like I'd scored for Ireland in the World Cup, and I look for my family. For the first time for more than a decade I see smiles on their faces, and I make to get down from the dock and go to them. There'll be no more locks and bars now, no more screws, no more handcuffs.

But my way is blocked.

'You got to go back down,' says the screw with us. I won't take an order from a screw! I won't let that bastard take any more liberties with me. But that's prison talk, and I'm no longer a prisoner. So I do it. I go with the others back down, where there will be forms to sign, property to be repossessed. The screws are all down there, looking at us, nervously.

'What are these four bastards going to tell the world about our system?' they are thinking. The ones who *can* think.

Blow the lid off it, Mister. Sky high.

Their eyes try to be smiling at us, but I can see behind those thin disguises the thoughtless cruelties. They pissed in my food. They tore my mother's photograph. They gave me injections of pethidine. They kicked me around the block like a football.

And I can read the slogans which take the place of thought: POA VOTES FOR THE ROPE – POA SAYS HANG THE IRA – DON'T COMPLAIN, YOU BASTARDS, BECAUSE YOU VOLUNTEERED.

I am the last to be called, so I sit and smoke. Then it's – 'Conlon!'

I walk down the passage feeling like Superman, past the row of cells. All the prisoners are at their doors, hammering and kicking and whistling me on my way. I float by on a wave of adrenalin. The screw at the desk says, 'Sign for your private cash.'

I sign where his thick index finger tells me to. Then he holds up a small, brown manila envelope. A prison wage packet. He swings it to and fro between his finger and thumb.

'There's £34.90 in this. Do you want it?'

If I had to break his fingers wrenching it from his grip, I'd do it.

'Course I fucking want it. I'm going to give this to my mum.' I snatch it out of his hand and put it in my pocket.

'Right. Which is the way out?'

He looks worried.

'Oh, well, we'd like you to just go back to the cells for the moment.'

'What?'

'Please go back to the cells, it's just for an hour or so. See, there's a huge crowd out there, and we'd rather wait until they go away.'

'Bollocks to that, Conviction's quashed by the Lord Chief Justice himself. I'm free. Show me to the door.'

There's a policeman behind me, coming up to me. He stretches out a hand as if to touch my shoulder.

'I'm sure you wouldn't mind waiting just a few minutes while we organize some transport, would you? Then we'll show you out by a rear door.'

I spin round and take a step away from him.

'No fucking way. No transport. No rear door. You put me in here through the back door. I'm going out the front door. Now open the door. Open the fucking door.' I'm thinking of my father. These are his words, and now they're running through my head, 'Don't forget son, they put us in the back door. When your day comes you go out the front door. You tell them what they done to us.'

Suddenly a screw opens the door and points down a little corridor, showing me the way out. Suddenly the door closes behind me and I'm in a corridor with six policemen, which terrifies me. Just as I start to panic the door opens and I see Helena Kennedy, Paul's barrister, and I run to her.

'How do I get out?'

'Come on, this way. There's a massive crowd outside.'

She took me along the passage and round a corner and there was Grant McKee and Ros Franey. I grabbed Ros and held her tightly, saying, 'Where is everybody?'

'Round here, just round here.'

Around another bend in the corridor people were milling around, full of excitement and triumph. I began to see some of the people who had worked so hard for this day. Sister Sarah, my sisters Ann and Bridie, Carol Coulter from the *Irish Times*, David Andrews, an Irish Member of the Dáil who had fought for years for us in the Irish parliament, and Tom McGurk. Sister Sarah Clarke, who had been trying to tell the world of our innocence almost from the day we were arrested. Sister Sarah had tried, and tried again, to get permission to visit us, but the Home Office had always refused. So now, seeing her for the first time, I was amazed at the tiny little woman she was. Then my sister Ann said, 'Come on. Let's get out the front door.'

Everyone was excited. I hugged and kissed and was hugged and kissed, and then I saw Gareth. I called out to her.

'I'm going out the front door. You come too.'

'No, this is your day.'

So I grabbed Ann and Bridie and we made for the front door. It was pulled open and we went out together, Ann on my right and Bridie on my left. When they saw us the crowd erupted, it was a roar like a football crowd. There were crash barriers out, and beyond them thousands of heads bobbing up and down, cheering and throwing their arms up. There was a building site opposite and all the workers were waving their hard hats. Passers-by were being caught up in it. I felt the rush of happiness and warmth coming out of the people and I was carried out among them on a surge of joy. I suppose when you die and go to heaven you get a feeling like that.

Walking around on his own inside the barriers was a man in a tweed jacket talking on a cordless telephone. I'd never seen one of these, and I thought he must be Special Branch using his walkie-talkie.

'Get me away from him, he's police.'

'No, no,' said Ann. 'That's Chris Jamieson from ITN. He's a good guy. He's got a car for us.'

Then she pointed to the battery of TV crews and press people.

'Come on, do you want to say something?'

I went over to them. I hadn't prepared this, I just opened my mouth and spoke.

'I've spent fifteen years in prison for something I haven't done, for something I knew nothing about. I watched my father die in prison for something he didn't do. He's innocent, the Maguires are innocent, the Birmingham Six are innocent. Let's hope they're next.'

There was a huge cheer and that was it. I was pleased, because the words came out exactly as my father would have wanted. Then we drove away.

1

First Memories

My mother says I was born such a delicate child, with such thin blood, that the doctor prescribed me a bottle of Guinness a day. So while the other babies were suckling on their wee bottles of milk, I was already being introduced to one of the great Irish traditions. But the first thing I can truly remember is when I fell backwards into scalding water, coming in from the yard at the back of our house. I was about two. I tripped over the back-door ledge, fell backwards into this bucket and boiled the arse off myself. You could say I've been getting in and out of hot water ever since.

The first boundaries of my world enclosed six small streets off the Lower Falls Road in West Belfast: Mary Street, Peel Street, Colin Street, Ross's Street, Lemon Street, Alma Street. In my first four years I never wandered outside these streets, but that was an interesting enough world for me. I'd be out on the street all day, from eight in the morning, sitting out on the cribee (*the kerbstone*), with my feet on the road, and all the women in the street would be on their hands and knees with buckets and scrubbing brushes. These women would be grannies, married women, widows and young girls. They'd all have flowery printed aprons and scarves round their heads. They'd all look the same, except their aprons were different colours. Kneeling on their little cushions, they'd take so much pride in getting their bit of the pavement clean. The women would be chattering away: 'Has your Johnny found work yet?' 'Is your Joe's chest all right?' 'Are you going to bingo tonight, Sadie?' Each of them would be scrubbing the paving stones in an arc around their doorsteps so that there were always these neat scallops of clean pavement outside every door. Meanwhile the older boys would be playing handball, and the girls would be skipping and playing at hopscotch. The girls would be singing a little song, 'Mary Ross peeled a lemon', a song about the streets they lived in, while they dived in and out of the skipping patterns.

I'd be watching and waiting for one of the women coming out, calling me to go a message. I'd have to get a quarter pound of butter and a loaf and they might give me twopence. Then I felt I had all the money in the world and I'd be round Lena's sweetshop, or John Kerr's, buying aniseed balls and gobstoppers and penny whoppers. Nothing was ever saved, all the kids shared. Even if you had two shillings you just couldn't spend it quick enough, in case it fell out of your pocket. You spent it and shared it.

In the summer nights I'd move back from the cribee to the doorstep, because my ma wouldn't let me dander too far once it was gone seven o'clock. I'd watch the men off to the pubs. There were three pubs, Paddy Gilmartin's bar which was called the Laurel Leaf, Peter Murray's directly opposite, or further down on the right-hand side was Charlie Gormley's, across from Finnegan's, the butcher shop.

Paddy Gilmartin's was probably the most salubrious of the pubs. He'd built a little lounge with a sliding door, that had been veneered and varnished. When I was a kid, I always longed to slide that door back whenever I went in. When you opened the door, the *noise* of people singing – sometimes my mum, sometimes my father, friends, neighbours – overwhelmed you. It was really warm and friendly and I know that if I could sneak in there, I'd get potato crisps, lemonade and no doubt a bit of money. Mind you, you would never see a woman drinking on her own and never in the week in any bar on the Falls Road. It just wasn't done. The women would be taken out on a Friday or Saturday night.

In comparison, Charlie Gormley's was where most of the young fellas went. They'd take over the lounge up the stairs. Charlie had little thin blue plated bars on the windows – probably somebody had been thrown out the window sometime or another. Charlie also served afters – drinks after hours – to his regular clients. Charlie was good that way, he'd also give you credit. It was some pub for the crack.

Everybody would be slagging each other – if you went in there with a clean shirt on, you'd get some joker saying, 'Did your ma steal a box of soap powder? Would she do mine?' People would be drinking pints of Guinness by the lorry-load, cider, Harp and every short you could name. It was a great place. You'd go there when you were seventeen 'til you were about thirty, and started getting a bit of sense. Then you'd get into the habit of going along to Paddy Gilmartin's or Peter Murray's.

Three great bars within fifty yards of each other – and they'd be bunged at the weekends and everyone would have a carry out when they were leaving them.

And then I'd see Francie Teague, who lived just up Mary Street from us, coming lighting the gas lamps. He was a tall man with great big hands, and he'd have a little V-ladder with him, which he'd prop up against the lamp-post and climb up to light the gas. There was a great tradition in Belfast for getting ropes and tying them up on the bars of the lamps and swinging round on them. Gradually the rope would slip off and as the wee girls carried on swinging the ropes would be sliding down. As Francie Teague came along to light the lamps, he'd get the girl's ropes and tighten them back up again.

The houses were two-up, two-down, very condensed, and the street wasn't wide enough for two cars – not that anyone had a car when I was a kid. People were packed very closely together, the doors were always open, so I remember we used to run in and out of the houses playing hide-and-seek behind the front doors. It didn't matter whose house it was, nobody minded. There was an earthiness about the place which was born, I suppose, from the poverty, from the fact that the men could hardly ever find enough work, but you never met warmer people in your life. There was an abundance of skill and craftsmanship where I lived that wasn't being used – skills were never given a chance as jobs were so hard to find if you were a Catholic. But the individual tradesman's loss was the community's gain. You'd have the likes of Andy McDonald of Mary Street – a great spark (electrician) – where if something was wrong in your house with the wiring, Andy would be down rewiring your house for you. So instead of the £40 which you could ill afford to get the wiring done, you'd give Andy a fiver, and he'd be absolutely delighted. If slates came off in the winter, Dan Lindsey would be round with the ladder putting Bangor blues on and he'd say, 'Buy me a drink when you're flush.' He wouldn't charge you. That was typical of the community spirit – everybody helping out.

The poverty though was obvious, even to my young eyes. I remember calling for a mate of mine one day and his mother coming to the door. When I asked if he was coming out, his ma said, 'No, Gerry – his brother Jim's wearing his clothes today.'

We were all Catholic around the Lower Falls, and this was one of the many families where the number of kids went into double figures. My parents had only three children alive, I was the only boy, but I never saw my mother throw out any of our old clothes. She would always give them to somebody who needed them, some woman with fourteen or fifteen children. For most of her life, my mother worked in a rag store, sorting out old clothes, and she was always asking them could she bring home pullovers, and those little T-shirts we used to call sloppy joes, to give to one of the really poor families. It was the same with food. If there was a big pot of soup on the go in one house, or a big stew, and if only half the pot was eaten, someone would be out looking for other people to give it to.

Our family was never as poor as some were. We were what you'd call fortunate, which means we had meat and shoes on in winter instead of those plastic sandals that cost one-and-ninepence and left your toes cold. The reason we had shoes on our feet was entirely due to the women of the family, my mother Sarah, who I never knew to be out of work, and her mother Mary Catherine Maguire, in whose house we lived.

My grandfather Vincent Maguire died when I was about one. The first photograph taken of me was with him, sitting on his lap when he was bedridden, just before he died. I suppose he was very ill then, but in his heyday Vincent Maguire was a real character. He pinched my granny off another man during the First World War, a man she was betrothed to. Both men were away in the trenches in France but my grand-da somehow slipped out of the fighting and got himself back to the Lower Falls. One night he met my granny, they had a whirlwind romance and when the other poor man came back on leave she was already Mrs Maguire.

Vincent or Vinty, as we called him, was a great performer on the penny whistle. So he'd love winding up the hardcore nationalists down on the Lower Falls come July the 12th, which was the day the Orange Order used to celebrate the Battle of the Boyne with marches and bands. Vinty would put on a bowler hat and a sash and he'd be out there with his tin whistle dancing up and down, playing 'The

Sash My Father Wore' and 'God Save the King' all along the Falls – just having the crack with all the diehard Irish republicans, who took it in good humour. He got away with it. You wouldn't today, but things were that little bit different in the forties.

As I've said, it was partly due to my grandmother that the Maguire family were comfortably off. She was the one with the clever head on her shoulders. She knew how to make a shilling or two. The way she'd do this was by spotting bric-à-brac shops that sold everything from plates and light bulbs to oilcloth. Her opening line would be, 'Do you do credit, Mister?' And if he said yes her next line would be, 'Where I live, I know a lot of people looking for a bit of credit.' In some ways it was a sting, but people were getting stuff they needed on easy terms. She would start off by getting people who genuinely needed things to take out credit at these shops. They'd be pleased to be getting credit, the shopkeeper was pleased to be giving it and my granny was delighted as she'd get certain items out of the shop as her commission.

So my granny's house was always full of bustle, with people coming in to pay their credit, the teapot always on and maybe I'd be lucky and get a sixpence if I placed myself in the right position. I'd see Mr Shah Deine, the Indian shopkeeper from Agnes Street up on the Shankhill, who had an informal partnership with my granny, and who would be in every week, Friday night or Saturday morning.

Shah Deine was the only Indian who was ever seen in the Falls then. He had a strong Indian accent and hadn't really got the ear for the Belfast accent. So people like my grandmother and her chums would run rings round him. They'd give him a story, and he wouldn't understand. The only thing him and my grandmother would exchange were smiles, never any money. Nobody could understand how all he came out with were smiles. 'Jesus Christ,' they'd say, 'isn't he a lovely man, that Indian. Very understanding.' He always got paid but never what perhaps he thought he was going to get when the deal was made.

Then there would come Sam Daly the Jewish moneylender, who had his offices on Royal Avenue. He later became a Councillor at Larne, or even possibly the Mayor. Sam was very Jewish, and I was always so impressed by how clever the man was. He came every Saturday in his trilby hat and a shirt and a tie. The tie was a mark of respectability. People round the Falls might wear a cravat, maybe with a matching handkerchief when they were going out. Ties were only used for weddings and funerals.

Apart from being a centre of business, my granny's house was also a great social centre. One of the reasons for this was we had a radiogram, so after pub closing time at ten o'clock people would bring in bottled beer and maybe a bottle of brandy and have a party. The people holding the party would be expected to provide the food. The food would be a big pot of vegetable soup: carrots, parsley, onions, peas, lentils, boiled potatoes and a bit of meat. You could eat until your nose bled – that's a Belfast expression for you could eat it forever.

They might go instead to my Auntie Kathleen's house, or to Lily McCann's, but I always hoped they'd come to ours because there was twopence on the empty beer bottles, and that might be worth as much as four shillings to me.

Getting little bits of money was one of the great preoccupations of the children, I suppose because of the general atmosphere of poverty which surrounded us. Being in the right place at the right time was very important – for instance I would never want to miss Sam Daly when he came over on a Saturday, in case he tipped me a sixpence. Other opportunities depended on the seasons. In winter you were praying for snow. You'd always be going to bed and tacking on to your night prayers, 'Dear God, make it snow tomorrow, so I can clean people's doors and get a shilling.' Then, if my prayers were answered, I'd be out with my friends, a kettle of boiling water and my granny's coal shovel, up and down the street, knocking on the doors saying, 'Do you want me to clean your door, missus?' Other kids wouldn't always have a kettle of boiling water, so we were a lot quicker, making twice as much money.

Apart from my granny with her clubs, the one completely reliable source of income for our family was my mother. She has always been a great worker. She's worked since she left school at the age of twelve, very ordinary unskilled work, but with long, hard, physically tiring hours. She's only had three jobs. She started at Greaves's mill, a linen mill in 1938, spinning the yarn to make the linen. The tiles on the floor would get so hot that you couldn't have shoes on. The spinning-looms were forty feet long. You put the yarn on wet, and it would then be spun on to the spindle or a reel to straighten it. The friction would dry it out partially. The room would be filled with fluff, so you were always breathing the fluff in with the air and everybody would be coughing away. My mother stayed there till she was seventeen. She then joined Harry Kane's scrap-yard in Cyprus Street, and her job there was sorting out the old clothes, which would be baled up and shipped off elsewhere. The only other job she's had is at the Royal Victoria Hospital working in the kitchens, a job she's held since about 1970.

That is how I remember her best in the early days, always at work, and also teaching me to say my prayers and the rosary. Without fail we said the rosary every night, as a family. Wherever I might be playing football, my sister would always be sent to call me in for the rosary – and until I was fifteen I'd always come.

My mother is very religious. Her whole life has revolved around God – mass, Benediction, keeping the holidays of obligation, doing novenas, observing the fasts. For years her annual holiday consisted of going down to the shrine at Knock in County Mayo, where there was once an apparition of Our Lady, and praying for three or four days. That may not be many people's idea of a holiday, but it is my mother's.

My father's name was Guiseppe, not because we were of Italian blood, but after a godfather of his who was from Italy, Joe Raffo. He owned an ice-cream shop in Divis Street and was always very good to my grandparents. So they christened my father Guiseppe, the Italian for Joe: as a mark of respect. My father was embarrassed at having the only Italian name in West Belfast, where as I've said people would have the crack about things like that. So he went along to the local priest when he was about thirty and asked if he could change his name to Patrick Guiseppe. But even though he did, everybody carried on calling him Guiseppe. He'd try and say, 'But my name's Patrick now' and people would say, 'Oh, oh all right, Guiseppe.' My father was a very lovely, gentle, loving man and I was his pride and joy. Wherever he went, he took me along if he could.

One time he was a labourer with a road surfacing gang, over in a place called Cherry Valley. It's only a middle-class suburb, but to me the place sounded like a different world, as if it should be in America or some place far away. So at weekends, if he was working overtime in Cherry Valley, he'd let me come with him.

It was exciting being woken up and having my breakfast early. I always had coconut scones and tea, but I only ate the coconut and icing off the top of the scones, and drank the tea, and then we'd be off on the bus to Cherry Valley. There I would see how the well-to-do people lived, with trees in the streets and cars in the driveways. My father's workmates would be sitting together in a little workman's hut in tar-encrusted jeans and flat caps. A coke fire would be glowing in the middle and a teapot stuck on top of it, with the smell of the bitumen all around. I was probably about six or seven and came in very noisily, very cocky, feeling very grown-up to be one of the workers. Some of the men would be looking tired and half asleep and they'd regard me a bit grumpily, suffering from what I now know must have been terrible hangovers.

By ten in the morning they'd pack me off to the shop on the corner with a wee list they'd written out – packet of fags, couple of Barney Hughes's baps, copy of the *Irish News* – and when I'd be back with the things and their change they'd just say 'You can hang on to the change, son', which might be as much as seven-and-six. To a seven-year-old this was a fortune. It was an amount you could normally only dream of getting, because it was enough to buy the most desirable thing any boy my age could own – a football.

Football was the great obsession. We were desperate to play football. If we couldn't get a ball we would use a rolled-up jumper with wet newspapers inside it (the wet newspapers made it heavier). It was through playing football we first came into conflict with the police. Black-bastards we called them: black after the colour of the RUC uniform and bastards because they liked nothing more than to come up the Falls and break up whatever was going on in the street – card games, football games it made no difference. They cruised down on their motorbikes or in their black Zephyr squad cars, with the tall aerials sticking up, and everyone would scatter. But the great fear was of them getting our ball; the ball was paramount and the coppers knew it. If they got hold of a proper ball you'd see them pull out a penknife and stab the ball and rip a great cut in it and throw it into the street. So it was important to have someone brave enough to go in and retrieve the ball and kick it back down the street, even if it meant getting grabbed by the hair and hit a slap round the face or kicked up the arse.

Street-corner card-schools were a great feature of our area. Everywhere you went you'd see men down on their hunkers playing cards, always for money – pontoon, brag, poker. Sometimes in summer there would be as many as four games going on in a single street, each with a little crowd of bystanders watching the game. They put two sheets of newspaper down and weighted the corners with stones and the money and the cards would go on to that. I remember one lad had a hole, or cavity, in the sole of his shoe just big enough to trap a coin. So he'd be watching a card game and he'd deliberately stand on a loose half-crown which had strayed near the edge of the paper. Then he'd shuffle backwards with it, bend down to tie a shoelace and pocket the money.

There was good reason to hold the games on street corners, because it offered more ways to off side from the coppers. The men used to refer to motorcycle cops as derangos, for some reason which I don't know, and if one of these derangos was circling our area and saw a game going on he'd put on his siren and blast up the street towards it. So a card-school would post a look-out who had a special warning, a cry meaning free-for-all, save what money you can and run. He'd shout 'Vee-oh', and I used to try to get in between the legs of the bystanders, not just so I could see the play, but just in case somebody shouted 'Vee-oh'. Then everyone would dive in and grab what they could, and I might get a couple of half-crowns if I was lucky.

Thanks to the look-outs, by the time the derango arrived everyone would have disappeared, though there might still be some money lying on the pavement. So the copper would just stoop down, slip it into his pocket and roar off on his bike. Of course, there were lots of deliberate false alarms. People would shout 'Vee-oh' so that the game would scatter and someone could dive in and get the money even though the cop was still down in the barracks.

By this time, of course, I was at the primary school in Raglan Street. The head teacher was Miss Noblett and my own teachers were Miss Corbett and Miss McVeigh. I can vividly remember my first day, which I found very frightening. First of all I was surrounded by strangers for the only time in my life. The school was no more than fifteen streets away, but I didn't know anyone. Then they gave me one of those little bottles of milk and a straw, neither of which I had ever seen before, and in any case I was used to drinking tea. Later we sat down in neat rows in little desks and sang 'Baa, Baa, Black Sheep' and recited the alphabet. I could not imagine what was going to happen next. All was utterly foreign. I had spent my entire short life playing in the street and I wanted to run back to the street, and to my granny, because this wasn't fun.

In the end I came to enjoy primary school, and look forward to it very much. I didn't find the work terribly hard, although I was idle and lazy about it. But the real reason I came to like school was the same for which I was originally frightened of it. At school I got to know all these new people, made all these new friends. And making new friends I've always found to be one of the greatest and most rewarding pleasures of my life.

2
Growing Up

So I had a happy childhood. My parents loved me and the community in which I grew up was an affectionate one. But by 1965, when I was eleven and just about to leave the primary school for St Peter's Secondary, something happened to my father which casts a long shadow over the story I have to tell.

I need first to say a little more about the kind of man Guiseppe Conlon was, and I can best do this by telling the story of his war. He was born in 1923, so the Second World War was in full spate just when my father was of an age for military service. At that time he was working as a labourer in London, and sure enough he got his call-up papers. So they gave him his basic training and told him he was due some home leave before his career as a fully fledged soldier would begin. My father was appalled at the idea. He took himself back to Belfast to be close to his childhood sweetheart Sarah Maguire – they'd grown up half a mile apart and met as schoolchildren – and when he was home he convinced himself that the Second World War was nothing whatsoever to do with him. He was a completely non-violent man, a natural pacifist, who hated regimentation of the kind they imposed on you in the Army. So, when the leave expired, my father just stayed where he was, where it was natural for him to be, at home.

But on his way back to the house one night he found an Army jeep waiting outside, with a bunch of soldiers who jumped on him. He was arrested for being AWOL, and brought handcuffed on board the boat to England. It was not until they were under way in the middle of Belfast Lough that they took the cuffs off him. So he stood at the rail, watching Belfast slipping away, and suddenly thought he might as well die in Belfast Lough as in Germany or somewhere else. So he pulled off his shoes and dived over the side. By the time he'd swum the half-mile to shore the ship was over the horizon, and he simply hitched a lift back home in his wet clothes and bare feet.

The British Army must have decided he'd drowned because they never came back for him. Guiseppe Conlon was left in peace to settle down at home and, in 1947, he married Sarah, my mother.

In one of his longest periods of employment during the fifties my father worked at the Harland & Wolf dockyards, where the only job he could get was red-leading, spraying the steel hulls of the ships with red lead. I can remember him coming in one Thursday night and telling my ma, 'We keep asking for masks. We got no masks.'

With no protective masks worth the name, the fumes were eating away at his lungs and from that time onwards breathing was always difficult. Then, when I was eleven, he started coughing blood. Because of the bad housing conditions, Belfast had the highest TB rate in Western Europe. The little two-up and two-down houses I described earlier had terrible problems with condensation. They were built in Victorian times: back-to-back rabbit-warrens of streets. There were no baths, but plenty of water was running down the walls taking the wallpaper off with it. There wasn't anything that the residents could do about this, they ended up with damp, unhealthy houses. Rickets, whooping cough, TB – all things that seemed to belong to a previous century in Britain – were rife in Belfast while I was growing up.

We all had to go down to Durham Street to the chest clinic, which wasn't far from where we lived, and have tests. A few days later my father and my two little sisters, Bridie and Ann, were diagnosed as having pulmonary tuberculosis. My mother and I were clear. My ma sat me down and explained that my dad and my two sisters would have to go into the hospital, and all I could say was, 'Why don't we have to go into the hospital too?' My mother and my granny must have been very worried, but they put on a brave face. 'Oh,' they'd say, 'it's only for a few tests, they'll be out soon enough.'

But they weren't out soon. I thought it would be only a couple of days they'd be away, so by the time we went down to see them at the end of a week I was desperately missing my father. We went down in a blue coach to Whiteabbey, the sanatorium where they were being kept. It was way outside Belfast, which seemed a huge journey to me, and I remember sitting in the coach watching the countryside go by, with bags of grapes and pears on my lap. The grapes and pears were a special luxury, but all I could think of was seeing my father. But when I did see him I wasn't allowed near enough to touch him. He was also kept isolated from my little sisters, Bridie, who was then eight, and Ann, who was only six. They were living in two huts which were ranged alongside each other, but on a slope, so that my father's hut was lower than theirs. He was living just a few feet away, but he wasn't allowed near them. The best he could do was to bang on the window and call up to the girls through the glass.

This was a tremendously difficult time for my family, especially for my mother, who knew how serious it was. She put a very brave face on the worry about my father and my sisters. She also had real financial worries with all the travelling back and forth to Whiteabbey and buying little bits and pieces, sweets, biscuits, toys for my sisters and fruit for my father. She would have to get to work at Harry Kane's by eight-thirty, so she would be up at seven, make me my breakfast, her and my granny would clean the house, make sure I had my dinner money and go to work. She did overtime every Tuesday and Thursday, when she left at eight pm – with half an hour for dinner and half an hour for tea. Normally she left at six, when she'd come back home where my granny had made me my tea, tidy up and do the laundry, have her own tea and the three nights a week when she wasn't doing overtime she would go with me to visit Whiteabbey. She never complained, I never saw her cry; she even used to say she wished it was her in the hospital being sick instead of my father. All I can say is that my mother is an extremely strong, loyal and hard-working woman with unbelievable strength of character. Family is the most important thing in her life: she carries herself with tremendous dignity and would never think of burdening other people with her problems.

I missed my father and my sisters, but I strongly felt the loss of my father, who idolized me. So I would complain to my mother about missing him, cry every time we left the sanatorium after our visits. It was a terrible time.

I remember that the treatment consisted of endless injections – five or six a day it seems to me now – and when I saw my sisters' arms I was horrified at how black they were from the bruises caused by these injections. Bridie took it very calmly. She was missing us, but she kept it all out of sight because she knew she had to look after my sister. Ann was very vocal. She kicked and screamed and yelled not to have the injections but to be taken home. She remains a great fighter to this day, for which I've since had good cause to be thankful. Bridie was always the steady one, and that quality, too, would be much needed by our family in the following years.

In the end they were away for many months, leaving the house desperately empty. When they did at last come back my sisters were cured, but my father was never able to work properly again.

St Peter's Secondary was a large school, with six classes in each year, and even though our family had been cut in half by the illness, I found school a thrilling adventure, full of unexpectedness, frightening and exciting at the same time. I was put into class 1C. On the scale of ability, class 1A were the geniuses and 1F were the thickoes, so I was at the top of the middle. But 1C was a bad class to be in because there were no characters in it. Most of the kids were too studious for my liking, taking their lessons too seriously. The people I wanted to be in with were in 1D, where I knew they liked having a laugh and a joke, because I could hear them through the wall. So after a few months I arranged to be kicked out of 1C and relegated to the lower class.

There's one more thing I should say about moving from 1C to 1D: part of the curriculum in classes 1A, 1B and 1C was learning French and more importantly Irish. The history was also very Irish-oriented and if I had stayed in that class I would probably have had a greater awareness when the troubles started – I would have known the history of Ireland, which is very evocative. Perhaps if I had stayed in 1C, I would have had a more defined republican attitude at a very early age. The fact that I did go down a class where they didn't teach Irish history and such made the difference between me being what I am now and the kind of person who might join the IRA. The vast majority of people who ended up in the IRA had been taught Irish history and Gaelic.

When you looked around, at least amongst us, the Catholics, it seemed that education was not a passport to success. However many certificates I got or exams I passed, I would probably have a life on the dole, as did most of the men who lived where I lived. Like mine, most of my friends' mothers were working while their fathers were unemployed. Women's work attracted a lower rate of wages, so the factories naturally preferred them. The men worked when they could and played cards at the street corner when they couldn't.

At the same time I was fast developing an important extra-curricular interest, gambling on horses. That probably came about because my father started working in Walsey's, the bookie's shop on the Falls Road. For years the job was done by his brother, my uncle Mickey, so when Mickey died it seemed natural for my father to succeed him. He was the board-marker, a type of person that has ceased to exist since betting shops went electronic and began looking like mission control at NASA. But in those days the marker was the man most closely watched by the punters, marking up the changes in the odds as they came through on the blower. So when I used to run down to the shop, about thirty yards from our house, with my father's tea and sandwiches I saw it as a rather glamorous position, the centre of attention. I noticed how the punters regarded him as a lucky marker, for some reason. 'Come on, Guiseppe,' they'd say, 'mark us up a good result.' And you'd see people tip him a few quid if they'd had a nice touch.

Then one Saturday I was with Tommy Moore, and we found a betting slip in the street. It said *Thirty-bob win, Kentucky Fair, thirty-bob win Blazing Sand, and thirty-bob win double*. We went in and looked at the board and saw my father had marked Kentucky Fair in first place, at 9 to 4 favourite. Then I looked down the blackboard. Blazing Sand was also a winner.

Jesus Christ! We couldn't believe we'd found a docket with a winning double on it. It had won a fortune, well over a tenner. Our problem was, how to get the bet lifted. We couldn't do it ourselves, being too young, so we approached some guy and he agreed to lift it for us. He knew it wasn't our bet, because two kids of eleven and twelve weren't going to bet four pounds ten, so he just gave us a fiver out of the winnings and kept the rest. It didn't matter, we had a fiver! It was so much money we thought we could never spend it and it would last for ever. We went straight down to Morelli's ice-cream shop between Albert Street and Lemon Street and bought two big 99s. Then we went down to the Broadway picture-house and saw *The Sound of Music*.

After that, a year or two later, I began to take a serious interest, looking at the racing page in the *Irish News*, picking out a horse I fancied, putting my dinner money on it. I'd wrap a half-crown in a bit of paper and stand outside the betting shop and ask some man going in to put the bet on, and if he wanted to know who it was for, I'd say for my dad or my ma, or even my granny.

The only other thing that really mattered to me then was football. The one thing I wanted to be in life was a footballer, a George Best or a Jimmy Johnston, real footballers who could control the ball and beat five or six men. We played every spare minute. In summer we'd be out from two in the afternoon through to five, go in and get a quick cup of tea and a sauce sandwich – two bits of bread and butter with HP sauce in the middle – and be back out playing from six till eleven. We didn't time the matches, we went on until a certain number of goals had been scored. So half-time came when a team had scored twelve goals and full-time when it reached twenty-four. So these games were marathons, lasting hours. Our team came from Peel Street, Lemon Street, Mary Street and Colin Street, and was known as the Comanches, because we were classed as wild kids from all these big, impoverished families.

We had no football pitches, so the games were played in the street, of which our home ground was Peel Street. We'd have to dribble round cars and stop when people crossed the road coming out of Hughie Finnegan's the butcher's or staggered out of Charlie Gormley's pub. We challenged teams from other streets, and played home and away fixtures. Now and again, before the Troubles started, we'd play against Protestant teams. We'd go up what, in the Lower Falls, was called the Black Pad, which was North Howard Street. This was a no man's land, the connection between the two parallel roads, the Shankill and the Falls. Today half way along it is where the peace barrier separates the Catholics from the Protestants – Belfast's Berlin Wall.

At that time you were safe going up the Black Pad, though you had to be careful. On the rare occasions when we played a team from the Shankill, there would inevitably be Protestant supporters coming down to watch the game, and they'd all get behind the goal at the Shankill end. So if you had a big crowd coming down, you didn't want to end the game kicking towards the Falls. If you did, you'd be liable to run a gauntlet to get back. So we'd have an agreement when we played Protestants that we'd kick towards the Falls in the first half and play with our backs to it in the second. Then, when the game finished, we could sprint down home safely.

Among semi-professional teams we supported Distillery, who played all in white like Real Madrid, although there the comparison ends. We supported the Whites not because they were a brilliant team, which they were not, but because the other local side, Linfield, discriminated against Catholics and wouldn't play them in their team. So naturally we shouted for the Whites team, half of which was Catholic, and would even have the odd player from our part of West Belfast.

At the age of about twelve I started going across the water to Glasgow, to support Glasgow Celtic. Celtic were the greatest team in our lives at that time. Manchester United were important too, because George Best played for them and not only was he the most exciting man in football, he came from the streets of Belfast. But we identified most with Celtic as a team, because we saw it as a Catholic team and because their great rivalry was with Rangers, who were exclusively Protestant. So it was a tribal thing, Distillery versus Linfield all over again, except this was big-time, all-professional football.

When we went over to see the bhoys (the Celtic team) play, we used to bunk the boat. We'd buy sailing-tickets for half a crown, which got you on to the boat but, in spite of the name, didn't entitle you to sail. You were supposed to come off half an hour beforehand. But we used to hide on the boat, a bunch of young lads from my school: Mickey McParland, Brian Donaghy, Big Joe Boyle, Paul Hill. Then we'd be on our way to Parkhead (the Celtic ground) – into paradise, into the jungle.

When I was fourteen I got so pissed off with school I started going on the hike with a couple of other boys, mitching school (*playing truant*). They told me they'd been doing a few houses, and if I was going to be on the hike with them, I'd have to be doing a few houses too. To me, this didn't represent a problem. That was how I came to break into a house for the first time.

The house was in Amcomrie Street. We got in through a window, and the other two were downstairs, looking for watches, jewellery, radios, or anything we could sell to the traders over in Smithfield market. I was up the stairs, and I opened up a woman's handbag that I'd found lying on the bed. It had a whole bundle of unsealed envelopes in it, and when I peeked inside the first of them I saw it was stuffed full of cash. I yelled to the others to come up the stairs and when they came I had all these envelopes laid out on the bed. There was more than £600 inside them. We split up the money and were off.

I couldn't spend it fast enough, it terrified me. I bought fish suppers for all my mates, took parties of them to the cinema, anything to get rid of it. But by now the school board was on my trail. They wrote to my parents saying they thought I was mitching. So my parents got me to go back to school again, while my two partners in crime went on with their housebreaking. Then, one morning about seven, an unmarked police car drew up outside our house. I was taken out of my bed by two CID men and off to the police station, and I remember my parents calling after them 'What's he done? What's he done?' and the policemen not telling them, and not letting them come down with me.

Eventually I learned that the two kids I'd been on the hike with were caught doing a burglary. In their statements they admitted to all the other burglaries, and involved me in Amcomrie Street. We were all up in court and bailed, and eventually they got two or three years in an approved school, while I was sentenced to twenty weeks of community service. My father was with me in court. My mother was naturally working but she asked in a letter to the magistrates if she could pay restitution of the money I had stolen. I thought at the time she was mad. But my mother is like that.

3

Us and Them

My family has always been proud to be Irish, but they have never been more than passive nationalists. My mother's father, Vincent Maguire, would laugh at the republicans, telling them not to take themselves too seriously. For my mother, religion and respectability were more important than politics and to my father any form of violence was anathema. These were the values passed on to me by my family. And the values would be obvious as soon as you walked through our front door. All the houses in our street were identical, but you could tell someone's attitude just by looking at the walls. People like my mother had pictures of Jesus, the Sacred Heart and Patrick Pio (an Italian saint who bore the marks of the stigmata) all around. If you went to other people's houses, there'd be pictures of Patrick Pearse, James Connolly or a framed declaration of the Republic. There'd be pictures of Our Lady too in these houses, but these republican emblems would be mixed in as well. On the street, the feelings you formed were more simple, more tribal ones. It was Us and Them.

The great tribal event in a Catholic kid's year was the Feast of Our Lady's Assumption into heaven, on August the 15th. That was adopted by the Catholics as our answer to July the 12th. The Protestants used to light huge dramatic bonfires on the night of the 11th, turning the sky red and black from the flames and the smoke, and on top of the bonfires they'd burn effigies of the Pope. So on August the 15th we'd try to have even bigger bonfires. We'd spend weeks collecting stuff, each street vying with the others in intense rivalry. We'd go from shop to shop asking for orange boxes. We'd look in empty houses for floorboards and skirting. We'd go along the Falls and steal tyres out of the backs of garages, and then up to McQuillan's quarries, where there would be massive, ten- or twelve-foot lorry tyres, which we'd spin home, taking turns to curl up inside them and be wheeled along. It was very exciting and fulfilling.

But the sense of Us and Them was nowhere more apparent than at certain Irish League football matches. Grosvenor Park, the Distillery ground, was in a predominantly Catholic area and in the late sixties, when they played home matches against Linfield or some other sectarian team like Glentorran, the Protestant fans came down in a great show of strength, with hundreds of Union Jacks and Ulster flags. As they had the best players in the Irish League, they usually saw their side give ours a thrashing on the pitch, and would then march away triumphantly down Distillery Street, waving flags, blowing their tin whistles and smashing all the windows. Then they'd be looting shops and stealing things from people's front rooms. They'd chant 'Fuck the Pope' and filthy slogans about the Virgin Mary, and the R UC would just stand by and watch them.

When I first heard these cries I couldn't understand what it was all about, what they had against the Pope or Our Lady. Nationalism meant nothing to me, because Irishness meant nothing. No doubt I heard people singing Irish rebel songs in my granny's house during our Saturday night parties, and heard stories about the atrocities of the Black and Tans. But they were just songs and stories. They had no mystical significance, because there was no one instilling Irish patriotism in me, the way some families did. The world I lived in – those few street corners in the Lower Falls – was a very small one. What I felt was what absolutely everybody felt, a fierce loyalty to that community.

As you grew up you couldn't miss the attitude of the coppers towards you, and the different ways they behaved with the Protestants. I remember going up to Shah Diene's every Friday with the club money, the instalments for whatever had been bought by my granny's customers. She'd give me half a crown plus the bus money, but I used to save the bus fare. This meant I had to walk up Northumberland Street, a totally Protestant area, and then across the Shankill into Agnes Street.

I could see that those streets were much like ours. The card-schools were out on the street corners, exactly the same as on our street corners. But now I noticed one glaring difference. Here the RUC would be standing around watching the card games, and having a laugh and a joke with the men there. Down where I lived they'd be breaking the game up and arresting the men for gambling, or they'd be scattering them and taking the money off the ground. Up here, they might even be joining in the gambling.

When I was thirteen I was standing in the hall of a chemist's shop in the Falls Road with a boy called Gerry McAnoy. We were waiting for a friend by the name of Kieron O'Neill to arrange a football match with him, and it was pissing down with rain. Suddenly this big black Zephyr car drew up and two RUC men got out and asked us what we were doing. When we told them, they said.

'No, we think you're loitering with intent.'

And I said, 'What does loitering mean, mister?'

I wasn't taking the piss, I really didn't know the word. But it can't have helped matters, and they arrested us. We were taken down to Hasting Street barracks and asked our names and addresses, and what we were doing. We told them again, but they wouldn't believe us, and they were pushing us around, one of them pulling Gerry round the room by the ears.

I said, 'I'm going to tell my ma and dad about you.'

And he just punched me on the nose. Immediately there was blood pouring out of it. Then he hit me a great kick up the arse.

After about an hour and a half they'd had their sport and they threw us out on the street. We went straight to Gerry's sister's house at Ormond Place, and I remember her saying as she tried to clean the blood off my shirt, 'Them dirty black-bastards, never leaving people alone.'

That was how we all felt about the police.

When I was sentenced to twenty weeks' community service for the housebreaking offence, it was held at Millfield Tech, which was situated between the Falls and Shankill. So offenders from both communities would be down there on Saturday morning, and the first thing I noticed the first day was all of us standing in two cliques, glaring at each other. It seemed like pure hatred coming out the both sides.

We were set to doing woodwork, and all the Catholics were down one end of the room, and all the Protestants were crowded together down the other, and bits of wood and chisels would occasionally fly down the room, and they'd say 'Fuck the Pope' and we'd retaliate with 'Whose fucking the Queen tonight, then?'

The people in charge were good people, with genuinely good intentions. One of them was Billy Johnson, the Irish League footballer who ended up manager of the Crusaders. He'd take us for physical exercises, and when he gave us circuits to do he'd try to pair Catholics with Protestants. I suppose he was hoping we might to get to know each other, break down the barrier a little. It was a waste of time. One of the pair would always either lag behind or streak ahead, anything but go round with the other guy. Or if it was a game of basketball, he might try to mix us up. But when the teams were chosen it was always the same story: Catholic against Protestant, Distillery versus Linfield, Celtic versus Rangers.

The idea was to teach us a bit of common sense, I suppose. But we all knew it was a waste of time. We weren't going to mix.

By the time I left school, in June 1969, the civil rights marches had been going on for a year. I knew that these demonstrations, which started first of all in Craighaven and then Derry, were trying to get a better deal for Catholics throughout Northern Ireland, both political rights and jobs. But I hardly understood the details. I didn't know that gerrymandering was rife throughout Ulster – I didn't even know what the word meant. What I did know was that the people in the Bogside in Derry were Catholics, like us, and that the RUC were giving them a hard time, like they did us. So when that summer the Bogside erupted into rioting and the police were baton-charging the crowd, firing CS gas and hosing them with water cannons, there was a sense of outrage in West Belfast, as if we were under attack ourselves. Soon we were.

People started agitating and demonstrating outside RUC stations in West Belfast in support of the Bogside. The first time I was in a riot I was in Hasting Street with a crowd of several hundred, and we were sitting down outside the barracks. So the RUC came out and tried to move the people away. Some refused to get up and the police were hauling them along, even pulling them by the hair. So a peeler got chinned, then another got chinned and then one of their cars got turned over.

I was fifteen, and of course I found the riot intensely exciting. The RUC was such a hated symbol that it felt good to be able to retaliate, throwing stones, bricks and bottles. All the hostility that had built up over the years had found an outlet.

The next thing was that the B Specials were called in, because now there weren't enough RUC to cope. The Specials were a force of uniformed auxiliary policemen, exclusively Protestant and very brutal. They thought nothing of taking reprisals against Catholics, beating up bystanders, trashing houses, looting and burning. Shooting people even.

My Uncle Willie McCann lived in Conway Street, one of the streets which connects the Falls with the Shankill. Willie was a seaman, and married to my mother's youngest sister Annie. At this time he was working as a steward on the *QE2* and so he was away in New York when the violence in West Belfast started. So the night the Specials came down Cooper Street and Conway Street, with a mob of Loyalists at their back, my aunt was alone in the house with her three young daughters, the oldest of them no more than six. I really don't know if they picked on her deliberately or chose the house at random. She was no kind of political agitator or activist – I doubt if she had a political thought in her head. But they put her and the children out in the street, smashed the windows, stole the furniture, stole whatever they could find to steal, and petrol-bombed the house.

We were living in Leeson Street by this time, and the family took refuge with us. The house in Conway Street was burned to the ground and they had nowhere else to go to. All they had left were their lives and the clothes they had on. And that night we saw policemen and B Specials standing around drinking with these Loyalist mobs in the ruins of Catholic houses they'd bombed. It was so easy for them. We had no guns in the Lower Falls in 1969. The IRA didn't exist there at that time, that was when the initials still stood for 'I Run Away'. So it was easy for the Specials to come in their Short & Harland armoured cars with the machine-guns mounted on the top, and take pot-shots down the Falls Road. That was the night, in the blink of an eye, when the whole of the Lower Falls was changed. We came out next morning and saw it: houses in Conway Street burned, Cooper Street burned, the Mercedes car showroom burned out, the blackened shells of buses, the bank in Balaclava Street a smoking ruin, the Co-op next door to it ransacked. The whole place seemed strange. Everything that was familiar and comforting about it had gone.

Over the next few months the population of West Belfast began to swell, as Catholics were moving in from all over the city where they'd been burned out. They were moving for protection, to where there was safety in numbers. So we built barricades for ourselves and became a community under siege, a walled ghetto.

For a young lad, the time which followed was a wild time. Looking back, it was like anarchy. Everywhere there were these vigilante groups, posted as look-outs against the police or the Specials. These groups had their own little huts, built out of metal and canvas, and at nights they'd sit outside them round their fires telling stories. And I'd be hanging around near them with my mates, too young to join, but sitting out all night listening to these stories about their exploits.

With all the new people coming in, there was also the chance – for the first time – to meet girls from families my parents didn't know. To impress the girls I'd be passing on these stories, only now I'd be in them, trying to impress, trying to be macho. It was a time when we seemed to lose our inhibitions, when the law no longer mattered, the police were not there. It was a time when you stayed out all night drinking and smoking and lumbering with (*running after*) girls, a terribly exciting time. From that time I never went back to my house for the rosary.

When the British Army first came in on 14 August 1969 it was welcomed in the Falls Road, as the protector of the Catholic population. People were out giving them cups of tea and sandwiches, as if to thank them. For months Catholics would help the troops in any way possible, go messages for them, let their daughters go up the barracks to dances, anything. Of course, we exploited them if we could. I remember a couple of my mates being given a fiver by some soldiers and asked to bring them down some cigarettes and a bottle of pop. Instead we went straight into the bookies and had a bet.

Gradually the Catholic people's friendliness towards the troops dropped away. Things had changed. The first member of the security forces, a man called Victor Arkbuckle, was killed (by Loyalist gunmen, as it happens) in October 1969. Everything got very serious. A curfew was imposed on the Falls Road on 3 July 1970. This was resented by everyone, particularly as no curfew was imposed in the Loyalist area. The IRA began to get organized as the feeling of resentment developed. Everybody started making decisions then. The die was cast and people started taking sides in a way they never did before. Nothing was ever the same again.

I fell foul of the curfew one night about a year later, with a Scotch feller named Joe Duffy. We'd been into town for a drink and started coming back about ten o'clock. On the way we saw a great crowd of people outside the funeral parlour in Albert Street, and across the way was a bunch of soldiers with flak-jackets on and armoured cars. We could hear gunfire and bombs of some kind going off, all happening where we lived.

Someone said, 'Don't be going up the road.'

'But we live there.'

'Don't go. It's bad.'

So we sidled over to these soldiers. They were from the King's Own Scottish Borderers.

'Any chance of getting up the road?' says we.

'Yes, certainly son. Come across.'

So we came across and they arrested us.

They kept us standing up against a wall for about half an hour, with another guy named Mo Short, and we were yelled at and given a right slapping standing there. After that they put us to sit in an Army lorry, and Joe Duffy was saying, 'I want to see my lawyer.'

And the soldier who was guarding us was pissed, and just yelled at him, 'See your fucking lawyer!'

Then he started swinging the butt of his rifle at Duffy's head, and Joe kept ducking, and this Mo Short, who was sitting next to him, kept getting it in the side of his head.

When they'd got the full lorry-load of people off the street, they took us over to Musgrave Street, the police station behind Chichester Street Court. We were charged with breach of the curfew and disorderly behaviour, and remanded to prison.

There were hundreds of people arrested that night, and they all ended up in Crumlin Road prison like me. I was very scared. I spent my first night in a cell all on my own with only the Gideon bible. But after a while I heard singing. It was all the other prisoners who'd been brought in the night before singing out of their windows. Then I felt better.

The next day was Sunday and we all went to chapel for mass. It was crammed with all the people arrested on the Friday night. The screws were shitting themselves. They'd never seen anything like this, the sheer volume of Catholic prisoners in one place. At the end of mass we sang the hymn 'Faith of Our Fathers', which is a kind of Catholic anthem, and everybody was bellowing out the words, and the whole prison was reverberating. The roof shook from it.

Then next day I was in court, up in the dock in Chichester Street. My father had got me a solicitor, with the result that I was given unconditional bail. I was in a daze. I started walking down the same stairs, back down to the cells. And then the man said, 'No, no. You don't go back down there.'

So they opened the little door at the side of the dock. I went down a few steps and there was my dad.

4

State of War

When I left school in June 1969 I had no notion of what I would do with myself. Although I was lazy and not especially honest, I was not averse to trying out a job for size. Besides, it was what my parents wanted for me. Eventually, just before all the riots blew up, I landed a job with a firm of hairdressing suppliers by the name of H. J. Christies, of College Street Mews. I had to ride a bicycle round all parts of Belfast, delivering scissors, combs, rollers, curlers, shampoos, parts for driers. The storeman would load the basket so full of stuff that one man could not have lifted it off the floor on his own. The pay was £3 15s for a forty-two-hour week, a minuscule return even to a fifteen-year-old. I deeply resented the fact that the storeman was getting six or seven times my wage, and all he did was load the basket.

So – perhaps inevitably – I began petty pilfering to supplement the wage, bottles of this and packets of that, which I'd sell cheap to a barber here or a hairdresser there. Then after only a couple of months I broke my thumb falling off the bike – the load was so heavy it twisted the handlebars round and I came off. As I could no longer ride the bike I had to chuck it in.

My next job was at Ross's a very large textile mill with its main gate on the Falls Road, and a rear gate up near the Shankill. Most of the workers in the mill were Catholic, and most of them were women. But it was a ritual that any feller who started working in the mill got a greasing. The women'd grab hold of you and pull your trousers and your underpants down, get a load of grease and slap it round you. That was the initiation. But I was terribly embarrassed about it and whenever, after that I went in among the women in the mill I'd blush a deep red.

I was Ross's gate-boy and again my job was running messages, but this time it was an easy thing. I had to make me and Tommy O'Neill, the gate man, our tea and a bit of breakfast, maybe butter the baps or do a couple of boiled eggs. Tommy was a very good man and very kind to me. Then we'd read the paper and he'd tell me a few yarns, and it would be time to bring the letters down to head office to be mailed. I also had to go all round the spinning and weaving rooms in the mill itself, into the bathrooms putting liquid soap in the dispensers, and keeping them stocked up with toilet rolls and Swarfega for the workers to degrease their hands. I also had to take clothes down to the dry cleaners every Friday for the office people. So I'd be cycling round about the mill on my bike, with plenty of time to get into the betting shop or go out for a ride, if I wanted to. It was a pleasant job.

My downfall was my feud with one of the office women. Most of the administrative staff were Protestants and at half past nine they came in to work by the back gate, which was up near the Shankill. It was my job to open the gate to them, but I was always concerned about hanging around by that gate, because by now the Troubles had started and I didn't want to be attacked when I was up there. So I'd always close up the gate as quick as I could when I thought everybody was in and be off back to Tommy O'Neill in the lodge for my breakfast. But one particular woman was always being late, and she'd be ringing the bell for me to come back again and let her in. So I used to exchange words with this woman, saying, 'Why can't you come in at the same time as the rest?'

She would make veiled threats, such as didn't I know she was the wife of the personnel manager. And she'd be having a word with him about my cheek, so she would.

I got so angry with this woman I decided to leave. I put in my notice one Friday morning and one of my last messages was to ride down to the cleaners to collect the staff's clothing. When I looked at the tickets on my way down I saw most of them were clothes for this woman and I just said fuck it. I tore up the tickets, dropped them down a manhole and went into the betting shop with the cleaning money. I was so angry I never went back to Ross's.

These were the first two jobs I had in Belfast. I went for another a few months later at a heating engineers in Corporation Street. I did a test in the morning and was told OK, I qualified and the rest was a formality. But when I came back that afternoon, I had to fill in a form saying what school I went to and this revealed for the first time that I was a Catholic. After that they couldn't get rid of me fast enough, and the job went to somebody else.

So now I was on the dole, but my real money was coming from other sources. I remember once going down to the dole office and meeting a guy whom I shall call Mitty.

'Where you going, Gerry?' says he.

'Down the dole, Mitty.'

'Come on and walk with me. You can give me a hand when I walk back.'

I didn't ask what he meant, I just nodded my head. So we went round to the dole office and we got our money. Then we were coming back up Great Patrick Street and at the start of York Street we came to the Co-op. Mitty said, 'I've got to go in and pick up something for my ma.'

So in we go, up to the electrical department. Next thing Mitty got a two-wheel trolley, and all of a sudden he'd pushed it under a washing-machine, hoisted the thing clear of the ground, and wheeled it straight into a lift. I said, 'What the fuck are you doing, Mitty?'

'This is my ma's washing-machine, Gerry.'

'That's fair enough.'

When we got down to the ground floor, Mitty pushed the washing-machine out into the street and wallop, he'd run it down to Smithfield and sold it for £50, a brand new Hotpoint.

I said, 'But I thought it was your ma's.'

Mitty just burst out laughing and slapped a tenner into my hand. It was then I realized if you had enough of a brass neck there was nothing you couldn't steal. There was a well-known shop-lifter in Belfast who inspired a whole generation of kids who were of a criminal mind. He had a catch-phrase: 'All you need in life is an overcoat and a fast-clutching hand.' The overcoat would be draped over one shoulder and all illegal purchases would be snatched and tucked up under the arm. He inspired us because he had a lot of panache, a very funny, lively character and we couldn't help noticing he always had very good clothes. His nickname was Fagin and he was about four or five years older than me. He had this devil-may-care attitude and was generally very influential.

After six or nine months' practice I was doing it myself all the time. People would ask me to get them something, we'd negotiate a price, and I'd already be in the frame of mind that I was just collecting something that belonged to me. I'd go into the shop, and if it was possible I'd take the thing then and there. If not, I'd go back an hour later, walk over and lift it, and just walk out.

I'm amazed now that I was never pulled. I'm also embarrassed and ashamed. At this time in my life, I was adrift, aimless. I had no prospects and bitterly resented that I would get no job of any quality. For want of anything else stealing was becoming a compulsion. Once I was in Stonedry's with two friends and we went over to the trouser rack and just pushed all the trousers together, I lifted them up by the coat-hangers, covered them with my overcoat and strolled out. Later on in the pub toilets we sold sixty-five pairs of herring-bone trousers in twenty minutes, for 55s each. Another time in Haslett's in Ann Street I turned on all the television sets to make sure which one had the best picture, called over the girl to tune it for me, and when she walked off I just picked it up and left. People looked at me, but no one said anything. No one ran after me saying 'Stop thief!'

We gave Haslett's such a hammering that they started chaining the goods up. We'd taken a whole string of orders for radio-cassettes and we went there and found all these security chains. We said, 'This is definitely not on, they're taking a liberty.'

So somebody said, 'We need a chain-cutter. Let's go round to Smiths and steal one.'

So we went in and stole the chain-cutter, came back to Haslett's and lifted the radios.

It was easy. Easy work, easy money. I was getting a £100 or £150 a week, far more than I needed. Most of it went on drink and horses, and I'd always give some of it away, the same way all of us did.

The only person in my family who might have even suspected anything was our Ann. She was ten or eleven years old, and she used to go through my pockets when I came home drunk. So she'd find money in my pocket, more money than I should have had, and she'd blackmail me.

'Give me ten bob, Gerry, or I'll tell my Ma about this twelve pounds you got here,' she'd say. Or twenty Number Six I'd give her, to buy her silence. If my mother had ever found out she would have gone absolutely mad. I'd been surrounded by the love of two very law-abiding decent Catholic parents. Now I'd turned into a disreputable chancer, and must have caused them a lot of heartache. At the time, of course, I reckoned I was a very fly man. Now I blush a bit at the dishonest and ungrateful wee kid that I really was.

As I said, the police didn't come into the Lower Falls any more at this time, and it was the IRA – the Ra we called them – who were beginning to fill that gap. There were still two wings of the IRA around at that time, the Officials or Stickies, and the Provisionals. Each had its own organization, its own command structure and its own youth movement, known as the Fianna.

As far as the British Army was concerned, when I was sixteen or seventeen the security problem was getting very serious. They were getting blown up and shot, and there were regular shoot-outs with the IRA on the streets. The violence was escalating year by year.

The first time I had trouble with the Ra it concerned the Officials. It was over nothing at all, just a petty argument and a piece of macho posturing. I was with a group of mates on a street corner, Leeson Street and the Falls Road, having a drink, when this kid came over and told us to move away from the corner because we were annoying some people. When we didn't move they came back and started to jostle us, and try to punch us. In the end we came out of the skirmish on top and they slunk away, but in a matter of days we were paying the price for a small victory.

The next Saturday night I was on my way to a dance when a car drew up next to us with four guys in it. Bang, they hustled us into the car, and drove us off to a piece of waste ground. We were told we'd been arrested for fighting with members of Official Fianna, and we'd got to take a beating. Which we did. It wasn't a severe one, but it was a warning and my mother and father were very worried. Internment had just been brought in, and all sorts of people were being pulled by the Army and sent to Long Kesh. My parents saw I had no job and they probably thought the same might happen to me – I'd be interned, or worse, I'd be shot. So it was decided to send me over to England for a while to stay with my Uncle Hughie and Auntie Kathleen in London. I was delighted to go over to England. There was nothing for me in Belfast.

I worked as a scaffolder in the City Road, near the Angel. It was very good money compared with jobs back home, but I missed all my mates, and I missed the excitement. So by Christmas I'd had enough and I packed my bags and took the boat train home. Things hadn't changed. A few more people had been shot. A lot more had been sent to the Kesh, people I'd known at school, not all of them in the IRA by any means. Just wrongfully detained, picked up for something or nothing.

For me it was back to the old routine, relieving the shops of their goods. But in March 1972 I was suddenly repaid some of the tax I'd had deducted from my wages in England. It was more than £200. That day I met my cousin Tony who was on the hike from school, so I took him down and cashed the cheque and bought him and his mate a whole lot of things, Ben Sherman shirts and suchlike. Then I was seen in the betting shops splashing money around, and it seems that the Officials, who I suppose had their eyes on me, assumed I was burgling people's houses. So one Sunday afternoon three of them made a dramatic appearance at our house in Cyprus Street looking for me. They were obviously going to teach me a real lesson this time.

It was my sister Ann who answered the door, and she said yes, I was in, and what did they want me for. They said they just wanted to talk. So Ann came in and spoke to my mother who went out and told them, 'My son's not going with you.'

They went away. But half an hour later they were back, asking my ma would she bring me up to the Citizens' Advice Centre on the Falls Road.

'What for?' says my ma.

'There's some people complaining their houses have been broken into, and your son's been seen around with a lot of money. He's a suspect for the houses.'

This was something I would never have done, break into houses in the area where I lived. For one thing I didn't want to steal from my own people, and for a second it was self-preservation. Even when you went shoplifting in the city centre it was dangerous to bring the stuff back to the Falls. The IRA had such a down on anything like that – it was out of order. Almost everything we lifted we sold before we came back, in pubs like Kelly's Cellar and the Bank Bar.

On this occasion, luckily, my ma was able to prove I hadn't got the money from doing burglaries in the Lower Falls, because I still had the certificate about the tax rebate and she was able to show it to these three Stickies. So they went on their way satisfied.

But I continued to have run-ins with the Ra over my antisocial behaviour. I got another beating for being part of a fight one Friday night, again it was a street-corner affair on the Falls Road. It started as an argument we were having with some Stickies, and then escalated when a bunch of Provisional Fianna joined in to help us. At the finish there was nearly a pitched battle between the Provos and the Stickies, with people pulling guns. I wasn't pulling guns. I never had a gun, I wouldn't know what to do with a gun. But, because I was in at the start of the fight, it was decided somewhere inside the Provisionals that I, along with my mates, had to take a beating for being a part of this disorderly behaviour. It was an effort to smooth things over with the Stickies. So I was taken down and given a much worse slap than the last time – I got a busted eye and needed seven stitches. All I could do was accept it.

It was suggested that I should join the Provo Fianna, that it might bring me into line, because I was getting a reputation as a general layabout with my 'antisocial' behaviour. I was told to report to the Divis flats, and we were drilled to commands in Irish and taught about the history of the Irish struggle. We were given odd little jobs to do, counting British army patrols as they went past, or helping pick up the local hooligans and thieves and give them a questioning – exactly what had been done to me previously.

But they turned me out after I stole from a pub with another lad who was also in the Fianna. They gave the other lad a bollocking but let him stay in. Me, they booted out. I was told if I behaved myself for a few months and kept away from the Fianna kids, I'd be allowed to rejoin. But I never did. I only went in because it would've been dangerous not to. Now I was delighted to be informed my services were no longer required.

By this time West Belfast was in a state of war. Some weeks five or six people would be shot, and riots were occurring almost every other night. When the Army used rubber bullets we'd shout, 'Give us more bullets, give us more bullets,' because if you picked one up you could sell it to a tourist for a fiver. They also used CS gas, and we'd taunt them with shillings, throwing the money at them and shouting, 'Give us more gas, here's the money for your meter.' My family tried not to get involved. They were passive nationalists, that is, they knew they were Irish but didn't believe that violence was any kind of solution. They could never condone the use of violence by anyone.

I was out and about on the streets, of course, every night. I was seventeen, and wanted to go out with girls and generally enjoy myself. I remember one night I'd been to the public baths on the Falls Road, because nobody where I lived had a bath and I wanted to be good and clean for a night out. I was going out with some girl and we were both stopped by the Army. They asked me my name, address and date of birth and radioed in to see if I was wanted. My name was called over the radio: 'C for Charlie, O for Oscar, N for November, L for Lima, O for Oscar and N for November.' By that time I was used to all this, so I felt a mixture of anger, boredom and resentment that I couldn't get on with just going out with my girl. But while they were doing that, one of the soldiers put his hand up my girl's skirt, calling her abusive names. There was nothing I could do. I got even more angry – of course my name meant nothing at the other end of the radio, it was hassle. I was piggy in the middle – not a member of the IRA, getting harassment off them but being picked up and hassled by the Army too.

A few days later, I came home and saw a member of some foot patrol standing in the hall outside my house. He was standing there in case of a sniper attack, quite understandably. Thinking of the aggravation I'd had a few nights previously I told him to get out of the hall. My father came out of the house when he heard this and gave me a real bollocking. 'This is my house. You tell no one to get out of the hall. I'm not going to be responsible for anyone ending up getting shot. You let him stand there as long as he likes.'

My father understood me so he understood why I was angry, but his gentle nature was the guiding influence in my life. I might flare up but I would never resort to joining any organization.

Myself and Pat Kane went to work in Manchester for a spell at the end of '72, came back to Belfast at Christmas and worked on and off throughout '73 on building sites. And then towards the year's end I got into a fight over a girl, a fight which was going to have important, unforeseen consequences. She was a Derry girl and I'd been seeing her for a lot of months at the start of seventy-three, but now we'd stopped seeing each other. So I was in this dance hall, Shelley's Disco just off High Street, and I saw her with some man, who came over to me. He said, 'Do you know Ann O'Brien from Derry?'

I said yes, and made a few choice remarks about her, and he said, 'I'm her fiancé.'

'So, that's your problem,' I said.

'No, it's yours. I'll see you in the toilets.'

I didn't want to be backing off from a row, so I went into the toilets, and there he was with two of his mates, and he lunged at me, stabbed me over and over again, a lot of times. He had a knife and a broken bottle. It was luck I wasn't blinded. I held up my hand to protect my face and was stabbed in the wrist. I don't remember what happened next, but I was taken to the City Hospital in a very bad way.

I reported the attack to the RUC, and I was told I could be in line for compensation from the Criminal Injuries Board, because the stabbing had cost me some mobility in my right thumb, and also because it happened in a disco, a public place. I put in the claim and then forgot about it, just went back to my life of thieving and drawing dole. But several months later, in the middle of '74, I suddenly got a cheque for £200.

When it happened I remembered the beating I nearly had over the tax rebate. So now I thought, if they see me with all this money what'll they think? I'd be better off out of this. So it was then my thoughts turned again towards England, where I thought I'd find the freedom I needed.

5

Getting Away to England

People where I come from don't think too much about the English, but England is another matter. England is where the wealth is. England is where you have to go to get a job. London's a place where you can have the crack – by which I don't mean cocaine.

Everyone has relatives in England. There are Irish all over the country, but in a few places they cluster together – obviously in parts of London such as Kilburn, but also in Liverpool, in Luton, in Southampton, in certain parts of Manchester and Birmingham. The Irish come to England to work to get away from the poverty and they end up creating small, tightly packed communities, just like any other immigrant community.

Like almost everyone in West Belfast a lot of my family were in England. The most notable to me were two of my mother's three brothers, Paddy Maguire and his wife Annie, and Hughie Maguire and his wife Kate.

Hughie is one of the most gentlemanly people I know, he is courteous and kind to a fault. He has been in England continuously since the fifties, when he was fourteen. In the sixties he was the foreman scaffolder in the construction of the Telecom Tower. He is a large, robust, rumbustious man with a shock of grey hair and big, generous puppy-dog eyes. When I used to see him in London he loved nothing more than to go out to the Paddington Conservative Club, near where he lived, for a pint and a game of snooker. He was and is a great story-teller. Hughie never forgot his family in Belfast, and was always sending home money and presents like suits, dresses, cardigans and pullovers. That's the kind of man he was. Kate was a cleaner in cinemas and different places all around West London, a very handsome woman with a scatty sense of humour and, like Hughie, great fun to be with.

Hughie and Kate were the ones we always stayed with when we went over to London. Maybe it was because they were always so kind they'd never turn you away, and because they'd no children and had more room to put us up.

Paddy Maguire was a small, dapper man with a tremendous sense of fun. He had been in the British Army, the Royal Inniskilling Fusiliers, and had then settled in London in 1957, just after he'd married Annie Smyth. The Smyths, like the Maguires, were born and bred in the Lower Falls, just a quarter of a mile away from us in Abyssinia Street, but by the nineteen-seventies the Paddy Maguires had become very Anglicized. The children Vincent, John, Patrick and Anne Marie spoke with cockney accents and there were pictures of the Queen and Winston Churchill in their house. Paddy worked for many years as a gas engineer and when I knew him was a staunch member of the British Legion and – like his brother Hugh – the Paddington Conservative Association.

Annie was the strongest woman of her family, maybe because she had to be. She was very hard-working and the children were the most important thing in her life. Annie was a very good-looking woman too, kept her house spotless and always dressed well. I doubt she thought as highly of me.

My first memory of London was when I went there with my granny when about six years old. She used to be over every summer to see her family and look for bargains, and she would very often take me or my sisters with her. That time we were with another relative, my uncle Willie McCann and his wife, my mother's sister Annie, the same who would later be burned out of their house by the mob in 1969. They walked me round to the local shop to get some milk on this beautiful sunny Sunday morning. The shop was shut, but it had a coin-operated milk machine outside, the like of which I'd never seen before. So we were putting in the money to get the milk when a large six-foot-two African man appeared and stood waiting to get milk from the machine. It was the only time I'd ever seen a black man except for the tribesmen in Tarzan films back home, who were always trying to kill Tarzan or Jane. And as this man was black and as he was wearing flowing African robes, I immediately thought he was about to pull out a spear and do the business on us. I started screaming 'Tarzan! Tarzan! He's the one who wants to kill Tarzan!' I had to be picked up and taken away, screaming hysterically.

My private idea of England always had this exciting side to it. As a teenager, just after I left the job at Ross's in October 1969, I ran away to England with my two mates Skee and Anthony. They were in the same situation as me: they'd left their jobs and not told their parents. We'd a few pounds in our pockets, so we just bought one-way tickets on the boat to Liverpool. We had no lugguge, because obviously we didn't want our families to suspect. So we all put on two of everything and went down to the docks.

We felt very grown-up strolling around Liverpool on our own, with all these people with funny accents saying, 'All ri', la? and 'How's it going, wack?' Someone told us we could stay at the YMCA in Mount Pleasant, whatever that was, so we went down there near the main city post office and signed in using false names. It was well situated for us – the cathedral at the top of Mount Pleasant and the docks down at the bottom. There was a snooker table, I remember. All you did was put a penny in the meter for the lights to come on, so we thought here was a nice cheap game. But we'd no sooner broken the balls than the lights went off again. They were on such a short time-switch, that game cost about £2 before it was finished – all precious money but we thought, no problem, we'll be getting work tomorrow.

Next day we went out looking for jobs. We did what all the Irish do – toured the building sites asking for a start. But we were skinny little fifteen-year-old runts, so we were invariably told to piss off.

That was the height of the skinheads era, and we met a gang of them at Lime Street station. One of the skins admired my shoes, Oxfords, and wanted them off me. But instead of him stealing my shoes we got talking and they ended up showing us round Liverpool. Later in the day we were all walking past a parked car and there was a brief-case in the car, and one of the skins said, 'Let's have it, then.' So they smashed the window, lifted the brief-case, and we all scattered, running in every direction. I ran with Anthony and Skee ran with the skinheads, and we got back to the hostel first. When Skee came in an hour later he was pissed. He'd been drinking cider with the skins.

After a week of getting nowhere we took off for Manchester, hitching up the East Lancs Road. We slept the night in a field near St Helens, waking up covered in dew and freezing cold. We got to Salford and I'll never forget the café we went into in Eccles New Road for our breakfast. We hardly had any money left, but we were starving, so we treated ourselves to the works: sausage, egg, chips, beans, bread and butter and a mug of tea for three-and-ninepence. On the way out Skee stole a coat, a car coat with a fake-fur collar, and we took turns to wear it while we killed time at White City dog track. We had no money for a bet, but it was something to do. That night we slept in a graveyard, in a little gardener's shed full of tools. We'd have stolen the tools if we'd just known where to sell them for money. But we didn't.

After another day or two of walking the streets and sleeping in this shed the police picked us up, for which by then we were probably grateful. So they locked us in the cells, got in touch with our parents and it was my father, as ever, who turned up to get us. First he gave us a right lecture about the stupid thing it was to do, then he took us out for a slap-up meal in Manchester.

We had to go back to Liverpool to get the boat and I remember my father taking us all out to see *Where Eagles Dare* with Clint Eastwood and Richard Burton. He even ended up paying for one of my mates to go back home to Belfast. When he'd gone round to his ma to say we'd been found and that he was going over to get us and asked for the fare for her son to get home, she'd said, 'No, I'm not paying. He's an absolute menace. Leave him over there to torture those people instead of torturing us.' But my father brought him back anyway. After all, we were only fifteen.

When I got back home, I was trying to talk to my mother, but she wouldn't talk to me. She'd got the hump. Finally, after an hour or so, I asked her for some fags which was just a ruse to get her talking to me. She said, 'Fags? You've got a cheek asking for fags. What have you got to say for yourself?' I said, 'Ach, ma. Don't be getting angry with me. Here's a souvenir I brought you from Liverpool.' She says, 'What's that?' So I put my hand in my pocket and pulled out a Liverpool bus ticket. She just burst out laughing and that was all the tension out of the air. It felt great to be home – clean bed and being looked after by my sisters with cups of tea. My sisters thought I was quite a character. They used to say, 'Jesus, Gerry there's enough fresh air in your head to run a compressor.' I'd missed all of them and it was obvious they'd missed me. I knew everything was going to be all right.

When I next went to England it was 1971 and I was still only seventeen. This was the time I'd been given a slap by the Stickies, and I was being packed off by my parents out of the way. After a couple of months staying with my Uncle Hughie, I misbehaved myself in a very shameful way. I was a mad gambler then and one day I picked up my uncle's Giro, cashed it and had it on a dog which got beat. Nothing was said, but he must have been terribly hurt knowing what I'd done. I couldn't stay there any more – when I thought about it, I was too ashamed. So I just packed my bags and slipped away.

I had had one other spell working in England, in 1972. I went with Pat Kane to Manchester, this time lodging with the McCanns, who had moved there after losing their home in the '69 riots. We worked night shift in a rubber factory called Greengate & Irwell off Regent Road, living out the great Irish tradition of coming over to England for a job, working and living in digs, saving a few bob, then getting homesick and going back. We never forgot our family back home. At that time I had my arms tattooed at a parlour up by Alexandra Park in Moss Side. On my right forearm there's a dagger piercing a heart, and three names, 'Bridie', 'Gerry' and 'Ann'. On the other arm I have two linked hearts saying 'Mum' and 'Dad' with a swallow above it. I thought it was the right thing. It was what grown men had.

One way or another I'd been coming to England, either for holidays with Hughie and Kate, or working. So, when the compensation money came through in the summer of 1974, I was beginning to feel sick and tired of Belfast again. I needed more space around me, more strangers around me, more scope for my activities. But here I was just dodging bullets and bombs; I had the Provos breathing down my neck over my stealing, and my family breathing down my neck to get myself some work.

I'd been going with a nice girl called Eileen McCann, who lived in the Lower Falls. She seemed to like me, and she made me feel good too, so I said to her one Thursday, 'Do you fancy going to England?'

She said she did. It was the 2nd of August. On the next day, Saturday, 3 August, we boarded the *Duke of Lancaster*, the night boat to Heysham.

6
Southampton

There was no plan. We were just going to London to find what we would find, until on the boat we met Mickey McQuaid. He was a chef on the ferry and his family came from Peel Street in the Lower Falls, the same Peel Street where I'd spent my early years sitting on the cribee and playing hide-and-seek in the houses, the same street that was home ground to the Comanches. I must have been in and out of Mickey's house hundreds of times before I was ten years old. So Mickey fixed us up with a free cabin on the boat, and we had a few beers with him, and he said, 'Where you going to in England, Gerry?'

I told him London, but not to my uncle Hughie's. I was steering clear of the family, because I'd Eileen along. So Mickey McQuaid said to us, 'If you can't find nothing in London that suits you, why don't you go down to Southampton, where my brother Danny is. He'll get you a job and he'll get you a place to stay and that there. I'll give him a ring myself, tell him youse might be in touch.'

So he gave us his brother's number.

We arrived in London on the Saturday, the worst day to be looking for anything. Eileen had never been there before, and already she didn't like it. So she said, 'Why don't we go down to Southampton, like Mickey said?'

I said OK, I didn't mind. So we rang Danny McQuaid and I told him I knew his young brother Mickey, and that I used to live in Peel Street the same as his family, and could he find us anywhere to stay. Danny was at least fifteen years older than me, and he'd been in

England for all that length of time, so he didn't know me personally. But he said, 'No problem, Gerry. Come down to us.'

He and his wife Mary were very kind to us. We stayed in their flat for a couple of weeks, then Danny found us a flat over in Portswood – 39 Shakespeare Avenue – and got me a job with McAlpines, working on the Southampton–Portsmouth motorway link. We thought at first we had it made. Eileen was working in a café, I had the motorway, we were both earning good money and quietly enjoying ourselves. I used to see Danny and his mates for a drink a couple of times a week, go out with Eileen a couple of times and for the moment I didn't even think about stealing.

Then one night about a month later I phoned Danny to arrange to go out with him and Mary, and he said to meet him at the Crown, a pub in Shirley. When we got there, Danny was outside the door. He said, 'Gerry, there's a feller in there says he knows you.'

'Who's that?'

'Say's he's from Belfast. Young lad called Paul Hill, about the same age as yourself.'

I looked in the window into the bar, and I saw this skinny, long-haired guy sitting with his pint, and I said, 'Oh aye. Me and him used to knock around together back home. He's a friend of mine.'

I knew him as Benny Hill. He lived on an estate out at New Barnsley, but his granny was in No. 12, Cairns's Street, which was round the corner from us, only about thirty-five yards away. So I probably got to know him when he was eleven or twelve, coming round to see his granny when maybe he'd stay the night there. We were also in the same school, St Peter's Secondary, but though we're almost the same age, his birthday must have fallen on the other side of the divide from mine and he was in the year below. Anyway, we played a lot of football and handball together, did a lot of drinking together. He used to be in the group of lads I'd bunk the boat with to get to Glasgow and see Celtic play.

There were two things about Benny that made him different from me. The first was he never joined in the shoplifting scene that I was in. He didn't steal, though he was always hard up, always scraping along on his £6 a week dole money, and he often benefited from the proceeds of our stealing. If we'd done well down in the city centre, we'd give him a tenner to go out with us at night. Or if we'd got a load of leather jackets, obviously he'd get one.

The other thing about him was, he came from a family like mine but as he'd been in 1C, and learned Irish history, he was probably more knowledgeable about all that mythology of the Easter Rising and the Black and Tans. Whereas I was more interested in the four-thirty race from Kempton Park, rather than James Connolly and Irish history.

At one time, he'd been arrested and interned at the age of sixteen. This had caused controversy and outrage in Northern Ireland and he was released a few days later. His mother, Lily Hill, who's a great woman, sent Paul over to England to stay with relatives and to keep him away from the trouble that was around us in Belfast. So, like me, Paul had been coming over to England on a fairly regular basis. I was pleased to see him but not terribly surprised.

Truthfully, by now I was beginning to feel a little pissed-off with the Irish scene in Southampton. It's a very old and close-knit community, clustered round Shirley or St Mary's near the docks, where there is that little market-place. I suppose it had its origins in settlements by Irish seamen, the trade Danny McQuaid had been in for years.

But it was very staid and I was beginning to think I could do better with my time than be spending it with Danny McQuaid and his mates. They were very good people, they were great to me. But I was twenty and they were all in their late thirties, all settled and married. They always congregated in certain pubs, the Kingsland and another called the George, amongst others, and they'd sit around drinking pint after pint of Guinness and chewing over the situation in the North. Of course they had republican aspirations, as have all Irish Catholics when they've sunk a few drinks and started to sing 'Danny Boy' and the rebel songs. I've been to America and met Irish Americans who are two or three generations away from Ireland and *they* can't stop talking about the North. It doesn't make them terrorists, or activists. Nor were the likes of Danny McQuaid. The most they would do was buy *The Republican News*, get a little bit pissed and a little bit maudlin, and say a few hard words about Ian Paisley and the British government and internment, and stagger off to their comfortable nests. I found it terribly predictable and quite depressing.

But now, with Benny Hill on the scene, I thought at last I'd have someone my own age, someone who talked the same language as me, someone to go out with, have the crack with (*enjoy the company of*). And we did have the crack all right.

Together we must have gone to every club in Southampton, got drunk, smoked drugs, touched for girls (*picked girls up*), met people, such a lot of people. I remember a guy called Joe, an Irishman who was forever in and out of Winchester Prison for fighting with the coppers, drunk and disorderly, having cannabis. And the three of us would be up and down Shirley High Road at two and three in the morning, singing and laughing.

We took some awful liberties. I remember breaking into a music shop when we were drunk and stealing electric guitars, which we didn't know how to sell. We were wandering up Shirley Avenue past Shirley Road police station with the guitars slung around our necks, wondering why they didn't come out and arrest us. We dumped the guitars in the garden shed of an Irishman we knew, hoping we'd be able to sell them the next day, but we never did. They're probably still in that shed for all I know.

Now that I was going about a bit I got friendly with another Irishman who was not at all like Danny and his mates. Tony had also been a seaman, but he was a rebel who'd been kicked off the boats, I believe for fighting. But Tony's tastes were different: American music, fashionable clothes. He was part of a small minority of Irish I found in Southampton who were not boring and conformist. Frankie, Jimmy and Eammon were others – outside the Irish mainstream, a little bit older than me. None of them were married, but they all lived with women. Tony was very well set up – fashionably dressed, his girl-friend was stunningly beautiful and in his flat the first thing you saw were four massive speakers for his quadrophonic sound system, bean-bags on the floor, everything at floor level. In the McQuaids' place it was the three-piece suite, the Axminster carpet and the colour telly. Tony had glamour, he had style. He also smoked joints.

This was new and exciting for me as a nineteen-year-old kid from Belfast. Any kind of drug was dodgy there. To the Catholic Church, any drug except alcohol has been produced by the hand of the devil, and the IRA were knee-capping people without a thought if they suspected them of drugs. But this character Tony knew seamen that were coming into Southampton from Morocco, South America, the Far East, and they would all be bringing him dope. At his flat, there was always a big lump of hashish in the middle of the table.

He introduced me to a new kind of crowd and we used to go and drink in a bar, the White Hart, just off Shirley High Street. Just going in there you got stoned on the marijuana fumes. Then you'd go to Fridays or the After Eight Club, or, if it was daytime, back to Tony's flat and sit in the garden and get stoned, listen to his blues records, talk to all these different people who came around.

Benny was only on the fringes of this, because he lived away out of town with his girl-friend Gina's sister, and they hadn't a phone. If he went out with me it took a bit of organizing. We'd usually start off seeing some of the more old-fashioned members of the Irish community in the pub. They made a great fuss of Benny, and insisted on seeing him, perhaps because he was the most recent arrival from Belfast and he didn't mind holding forth about the security forces and their atrocities – stuff which I found utterly boring. So I'd be dying for the landlord to call time, and for the old boys to be away to their mugs of cocoa and their beds so Benny and I could go down the clubs.

By now I was arriving later and later for work, or not turning up at all, and I was threatened with the sack. Eileen and I were seeing less and less of each other and she was getting very pissed-off with me. I'd be away out at night with Benny Hill, leaving her with his girl-friend Gina Clarke, when she might have preferred to be with me. Or I'd be off with Tony, leaving her on her own. So in the end Eileen split up with me and sooner or later went back to Belfast. I didn't blame her.

Benny still hadn't found himself a job, and he must have been under pressure from Gina. Anyway, one day he just said to me, 'We'd be better going to London. We'd have more of a laugh in London, Southampton's played out. We've been to all the clubs, we've done everything we can.'

This agreed with my own thinking. I'd had enough of Southampton. London meant bright lights, fun, different clubs and new people. So London was a great idea to me, the obvious next step.

7

Working in London

We arrived in London late on the Friday night and went to my Uncle Hughie's flat in Westbourne Terrace Road, near Paddington. We didn't phone them, we just turned up ringing the doorbell about eleven o'clock at night. No doubt they weren't especially pleased to see the two of us at that hour, but, as always, they welcomed us and gave us a bed.

It was obvious we couldn't stay another night there. The last time I'd created all sorts of problems, and I still remembered with some shame the business of the Giro. In any case the flat was small, and they'd already taken in a niece of Kate, Maureen, as their lodger. So the next morning we were talking about where we could maybe stay, and Kate suggested going to the Irish Centre in Camden, where the priest who ran it might find us somewhere. So off we went.

It was pissing down rain. We jumped from a bus and were running and dodging puddles, when my eye caught something down on the pavement. I ran past it, but a sixth sense told me I had to go back and look again. I grabbed Benny's arm to stop him.

'Hang on, I'm sure I saw something back there.'

Benny was pulling me to hurry me up.

'Come on, for Christ's sake, it's pissing down. Let's get into the tube station.'

'No. Wait a minute. I know there's something back there.'

I went back and found a pay packet that some prat had dropped on the pavement. I picked it up and checked inside. There was £75 there. I took it back to Benny and we split it. I was beginning to believe it was our lucky day. At the Irish Centre we told the priest we were just over from Ireland, and could he help us find lodgings or a flat. He was dubious. In the end he gave us the address of a hostel in Quex Road, Kilburn, run by a priest he knew. We got there about one o'clock.

The hostel was called Hope House, and the priest in charge was Father Carolan. It was a large place with a hundred beds, all occupied by single Irishmen. There are always thousands of guys like that floating around London, working on building sites and labouring jobs, staying a few days or a few months and then moving on, or out, or back. Father Carolan, I discovered later, was very reluctant to take us in, because he knew nothing about us. We could produce no letter from our parish priest back home, which was the normal passport you needed to a place like that, and we had no other kind of reference. But when he saw us looking like half-drowned rats from the rain he did the right Christian thing and said he would let us in.

I had never stayed in this kind of a hostel before, and to tell the truth I was no keener to start living there than the priest was to have me. It was run by the Catholic Church, which would hardly have agreed with the life I was leading, and the last thing I wanted was anybody trying to put me straight. I also thought the place would be full of country people, guys whose heads were in a different universe from mine. I considered I'd been developing some fairly advanced tastes under the eye of Tony.

Father Carolan allocated us to different rooms, Benny on the ground floor and me upstairs. When I saw my room-mates those first suspicions about the hostel were confirmed. They looked like a lot of Irish farmers whose only ideas about living were to earn a lot of money bending their backs for J. Murphy, Laing or McAlpine, to send half of it home to their mothers, and to have enough left to be out each night for a few jars. A 'few jars', by the way, means about fifteen pints in Irish terms.

Benny was luckier. He fell into a room with a Belfast man in it, Paddy Carey, and two others. I used to lock my stuff up and go down to Benny's room for the crack because I already knew Paddy Carey. I used to see him back home in Davitt's gambling club, in Dunville Street, playing cards. I also got to know one of Benny's other room-mates, at least to say hello to. He always wore a pork-pie hat and he had a fetish for green things. His suits were green, his overcoat and his socks were green, even his job was green – he was a greengrocer. I thought he was called Paul, Paul the Greengrocer. As it turned out later, Paul wasn't actually his name.

That evening, after we unpacked, we were going back to Hughie and Kate's for a bite to eat. So we walked down towards Kilburn Park tube to ride the one stop to their station, Warwick Avenue, and on the way we passed a pub called the Memphis Belle. There was a man standing outside wearing a Celtic scarf, and I turned to look at his face, thinking I knew it from back home. I later got to know the guy as Jimmy Goodall, who used to clear empties from the tables in the Memphis Belle. Standing in the hallway of the pub was a bearded guy with long shoulder-length hair and hippy-type clothes. I noticed him all right, but I didn't recognize him. Then he called out.

'Gerry!'

I looked again, but couldn't make out who he was. He said, 'Don't you know me?'

'No, I don't.'

'Paddy Armstrong, from Milton Street. Come in and have a pint.'

Milton Street was in the Lower Falls, off the other end of Murray Street from our place, so of course I knew Paddy immediately he mentioned his name. But his appearance was changed. He'd always been very well groomed, but now he looked like a throwback to the hippy period of the sixties: bare feet, a straggly beard and very long hair. He'd been at school with Benny and me, but Paddy was four years older so we weren't schoolmates at all. I remember him around our streets, though. Paddy'd be hanging around on the fringes of the street-corner card-schools, or lingering in the betting-shops. He was forever hard up, so he hardly had a bet, but there was always the chance of a bung if anyone else had a decent touch (*a lucky bet*).

I remember he was a great friend of my cousin Patsy Conlon, who got drunk one night on the boat over to England and bet someone he'd be able to do a balancing act along the ship's rail. Poor Patsy lost the bet. He went over the side and was never seen again. Paddy would never have done anything so foolhardy, he was a timid, mild man. Probably his most notable achievement in West Belfast was having a sister in Eileen Armstrong, one of the most beautiful girls in the Lower Falls. In Ireland I'd worked with Paddy briefly. We were both at Mackie's, a factory making machine parts, and a job which I'd only taken because the social security had threatened to cut off my dole money if I didn't. The work-force there must have been four thousand, but there were less than two hundred Catholics in the place. Paddy and I were in the mouldings shop and I can remember going into the canteen, with Paddy and one or two others, and being pelted with nuts and bolts by the other men there. It wasn't done in fun.

So Benny and I had the first of many drinks in the Memphis Belle. Paddy told us about London, how there were loads of Belfast people round Kilburn, how he used to go to all these dope-smoking parties and whatnot.

'If youse ever want to see me,' he said as we were leaving, 'or come to a party with the lads, you can always catch me in the Memphis Belle. Don't forget.'

The Monday after we moved into Hope House, we got a start on a building site in Camden where Benny's uncle, Frank Keenan, was already working. We were renovating an old pre-war block of flats at Mornington Crescent. The gangerman was called Tucker Clarke, a Limerick feller that was married to a girl from Ballymurphy in Belfast.

It was good on that job. There were a lot of characters there, not exclusively Irish. I remember a couple of Scotch brothers, absolute lunatics. At ten o'clock tea break, we'd be drinking tea while they got out the whisky or vodka, then they'd be off up the scaffolding doing Tarzan impressions, swinging one-handed fifty feet off the ground and letting out the Tarzan yodel.

I knew there would be a lot of taking the piss, especially for any new men. At the site I worked on in '71 I remember being sent to the store to collect two sky-hooks. I didn't know what sky-hooks were, but I was told I'd need a barrow. So I set off across the site with this wheelbarrow, with all the labourers behind me pissing themselves. It wasn't till I got to the store that I was told sky-hooks were paper-clips. So this time I was on the look-out for them taking the piss. The first job I got was to go a message, getting the food from a little café that was near by. And on the list they'd put rock-cakes. I'd never heard of rock-cakes. I didn't know this was an English term for currant buns, I just thought 'rock-cakes' sounded like a typical wind up. So when I came back they said, 'Where's the rock-cakes, Belfast?'

'No, you're not having me,' I said. 'Bollocks to that, there's no such thing as rock-cakes!'

I was not perfectly adapted for all the jobs on the site. At first Tucker set me working with a couple of chippies, but I kept breaking windows carrying lengths of timber. Somebody would call me – 'Hey, Belfast!' – and I'd swing round and smash the glass behind my back. So I was reassigned to the hoist, which seemed fairly easy work, just operating the start–stop button. The trouble was there was a guy there named Dublin Joe – the Irish always have a tendency to call each other by the town they come from – who used to bring a joint to work. And because I was up there smoking with Dublin Joe, I forgot to stop the hoist and it hit the ground with a full load of concrete on it. It hit with such a thump the hoist near buried itself and it took them a day to dig the thing out. So finally Tucker Clarke had me on the ground mixing sand and cement, where I couldn't do any more damage.

On the Friday we took our first week's pay packets down to the Memphis Belle. Paddy hadn't worked for months, but he used to pick up a little bit of cash in the pub clearing glasses off the tables. So we found him floating around the bar and he introduced us to some Belfast people who were in that night: Jimmy Goodall, John McGuinness, Brian Anderson, Sean Mullin, Paul Colman and some more of our people were in there, sitting at the back. It was great to see people from Belfast.

That night was Paddy's birthday celebration and I went up to a party at the flat in Rondu Road, where a lot of the Belfast crowd were living. I met Carole Richardson, Paddy's girl-friend, and Lisa Astin her friend, that night. They were nice young girls but they didn't make that much impression on me beyond the fact that they were very young and English. It was a nice crowd of people, good company, very happy-go-lucky. What I found most attractive about them was that they smoked a lot of dope.

Our life for the next three weeks was a fairly regular one. We worked Monday to Friday at the site, going down two or three evenings to Hughie's and having a few evenings with Paddy Armstrong's friends. With Hughie we'd have a very set pattern. We'd have our tea made for us by Kate, then go off to the Conservative Club, stopping on the way at the Bridge House pub for a couple of pints. At the Club there might be a card game or a snooker game, then we'd get back to the hostel about eleven.

One Friday night we went to a dance at the Carousel ballroom in Kentish Town Road, where a Belfast group called the Wolfhounds were playing. It was a very Irish crowd, with a lot of my family there, as well as Benny's uncle Frank Keenan. My aunt Annie was there, sitting with Hughie and Kate, and as they'd never met I introduced her to Benny. They sat beside each other half the night, just talking about back home, and how her family came from Abyssinia Street, and his came from Cairns's Street, and did he know her brother Robert, and did she know his aunt. They got on well enough, and at a later date a lot of the details that came out of my auntie's mouth were going to be repeated in a Guildford police station and written down as evidence that Benny Hill and Annie Maguire had met several times before this night, and not for social reasons.

We had been getting reasonable money, £11 per day plus our dole money, but Benny and I were always on the look-out for something better. After three weeks Benny said we would get £14 at a site just off Piccadilly, so we packed in the Camden Town job on the Friday and took ourselves to the West End early on the Monday morning. No luck. There was nothing for us, though we were told we might get something if we had employment cards, which it would take us a week to get. So now we would have to live on the dole and what our wits could provide.

On the Monday we walked round to Rondu Road to see if anybody was in. We found the place empty and the door open, so we walked in and took a few things, bits and pieces, which we sold in some second-hand shop. Then I kept us afloat with some good winners at the betting shop, including a 7 to 1 chance, Hard Attack, which the Irish jockey Tony Murray brought home by a short head for Captain Ryan Price. Benny sat in the pub – he wasn't much of a gambler – while I was in and out placing these bets, getting more and more excited because my luck was in. One time on the way between pub and bookie's I bumped into a feller I knew from the hostel. He was at studying the noticeboard outside the newsagent's: postcards with handwritten messages – LARGE CHEST FOR SALE or FRENCH LESSONS. He pointed these out to me, told me they were all advertisements for prostitutes. I'd never realized it.

'You're taking the piss,' I said.

'No, really. Every one's a whore.' And he tapped the glass. 'Them places is handy to break into. There's always a few quid lying around, so there is.'

Picking up his hint I copied down some of the numbers.

That night we had a few quid from my winnings, so we went out looking for Dublin Joe, who'd told us the pubs he used down Kensington. One was the KPH, the Kensington Park Hotel in Ladbroke Grove, but the barman there had never heard of him. We moved on to another pub Joe mentioned, the Elgin. We never found Dublin Joe, but I bought some dope off a black woman in the bar in that place. I got stoned.

We were talking about how soon enough we'd be flat broke again, and I remembered the idea about the prostitutes' flats. So I looked through my pockets till I found the scrap of paper I'd written the numbers on and I phoned one of the Large Chests, pretending I was interested in what she had to offer. I was given an address in Bayswater.

Benny just went back to the hostel to go to bed, but I took myself for a wee walk across Kensington Gardens and into Bayswater. I found the place, a basement flat. The windows were dark. Either she was asleep or entertaining a client with the lights off, or she was out. On the street corner I found a telephone box and dialled the number again, meaning to hang up if she replied. But there was only the ringing tone, on and on. These were the days before answering machines. She was out.

By now the time was about one in the morning. I slipped down into the basement area and took off the coat I was wearing, a Harrington jacket which belonged to Benny. I put it up against the glass and hit through it with my elbow. There was a crash of glass. I froze and listened, but heard no reaction, so I began widening the hole by pulling out jags of glass from the wooden frame. I cut my hand, but gradually made myself a hole large enough to go through.

I had no torch, the place was lit by the orange glow of the street lamps. Suddenly there was a little dog, a chihuahua dog, worrying and yapping around my ankles. It was a stupid dog, but it was obviously trying to do its duty, so I picked it up and tried to shoosh it, but it kept on yapping. So I tossed it on to the settee and tried to ignore it, pulling out the drawers, scattering clothes and papers everywhere. The dog would not give up, it was darting at my legs, snapping at my ankles. It was becoming a right nuisance, so I gave it a bit of a kick which knocked the wind out of it and shut it up. The dog then just lay on the floor, but seemed all right by the time I left the flat.

I looked around and wished I had a lorry to cart away all the stuff. It was a high-class place, full of plush carpets and expensive stereo equipment. But I went on rifling the place looking for something portable that would make this worth while. There was a small bedroom. I opened the wardrobe in it and found a bag, something like a freezer-bag. Through the clear plastic I could see it was stuffed with paper money. When I counted it, there was something like £700 inside.

These sixteen years later I am not proud of what happened that night. Exactly one year and one week after the break-in I was convicted by an English court on five counts of murder, of causing explosions and of conspiracy, and handed a sentence which the English judge said should be not less than thirty years. In reality breaking into a flat was the most serious crime I ever committed.

8

Arrested in Belfast

At some point in the summer of 1974 the IRA decided to mount a bombing campaign in England. Now, a lot of people I had grown up with in West Belfast had ended up going to prison for IRA activities. Some of them were people I'd gone to school with. The fellers I drank with would as likely as not be in it, and the people shouting for their horse beside me in the betting shop. Few, if any, of them would have known about the mainland bombing campaign, aside from what they read in the papers.

The decision to start the English campaign was made, as I now know, in the Irish Republic, not in Belfast. The people sent to do it were specially chosen for single-minded dedication, cool heads and the ability to lie low. When they came over (under assumed names) they looked for their targets – establishment places and anywhere with soldiers in – and one of the first they selected were two pubs in Guildford, Surrey, used by off-duty troops from training camps around the area.

So on the night of 5 October 1974, these men planted time bombs in two Guildford pubs: the Horse and Groom and the Seven Stars. It was a terrible atrocity. Five were killed and many more were maimed and horribly injured. I have a very good idea how bloody and horrifying it was, because I've had the accused man's privilege of seeing police photographs.

But when they happened, the Guildford bombings hardly made an impression on me at all. The first time Benny left to see Gina in Southampton was on a Saturday, and next day I was in the bedroom talking to Paddy Carey when Benny returned. I remember he said the train he came back on was diverted through Guildford, which the Ra had bombed the night before and he'd a Sunday paper with him. So we read something about the bombing. But coming from the street fighting in Belfast, Bloody Friday and McGurk's Bar and knowing all about Bloody Sunday in Derry, that kind of news didn't make much impact on you, least of all if you were someone like me.

I did the flat about ten days later. The morning after that, we counted the money and it was so much we began to feel a little nervous. I remembered how I'd left my fingerprints all over the place – I'd been so stoned and oblivious. So, as we'd no job to go to, I said to Benny, why not go up to Manchester with our money to see Willie and Anne McCann, my aunt and uncle. It would get us out of the way for a while. So on the Wednesday we went. First we went shopping in Camden High Street, and I bought an afghan coat and a pair of those clumping slip-on clogs which were fashionable at the time. Benny also bought an afghan, and some cherry-red and cream platform shoes. We walked – or rather we tottered – out of the shop, probably thinking we looked like a couple of rock stars – imitations of Marc Bolan and Gary Glitter.

Up in Manchester we had a quiet time, mostly going to the pictures, drinking and, me, betting, and by the time we got back late on the Saturday morning most of my money was gone again.

I was falling into the same rut that I had left behind in Belfast. If I was going to live like that I would rather be back with my family. London had not lived up to my expectations. No bright lights and glitter, instead I was sharing a room with two other people in a miserable hostel. I hadn't met anyone exciting – except for John Conteh in a café just after he'd won the world title, but he hadn't rung me up to offer me out for a pint. I was mixing with social misfits, and of course I was one at the time. I had stolen about £700 and here I was three days later – skint. I had made no real friends in London, just Benny and my family who I knew anyway. I was beginning to feel that Belfast was far richer, despite it's problems – I missed the crack. I was cheesed off and getting depressed, feeling tremendously lonely and vulnerable.

Benny went on to Southampton and I drifted into the Memphis Belle, had several pints and some losing bets and I was beginning to feel even more depressed when – out of the blue – somebody in the pub offered to sell me a tab of acid.

I'd never taken an LSD trip before. Carole and Paddy took it, so did a lot of their friends, and I certainly thought it was time I was initiated. But no one had ever marked my card, I knew none of the ground rules about the drug: how you were supposed to take it feeling happy and secure, and be with other people who knew what was going on. I just thought, OK, I'll do it, maybe it'll give me a lift. So I dug deep, parted with the rest of my money, dropped the tab and washed it down with a pint of beer.

If I hadn't been completely ignorant I might have been able to cope. But the effect of the acid was a horrible shock. After about forty-five minutes, I was suddenly confronted with moving walls and flashing lights, great bursts of colour in front of my eyes, and a sort of fizzing, electrical feeling inside. I was frightened I was losing my mind because it went on for so long, for hours – this feeling that my body didn't belong to me any more, everything moving around, everything distorted. I was badly shaken up, utterly confused. Beyond that, I don't remember much about the trip, but at some point I made the decision that I must get home to Belfast. I was very depressed, more than I'd ever been, very self-critical. London looked like a complete diaster. I'd come here for a bit of stability, but now my job was lost and I began to see myself getting caught by the coppers, breaking into some place or other.

The priest at the hostel later clearly remembered me that night in my afghan coat, acting very weirdly, very disturbed, unable to sit down or relax. I was in his office asking him would he give me back the next week's rent that I'd just paid him, so I could get my fare to Belfast. I was saying I wanted to go back to my ma, over and over again. He wouldn't give me it though, he thought I was on the edge of some breakdown. He offered to get me a doctor, but I just went to my room and lay down.

There was a new guy in the room called Paddy Hackett, a teacher from Southern Ireland. Later he remembered me badgering him for the money to get my ticket. According to him I said how I was cracking up and wanted to get away, and eventually he slipped me a few pounds. Then I went back to the priest. He gave me the last £5 I needed and told me be careful and be sure not to hitch-hike. He phoned up the station for me. The Heysham train had gone, but there was one for Holyhead which connected with the Dublin boat, and so I told him I'd get back to Ireland that way if I had to. I don't remember this conversation – I was so confused from the acid. I packed my few things and somehow got myself to the station in time. It was pissing down buckets when I left Hope House, just like it had been when I'd checked in, which to the very day was four weeks earlier.

At Holyhead, waiting to go through to the boat, I was pulled out of line by a Special Branch man. It was about one-thirty in the morning and by this time I'd come down from the acid trip. But I was left very sorry for myself, very down in the mouth, and I probably looked it.

'Name?'

'Gerry Conlon.'

'*Full* name?'

'Gerard Patrick Conlon.'

'Date of birth?'

'First of March 1954.'

'And what is your social-security number, *Mister* Conlon?'

I couldn't see the point of this question, but I told him.

'BT–07–54–12–D.'

He was writing all this down on a form. I was still nervous and twitchy, scared they would somehow guess I'd been on the acid.

'And where are you travelling from and to?'

'London to Belfast.'

He straightened up and looked at me.

'Belfast! Well that's funny, because this boat here goes to Dublin.'

'I missed the Heysham train, so I did. It's the only other boat that goes to Ireland tonight.'

'I see. Address in London, then, and address in Belfast?'

I gave him Quex Road and my parents' address. He wanted their full names as well. Then he said,

'OK, sonny. Just stand there.'

The man disappeared into an inner office, leaving me shitting myself the boat would go. At last, probably ten minutes later, the copper came back and said, 'All right, sonny. You're clear. Off you go.'

When I arrived back home with the afghan coat looking like some great yak, my sister Ann opened the door. She burst out laughing when she saw the coat, 'Jesus, Gerry, what's that you've got on your back.' When my mum saw me she said, 'Would you look at what the wind blew in? You look like the wild man of Borneo.' My hair was long and tousled, and the great shaggy afghan coat which I had been so proud of suddenly seemed ridiculous. When I went to sit down beside my granny she said, 'Gerry, I hope that coat hasn't got fleas on it,' and shifted away. Here's me feeling like the bees' knees in the coat one minute, and a dickhead the next. My dad was off having a pint at Murphy's so I didn't get to see him till later. He was delighted to see me, but of course he took the piss: 'So England was too tough for you, son. You've come back to a nice warm bed to be looked after by your ma and your sisters.' By this time the coat was hanging up; when he saw it he said, 'What in the name of Christ is that?' I said, 'Da, it's an afghan coat. It cost me a fortune.' When I told him what it cost, he said, 'You could have bought a better doormat and wore it for a cheaper price.'

Needless to say I didn't tell my family what I'd been up to in London. If I'd told my family how I got the money for the coat, it would have been holy-water time and off to confession.

Anyway, my first few days in Belfast were spent recovering my confidence, vowing never to take acid again. I was also trying not to bump into Eileen and her family, who didn't approve of us going off to England now that I'd let her come back on her own . . . I was too shook up to go stealing; I didn't even think about it, to be honest. I just signed on the dole, went out for a couple of pints, a couple of frames of snooker. I felt close to the edge, hours had gone missing from my life during that acid trip, I couldn't remember most of it. I didn't know what to do with myself, but I was now twenty years old, and maybe I ought to get some sort of order and purpose into my life.

I met up with Pat Kane again. He'd been in England the same time as me, and had even looked for me in Southampton. Considering what happened to me later, it was very lucky for Pat that he never caught up with me.

I was with Pat one night when the Army pulled us in after they'd seen us arguing and scuffling with a couple of other guys on the street, probably over some girls. This Brit patrol caught sight of us, slammed us into their Saracen and took us off down to their base. We just gave our names and ages, and were checked out on the radio. I hadn't mentioned I'd just been in England – and neither had Pat – but the sergeant came back and asked me what I'd been doing in England. I realized they must have had me on file from the night I came in through Holyhead. I then had to give the address I'd stayed at and they kept us hanging around for another half hour before they slung us out.

Two or three weeks went by, with me leading a very quiet life, getting out of bed late, loafing around. One Friday I was up around eleven o'clock when my father came in and said he'd just been talking to Lily Hill, Benny's mother, in the baker's shop in Leeson Street. She told him she'd had a phone call telling her Benny had been picked up by the coppers in England. She didn't know what it was for, though.

'Was you two up to something in England, Gerry?'

But I didn't think Benny's arrest could be anything to do with me. I said, 'No, dad, no. We done nothing.'

That night, the Friday, a couple of my mates called and asked me to go for a drink, but I had no money. My father had gone out to the Engineers' Club for a drink, my mother was on the late shift. It was my granny that was there. She now lived in the Divis flats but never a day went by that my granny didn't come down to our house.

'Go on out, Gerry,' she said. 'I'll give you some money for a drink.'

'No,' I said, 'give it me tomorrow.'

So I stayed in, which is how I came to be watching the news, about how they had detained a man for the Guildford bombing and him being hustled out of a squad car under a blanket.

I just looked and knew it was Paul Hill. I could only see him for a couple of seconds, the shoes and the trousers, but I knew from them, and the way he walked.

'That looks like Benny Hill,' I said.

I was laughing and joking about it, because I knew he couldn't have done what they said – I would have known, wouldn't I? My granny was still telling me go for that drink, and I kept saying, 'Would you stop it, granny? I'll take the money off you tomorrow night, so I will.'

Our Ann was there with her mate, messing about. I had the crack with my granny. She kept saying, 'I've got to go home.' This would be about nine o'clock at night. So I unzipped her wee slippers and threw them up the road saying, 'Now you'll have to stay the night, Mary Catherine.' Anyway, she did go home of course but she didn't stand me a drink the next night, or any night. I went up to bed and I never saw my granny in our house again.

At half past five in the morning came a pounding on the door. There was an RUC man and four or five Brit soldiers my mam let in asking for me. They came sprinting up the stairs and woke me up in my bed. I had to get out, bleary and half asleep, and face them. The copper asked me my name. When I gave it I was told he was taking me in.

'What's going on?' I asked, still in my pyjamas.

'Don't ask me, son. We just have orders to take you in.'

'Any chance of getting dressed, then?'

The copper left me alone in the room and I pulled on my clothes. I wasn't thinking at this time about England or Benny, I was thinking the worst they were probably lifting me for was for stealing. The copper wasn't taking the arrest too seriously, very casual about it he was, obviously not regarding me as a serious risk. So I just pulled on my clothes and sauntered down. I was put in the armoured car and they drove me away to Mulhouse Street Army barracks, where I was sat down on a bench by the desk sergeant and left alone, while he went about his business.

About forty-five minutes went by, with me watching the comings and goings in the barracks office. Then two men came in and for about ten minutes disappeared behind a screened-off area beyond the desk. When they emerged they approached me.

'Name?'

I told them.

'Right, you're our prisoner. Come on with us.'

'Where to?'

'We're going to Springfield Road. You're wanted for questioning.'

I was taken to a car handcuffed and pushed into the back, one of them on either side. One showed me the pistol in his armpit. He said, 'If you make a move to escape, Conlon, I'll be forced to fucking shoot you.'

I looked at him as if he was off his head. We sped along, with me looking out past the coppers. I caught sight of our milkman Joe McCann, driving his little milk lorry beside the Dunville Park – the

Wee Park, we called it. I thought, in a little while I'll be back out, doing a bet, watching the racing on TV. This was nothing, a routine check, the kind of thing that went on the whole time where I lived.

Springfield Road is the main police station in West Belfast. It was, and is, a fortified military command post, entirely encased in a cage of mesh, barbed wire and a razor wire. Armoured vehicles crawled around it, churning up the mud. It was about seven o'clock when a pair of massive corrugated iron doors opened to let the puny-looking police car in.

I was taken up to a top floor, an office with three cops in it. I sat there for half an hour. Two of the cops completely ignored me. The third strolled up to me at one point and said, 'Do you know what you're here for?'

'No. Do you?'

He shook his head.

'It must be something serious. The top man wants to see you personal.'

I was taken down to the desk where the sergeant on duty was told, 'This is Conlon. You know the instructions – no one to see him, no one to have any contact, until Mr Cunningham comes in. Just keep him in quarantine, OK?'

They took me to a cell, a windowless concrete box lit by a strip light let into the ceiling. It had a rectangular block in one corner, long enough to stretch out on, with a thin rubber mattress on top of it. There was no furniture of any kind. They took the laces out of my shoes and as I walked bemused into the middle of the cell, the steel door slammed behind me and the lock engaged with a heavy clunk.

9

Accused of Bombing

If you're a smoker, the first worry when you're alone in a cell is always cigarettes. Have you got enough to last you? Have you got any? Mine had been left outside. I looked around and found a bell-push beside the door. I pressed it.

'Can I have my cigarettes?'

'No. When you want a smoke you ring, and someone will come and light you one. No matches in the cell.'

The hours dragged by, but I couldn't keep track of them because I had no watch with me. There was nothing to do, except think about how I was missing the racing, and wondering what won the one-thirty race, the two o'clock, the two-thirty. Every now and then I rang for a cigarette, and I'd say, 'I'm going crazy in here. Can I have a newspaper?'

'Not allowed newspapers.'

'Can I go to the toilet?'

I was escorted to the toilet, and I noticed some of the other cops there giving me funny looks, as if they now knew something which I didn't.

'Would you mind telling me what the fuck's going on?'

But they'd just shrug their shoulders and tell me I'd know when the boss arrived. So I'd say, 'Well can you tell me, did United win today?'

'No I can't. Now, you're in overnight so get your head down, OK?'

I slept, and woke, and slept again.

It was the middle of the night, after midnight. Suddenly there were footsteps pounding along the corridor. I awoke and propped myself on my elbow, thinking, Shall I ring and ask for a smoke? I got up and at that moment I heard keys jingling and the door swung open. Two coppers came in; one was a large, heavy man, the other was of medium height and slighter build.

'Name?'

'Gerald Patrick Conlon.'

We had the rigmarole of my address and date of birth, and the smaller man said, 'Know why you're here, Conlon?'

'No.'

'Know Paul Michael Hill?'

'I know Paul Hill. I don't know if it's Paul *Michael* Hill.'

The smaller of the two men, a detective constable whose name was McCaul, produced a photograph.

'Do you know him?'

It was a standard police shot of someone with his back against a wall. He was wearing a canary-yellow crew-neck pullover and herring-bone trousers. He looked back at the camera, a face I knew very well indeed.

'Oh aye, that's my mate Benny Hill.'

McCaul pulled back his fist and just hit me a punch on the nose.

'So now you know what you're fucking here for.'

I clamped my hand on my hurting nose and stepped back.

'No I don't. I don't.'

As I testified at the trial, McCaul took a pace forward and kicked out, catching me on the shin, then drew back his hand again. But the large man, who turned out to be Detective Superintendent Cunningham, stopped him. He said, 'Then you've got ten minutes, Conlon. Ten minutes to remember everything. Be ready to talk to us.'

Then they left. My nose was trickling blood, and I just sat down there on the sleeping-platform, too shocked to think.

When the door opened, it was McCaul on his own.

'Come on, Conlon, tell me why you're here.'

'I said, I don't know.'

'Course you know. And we know, because your mate has told us.'

McCaul grabbed me by the hair, pulled me to my feet and dragged me along.

Suddenly there were two men standing behind McCaul in the doorway, one of them came into the cell.

'We're English policemen, Conlon. I'm Detective Sergeant Jermey and this here is Chief Inspector Grundy. We're investigating a matter – a very serious one indeed. And we think you can help us with this serious matter.'

I managed to say, 'I don't think so.'

Then Grundy spoke for the first time.

'Come on. Let's take him upstairs.'

McCaul still had hold of my hair. He dragged me out of the cell and towards the stairs. We passed a group of soldiers and McCaul called out, 'Look, this is one of the bastards who done Guildford.'

Guildford. It was the first time the town had been mentioned by anyone. But I had never been to Guildford – not to Guildford in Surrey, not even, for Christ's sake, to Gilford, County Down.

McCaul had me by the collar by this time. He pulled me up the stairs and into an office. They stood around me and Grundy took over the questioning.

'We have reason to believe, Conlon, that you took part in an IRA bombing attack that left five people dead in Guildford, Surrey. Now, what do you have to say?'

I must have staggered or my knees buckled, because they pushed a chair under me. I said, 'I didn't do it.'

I looked from face to face and they didn't believe me. I tried again.

'I've never been to Guildford in my life. I never bombed anywhere in my life. I'm not in the IRA, I don't even come from a republican family. Ask anyone.'

Grundy said nothing at first. Deliberately he snapped open his brief-case and took out a file with several sheets of paper in it. He pushed the papers towards me.

'If that is so, how do you account for this?'

There were about four or five pages, handwritten, and I recognized the writing of Benny Hill. I also saw my name cropping up here and there, with circles drawn round it. I started to read. It was like a fantasy, a complete fiction. The statement said I'd taken Benny to meet some IRA bloke called Paul and another bloke called Dermot who wore a long black coat and kept patting his side to show he had a gun. There was a lot of bollocks about a girl called Marion who taught me how to make bombs, and then a lot more about how he, me, Paddy Armstrong, two unnamed girls and this Paul had driven to Guildford in two cars and planted the bombs.

By the time I finished reading I was in a state of disbelief. I just said, 'Mister, he's telling lies.'

There was a terrible dig in the back of my head and McCaul said, 'But this is your mate; you said he was your very good mate. Why would a mate say all this about you if it wasn't true?'

'I don't know, Mister. I don't know.'

It was all I could say, but it seemed to make them mad. They were all firing questions at me at once, shouting and swearing at me. McCaul slapped me again, more digs in the ribs and back, dead legging me in the thigh.

Finally I was saying, 'When was it this happened? Tell me when this bombing is supposed to have happened?'

'It wasn't *supposed* to have happened. It did happen, and you done it, you lying bastard.'

'I wasn't there, I wasn't anywhere near there, I never done it. Just tell me when it was and I'll tell you what I was doing.'

'October.'

'I was in London in October.'

'We know that. You were fucking bombing London in October.'

'No, I was working. I did a bit of stealing, that's all. Then I came home. What day of the week was it?'

'A Saturday.'

Then I thought of my Uncle Hughie, I thought I might have been with him, as I'd been seeing him probably three times a week at that time. So I told them: 'Well I can prove it wasn't me, because I always went to the Conservative Club in Paddington with my Uncle Hughie. Just check in the visitors' book, where I used to sign in.'

It was a shot in the dark, because in my state of mind I couldn't have said offhand what I'd done on any particular Saturday night two months ago. But it had the desired effect. The two English cops backed off and looked at each other. They told me they'd check the information and see me later. I felt incredible relief to see them gone.

McCaul took me back to the cells but before leaving me he said, 'Stand against the wall in the search position. I want to search you.'

After this, McCaul then said, 'We'll be back for you bright and early, Conlon. We want no more of this shit. You better tell us what we want to hear.'

Then the door slammed behind him.

I was feeling very bad, spitting blood and trying to vomit. But I couldn't, because I'd had almost nothing to eat. I rang the bell and they got a doctor in to see me, a little bald-headed man whose name I now know to have been McAvinney. He asked me what the problem was. I said, 'I've got pain in the testicles and round my kidneys.'

So Dr McAvinney took my blood pressure and looked down my throat. He said I had a kidney infection and prescribed me some antibiotic tablets. After he left I lay down and tried to sleep.

The first people I saw the next morning were Cunningham and McCaul. I was thoroughly terrified by this time of McCaul.

'You're up to your neck in it, Conlon. We've known about you for a long time. Admit it, you're an officer in the Provos, but you lie low, you're a fly man, who only comes out for special jobs.'

It was absolute crap, laughable. But I wasn't laughing because now McCaul was hitting me again, slapping me all over the place, kidneys, stomach, head, asking me about all the IRA men on the Lower Falls. I just blocked his questions as best I could.

'I don't know nothing. I'm not one of them. I've had my own troubles with them – I can't help you.'

But he went on.

'You bombed the Co-op.'

'Of course I didn't bomb the Co-op. I stole plenty of stuff out of it, I never bombed it.'

And at one point I shouted out, 'Well if I'm supposed to be an IRA man, and you know it, why am I not interned in Long Kesh?'

And McCaul punched me again in the face, saying, 'Don't be fucking funny with me. You'll wish you *were* in the Kesh.'

'I do wish I was,' I said.

It seemed incredible to me then, and it is still incredible, that these Ulster policemen could cast me as a mainland bomber, as a member of an active-service unit, as any kind of fly man. The English coppers, of course, were ignorant about everything to do with Belfast, ignorant enough to believe anything. But this was the RUC's own patch. They only needed to put the word out and they'd have had the answer straight back, 'Conlon? He's half a hood – shop-lifting, likes a drink, mad gambler. Jesus Christ, the IRA wouldn't have him. He was kicked out of the Fianna, so he was.'

If they did put the word out, I can only assume they were deaf to the answers.

By midday I had still seen nothing of Jermey and Grundy, the English policemen. But I did see the doctor again, with no particular result. I never did get the medicine he'd prescribed.

Then Jermey and Grundy reappeared, and took over my questioning. And if I couldn't convince McCaul and Cunningham I wasn't in the Ra, how could I ever get through to these two? So they went on at me – stand up, sit down, against the wall – and more of the same – I just said I knew nothing about Guildford, and I didn't know why Benny was saying these things about me. Then suddenly they told me I was being taken to England.

'Will anyone be in your house now?' they wanted to know. 'Because we're sending for some fresh clothes, you look a fucking sorry sight, Conlon.'

I must have done. My blood-soaked shirt had been ripped off me by McCaul and another very vicious copper. My jeans were filthy and ripped, my nose was swollen and tender, my toes had been stamped on.

The fresh clothes were brought to me and I was taken to a wash-room at the end of a long corridor leading from the reception area. I took off my shirt and jeans and washed as best I could, watched all the time by an RUC constable standing behind me. My face felt bruised, my nose tender, and I was curious about how I looked. But there was no mirror in that place. I splashed water on myself. The water felt good on my skin and the soap had the scent of normality to it. I dressed in the clean clothes, knowing that my mother must have taken them from the drawer only an hour or two before.

With the thought of my parents fresh in my mind I came out of the wash-room and suddenly caught sight of them. Two small figures, they seemed, at the end of the passage beside the inquiry desk. They were talking urgently to the desk sergeant, trying to question him, and I called out and started to run to them. But in a flash the copper grabbed me by the hair and slammed me back in the toilet. He held me there until they had gone away, telling me not to be so stupid and not to do anything like that again, ever. My parents never even heard the commotion. I later learned they were told they had missed me, that I was already on my way to England.

I was in the back of a squad car, handcuffed to Jermey and with Grundy on my other side. We set off along the Springfield Road, turned up Cooper Street and into Lawnbrooke Avenue where there used to be a picture-house called the Stadium. We were stopped by a red light on the Shankill Road intersection, just by the picture-house, and there was a gang of Loyalist kids known as the Tartan Gang for their habit of wearing tartan colours. They were loitering in front of the Stadium, looking to my Catholic eyes real evil, vicious and capable of anything. Suddenly McCaul turned around leering and laughing and said to Jermey, 'Let's take the cuffs off him and drop him in amongst that mob. If we tell them what he is, they'll soon sort him out.'

And momentarily I reversed my feelings about going to England. Up till then I had thought – if I thought at all – that I'd stand a better chance here in Belfast, where at least they understood about the IRA. But now I realized the bigotry in my home town had got so bad that the RUC's minds were closed against me. The English police, I thought in my innocence, could never be so prejudiced.

We were off again to Aldergrove airport. We passed through a check-point and the car drew up at the departure hall. Jermey put his coat over the handcuffs and we walked through to the plane.

The last thing McCaul said to me will stick in my mind till I die. I was hauled out of the squad car by the cuffed wrist of Jermey and McCaul said, again with that leer of his, 'Conlon, they're going to put you away for so many years that, the next time you see Belfast, they'll be running day trips to the moon.'

10

The Interrogation in Surrey

Grundy and Jermey were Surrey policemen and they took me first to Addlestone, a small commuter town fifteen or so miles from Guildford. Surrey is as much the home patch of the English Establishment as the Lower Falls Road is of the deprived Belfast Catholic population which I come from. Surrey's lawns are rich, green and smooth as baize, its cars are shining new, it has row on row of solid, comfortable, respectable houses, so prosperous they make Cherry Valley look like a bog. So, although I was relieved to get away from the misery of Springfield Road, it now began to dawn on me that, here in Surrey, I was playing away in a foreign country. People had a hard time simply understanding what I was saying, let alone what I actually was.

I was sure of one thing though – I wouldn't be treated as brutally as I was in Springfield Road. All I needed to do was explain that I hadn't done what they thought, tell them everything I had really been doing on the day in question, and they would let me go. It never even occurred to me that I might be treated in the same violent way, despite my experience in Springfield Road. It couldn't happen here.

But, as soon as I walked through the door of Addlestone police station, any comforting thought about civilized Surrey was shattered. I saw the blue illuminated sign saying 'Police' on the front of the building as we swept into a car park at the rear. There were bright halogen lights at the rear of the building. It was starting to snow, and the snow shone against the light, gently flittering to the ground.

I was bundled out and uncuffed, then taken up some steps and into a large, elongated room where all the coppers in town seemed to be waiting for me, lined up like a gauntlet-run. As Grundy pushed me forward they inspected me up and down, not like a person but an object. I heard someone murmur, 'Irish bastard.'

Then a boot shot out and struck my ankle.

'Murdering Irish bastard.'

A blob of spit landed on my shirt, another foot hit my ankle a painful kick. I stumbled a little, Grundy gave me a second push and I made halting progress down the room, flinching at each kick and each insult. After about twenty-five yards I came to a reception desk. The sergeant there looked at me.

'Name?'

I said it almost in a whisper. He leaned forward and grabbed my shirt, pulling me towards him until I sprawled across the desk. My face was inches from his and he yelled, 'You murdering, Irish SCUM, you're an ANIMAL. What did I say? A murdering, Irish ANIMAL! Now tell me your name, your date of birth, and your address in words I can understand.'

I told him and he let go of me.

'Right, get undressed.'

I looked around for someone to direct me where to go. The sergeant just barked out.

'What you looking around for, animal? I told you to strip off, right here.'

I began to take my clothes off, shaking with fear. But my feelings were mostly disbelief. This couldn't be happening, not to me, not *here*.

When I was completely naked they made me stand there while they stood around jeering.

'Jesus, I don't reckon much to *that*.'

'Should have it cut off of him.'

'He'll have a long fucking wait before he uses that again.'

I started to cry. Some of them spat at me while the rest laughed and jostled me, or punched my back. Then I was taken down a short corridor to the holding cells, a door was pulled open and I was pushed inside. The door slammed and locked behind me, but immediately I heard the flap in the door go down so that they could watch me.

All there was in the cell was a wooden bench, and it was cold. This was the first night of December, and the two little windows high up out of reach had had their glass systematically broken. I sat down on the bench and shivered as the wintry night air blew into the cell. It was no good looking around for comfort, there was nothing in here, no blanket, no clothing, nothing soft.

I started to cry again, cold and frightened. I lay down on the wooden bench and curled up like a baby. But as soon as I did the flap opened and a voice screamed at me, 'Get up, you fucking murdering Irish animal. No lying down! No sleeping!'

I *was* like an animal, a zoo animal unfed, unwashed, nothing to drink. I would be hunkered down on the freezing concrete floor, or curled up as tight as possible on the wooden bench trying to keep warm. But they would come every five minutes and open the flap and yell and scream orders or abuse at me, 'Get up, stand up, scum! No sleeping! No resting! Not for you, you animal. You murdering mick bastard.'

Sometimes I was furiously angry at what was happening to me. 'I'm innocent,' I'd yell. 'I haven't done nothing.' They'd just laugh.

'Oh yeah? Only bombed and killed people. Only mass fucking murder.'

Disbelief still possessed me. I could not comprehend this. Around dawn I asked for my clothes.

'Clothes? You're joking. You get nothing from now on, nothing at all.'

It got light, it was morning, and I thought things must ease up now. In the light of day they would see they couldn't go on treating me like this. But it made no difference, except now it was a fresh shift of coppers who were doing it – yelling, abusing, banging on the steel door of the cell. Hours passed which might have been weeks. I was shaking violently, I felt filthy and weak. And then Grundy came back. He had fresh clothes on. He looked as if he'd had a good night's sleep and his behaviour was softer towards me. He gave me my clothes.

'How you doing, Conlon?'

'Mister, I'm cold and I'm frightened. What they've been doing to me here is wrong. I haven't done what they say I done.'

I asked for a drink of water and he got me one. As I drank it he said, 'Look, why don't you make it easy on yourself? Just admit you did the bombing, like your mate. Just tell us you did it and there'll be no more rough stuff, you won't be hit any more, you'll get some sleep, and some hot food inside you.'

I said, 'Mister, I haven't done that bombing. All I ever done is steal things. That's why I never joined the IRA. I don't know anything about no bombings.'

Grundy shrugged, put the handcuffs on me and took me out to a police car. I was driven off without being told where we were going.

It was another police station, in Godalming about twenty-five miles down the road. We arrived there about one in the afternoon and I was taken straight to an interview room.

It was Grundy and Jermey again, with the same questions over and over again.

'Your friend Hill says you were taught to make bombs.'

'I don't know anything about bombs. The only thing I've done is smoke pot and take acid.'

'He says you went to a house in Brixton where you were shown bomb-making.'

'Where in Brixton? I've never even been there.'

'Do you know a girl called Marion? Hill says she taught you bomb-making.'

'No, I don't know any Marion. Honest to God. I'd never have anything to do with bombs.'

'You're denying everything that Hill says is true.'

'I'm telling the truth, Mister. I don't know what any of this is about.'

'But he's your friend, you say he's your friend. And yet he says you were in it. Now why would he put you in the frame if it wasn't true?'

'I don't know. I don't know.'

'You're lying, Conlon. You're a lying, murdering little bastard – admit you are. Admit it.'

Suddenly I was hit a slap round the head, then another. Then suddenly Grundy says to Jermey, 'Sergeant, I'm fed up with this. You stay with him.'

Grundy marched out very tight-lipped, and came back a few minutes later. He spoke very crisply.

'Go and get Hill, Sergeant. Let's just show him to this lying cunt here.'

Jermey went out. I sat without moving, as if in suspended animation or a trance. I can picture that room in exact detail, even now. There was a window facing the door which looked out on to the station car park. I was sitting at the table to one side of the door and there was a clock on the wall on the other side. It was ten minutes to two. I was weak, exhausted. I had had no sleep, nothing to eat. They had not allowed me a cigarette, even. I must have looked rough and I must have looked terrified.

Then in came Benny, Jermey had him by the bicep of the right arm. Benny was smoking a cigarette, holding it in his left hand. His clothes were the same ones as in the photograph I'd seen in Springfield Road. They looked neat and tidy still. He hardly looked at me, his eyes just met mine and slid away to one side. Grundy pointed to me.

'Who's this, Hill?'

'Gerry Conlon.'

'Tell him what he did.'

'He bombed Guildford.'

I was sitting rigid, absolutely tense. Grundy had me by the collar. I almost shouted out: 'Benny, what are you saying this for? Look me in the face and tell me I done this. Look at me.'

But he wouldn't. His eyes were looking at the floor, and he said, 'I'm telling the truth. My conscience is clear. I advise you to do the same.'

'All right, that's enough,' said Grundy.

And they marched him out.

At my trial Sergeant Jermey testified I then immediately began to confess. The police claim was that, once Benny left the room, I jumped up, said I would tell them the truth and started babbling about Benny being able to make bombs not me, and us going off for a drive in a car at night with me stoned. I am supposed to have told them I read about the Guildford bombing the day after this drive, but didn't connect it with the night before. The police story was that they went on to tease a full admission of guilt out of me by skilful questioning and no use of force, which resulted in the first of my two confessions being signed that night.

What really happened was different. I did say I would write a statement, because that's what they kept on at me to do, make a statement, make a statement. I asked for pen and paper, and I laboriously wrote an account of everything I could remember about my time in England between August and October. It was probably confused and not very complete, because I was nearly exhausted. I still had had no sleep since Saturday night, and not much even then. So it seemed to take hours to write this statement, but at last I finished it. I handed it to them and they read it, and suddenly Grundy went mad. He ripped up my statement, ripped it right through and chucked it in the wastepaper basket.

'That's no good to me, you've been wasting my time. There's nothing here about Guildford. Nothing here about how you went there on an IRA bombing mission. That's the only thing I'm interested in reading from you, you fucking Irish murderer.'

'It's the truth I've written, Mister. Honest to God it is.'

'Well if that's the truth, Conlon, you'd better start telling us lies.'

The questioning and the beating began again. I was told to stand a couple of feet from the wall, and then put my hands on it. They bent down to my ear and yelled into it, punching my kidneys.

'You'll make a statement, because you're guilty. You're guilty, so you'll make a statement.'

'You can't hold out against us, Conlon. We can keep this going longer than you can stand it.'

'That's right. We can keep it up for another five days because the law says we can, and you don't have to see anyone. That's the law. We're allowed seven days' detention, and you don't have to see anyone.'

I watched them smoke and I longed for a smoke. Then Grundy said, 'How about a tea?'

'What do you want, boss, lemon tea?' said Jermey.

He went out and got two cups of lemon tea. I'd never heard of lemon tea.

'No tea for you Conlon. Nothing for you until you admit you did the bombing. No tea, no food, no smokes, nothing until you admit it.'

When I was slammed into a cell for the night I'd had two glasses of water the whole day, and no food. All night the night-shift were banging on my door with their truncheons to stop me from sleeping. I sat there on my bench with my head spinning.

At ten o'clock the next morning, Tuesday, the 3rd of December, I was back in the same interrogation room. I'd been given no breakfast. They went on badgering me, hitting me slaps, making me stand, sit, stand. Then Grundy said, 'Fuck this, go and get Tim. He'll make him see the light.'

Jermey came back with a thickset man who looked like a rugby prop-forward. This was Detective Inspector Timothy Blake. I was standing with my feet apart in the search position, leaning against the wall, and Blake grabbed me by the balls and wrenched them downwards.

They told me I could have it the hard way or the easy way and Blake was taking his coat off and rolling up his sleeves. I could see tattoos on his arms. He made out he was the happy sadist who preferred doing it the hard way. Then Jermey went to the rear of my chair, immediately behind me. He was feeling for two spots behind my ears, just where the lobes join the skull. For a moment his two middle fingers rested there, and then suddenly he drilled them into my skull and yanked me upwards, lifting me completely out of the chair.

The pain was indescribable. Jermey was pleased with himself. He was proud of this technique for inflicting pain without leaving a mark. He said he had learned it in the RAF. I was pulled up again and punched in the kidneys by Blake. I was screaming and yelling from the pain. I was like a child who's hurting and I thought, I'll be killed now, they could kill me.

Blake had these staring eyes. He told me he was a Catholic from an Irish family, but evil murdering bastards like me made him sick. He said he'd seen some of the victims of the bombing and it made him feel so bad he thought I should be shot or strung up for it. He was still saying things like this and hitting me the odd punch, wrenching me by the hair, when the door flew open. It was two senior policemen that I hadn't seen before, Assistant Chief Constable Christopher Rowe and Detective Chief Superintendent Wally Simmons. Rowe was tall and aloof, with a moustache, while Simmons was a slight, dapper man. Rowe took a look at me, poked me in the chest and said I was guilty and I'd better make a statement quickly. Soon after that he left. Simmons was acting very angry. He fired Blake out of the room and told the others to sit me on the chair. He sat on the table so he could look down at me.

'Now listen to me very, very carefully, Conlon, because if you don't you may regret it. I'm in charge of this case, and I'm convinced you are guilty.'

'I'm not,' I said. 'I'm innocent, you got the wrong man.'

Simmons leaned down and gave my face a terrible stinging slap, and just went on talking.

'I'm so convinced of your guilt, Conlon, that I am prepared to take steps – unusual but not unheard-of steps – to persuade you to confess. Do I make myself clear?'

I shook my head, so he just picked up the phone.

'Get me Springfield Road police station in Belfast, Chief Superintendent Cunningham.'

There was quite a long pause, during which Simmons went on talking to me.

'Is your mother called Sarah?'

'Yes.'

'And is she working at the Royal Victoria Hospital?'

I didn't answer, I just shut my eyes.

'And your sister Bridget, does she work in the, er.' He looked at a piece of paper he had with him. 'At a factory on the Dublin Road? That's a place where these sectarian murders commonly happen, the Dublin Road, isn't it, Conlon?'

He was right. The area of the Dublin Road was a no man's land, bodies were always turning up there full of bullets. You didn't have to be a mind-reader to see what Chief Superintendent Simmons was getting at.

By the time he was put through on the phone I was shaking and starting to cry. Simmons identified who he was and went on, 'This little bastard Conlon's not co-operating. You couldn't arrange a little accident at your end, could you, something to persuade him if he goes on like this?'

Simmons grabbed me by the hair and yanked my head over so that my ear was next to the telephone ear-piece. I missed what was said.

'Would you repeat that?' asked Simmons. 'It's a crackly line.'

'Yes,' I heard a voice say. 'I'm sure we can arrange something like that.'

Simmons pushed me back and said he'd call back later if he needed to. He hung up.

'Right, Conlon. It's make-your-mind-up time. I'll leave you to think it over.'

I was crying and shaking uncontrollably.

'What are you going to do? My family hasn't done anything.'

'What happens to members of your family is in your hands, Conlon. I'm not messing about with you any more.'

Then he left.

Simmons wasn't making an empty threat. He probably could have fixed an 'accident' to a member of my family, but the irony was I probably knew this better than he did. I lived in Belfast. I knew from everyday experience how bad the street violence was, senseless shootings happening every day and nobody being arrested for them. I could just see my mother or my sister being caught by a sniper's bullet, and it would be so easily put down as a sectarian murder against the family of an arrested bomber. The RUC, as everyone in Belfast knew, had links with a lot of people who could make this happen. They still do.

So maybe Wally Simmons was a cleverer bastard than he knew. The ploy got him the result he wanted all right, because now my resistance suddenly crumbled. Not in the afternoon of the 2nd of December, as the police maintain. I wrote the first of my self-incriminating statements now, on Tuesday the 3rd of December, in the afternoon. I made another the next day. When I signed them, I believed I would later be able to retract them. I believed they could never be shown to hold water. I didn't realize I was signing away my liberty for the next fifteen years.

11

Statements and Answers

I didn't know what I should write so I asked Jermey. It was like a kid with his English teacher. Jermey said I should start by putting that I was writing this of my own free will and that I had been cautioned. I did so. He then told me to describe how I came over to England, how I met Benny Hill, and how I moved up to London. Then he would get me Benny's statements and let me copy from them.

I wrote three or four pages of innocent stuff and then I thought I had best put in something about bombs, the IRA, or guns. So I made out that Benny was very deep in the republican struggle and that the bomb squad were watching his family in London. I wrote that Benny was wanting to do some IRA job, and that the ganger in Camden had something to do with it. I put him down because the Arlington Road building site had been in Benny's statement, where he said we'd had our jobs fixed up by the IRA. He also said we'd stored explosives in the cement store there. The gangerman was in truth completely innocent, and has never been prosecuted for anything we said he'd done but my repeating his name must have caused great suffering to him.

After I'd written this far I got stuck. Jermey showed me Benny's statement where he talked about the bomb-making lesson by a girl named Marion. He read bits out to me. Benny was originally saying the 'lesson' took place in a flat in Brixton, but in his second statement he changed this to a flat in Rondu Road, Kilburn. I realized he must have meant McGuinness's place, though he didn't name any of the Memphis Belle crowd who lived there. I then wrote a version of the same event, but said I was tripping on acid at the time and so didn't know where it was or what was going on. I definitely said that I did not know the girl.

I was stuck again. Jermey said I should describe the explosives that would have been there.

'I never seen any explosives in my life. I don't know what they look like.'

'Hill's statement says it was like brown sugar, but don't you write sugar. That would look like collusion.'

So I changed it to sand. I wrote some bollocks about a box with sand in it. I also remembered Benny had put down something about watches, so I wrote I saw a watch attached to the box.

Then I was stuck again. Jermey told me to write how I went on the Guildford bombing run. So I made up a yarn about how Benny was threatening to tell the 'boys' back in Belfast that I was on drugs. So I was afraid of myself getting done for the drugs I was taking, which was the reason I gave for going on that drive with him and Paddy Armstrong – Benny had written a lot about Paddy, so I thought I'd better bring him into it. I wrote that we drove for some distance and then Benny told me to go with some girl – I didn't know who she was – into a pub. I said the girl was carrying a bag of some sort, but I didn't know what was in it. Then I said how Benny warned me on the way back to tell no one where I'd been, and how I asked him why not.

A couple of times more, while I was writing, Jermey went out of the room to get Benny's statements so I could dip into them. When I finished I let the pen drop. The yarn I'd spun was that, yes, I was on the drive to Guildford, I did go into a pub with a girl that I didn't know, and we then left. But I never knew, never realized, it was a bombing. The statement wasn't meant to be convincing, but strangely enough at one moment I had a vision of myself actually in the scene of what I was writing. I shut my eyes and I said to myself, Jesus Christ, maybe I *was* there! I remembered my acid trip and how I'd blanked out most of what had happened to me. So, for a moment there, I had this horrible feeling that maybe I could have been on acid and gone to Guildford without knowing it. I was utterly exhausted by now, and hallucinating that the things I was writing were true. Then I came out of it, but maybe it gave the statement a ring of truth. The police were delighted with it, anyway. Jermey was cock-ahoop. He went away, had the thing typed up and I just signed it page by page, initialling all the corrected typing mistakes. I never read it through again. By then I was a beaten docket.

They took me down stairs and flung me in a cell for the night.

In my cell at Godalming the high, recessed windows were intact, and I was allowed to keep my clothes. Otherwise it was the same as Addlestone: a bare concrete box. The walls were painted in cold gloss paint, duck-egg blue. The floor was concrete and the light from the strip-lamp was harsh. They never switched it off. But at least there was a mattress on the wooden sleeping platform – I wouldn't give it the dignity of the name bed. The mattress was not much, a grubby, greasy slab of bare rubber, an inch or two thick. It was torn and pitted and smelt of vomit, and there would be nothing to cover me if I lay on it. But it was the only soft thing in the cell.

I did not attempt to lie down at first, I sat on the bed and tried to reflect on my situation. I was stiff in every limb. My nose and shins were sore, my lower back was hurting around the kidney area, sharp pains shooting out if I made a sudden move. My balls and stomach ached, my head throbbed, there was pain in every part of me.

I couldn't concentrate on what I had done in the interview room, the statement I had signed. Whilst doing it I tried to tell myself no jury would convict me of something I hadn't done, not something as bad as this. I even told myself it would never come to that, the police would return to their senses and let me go. Now I forgot all that, I was dazed. The past few hours had gone, they weren't important, they were meaningless. They had stopped beating me now, and that was the only thing that mattered.

But even now, even after I had co-operated, the terror tactics went on. Every so often the policeman on night duty came to the cell door and flipped open the spy hole. If I showed signs of sleeping he would start hitting the door with his truncheon, hammering viciously and shouting, 'Wake the fuck up! Wake up! No sleeping, you bastard.'

I got the feeling he would like to have my head on the end of his truncheon instead of the door.

I wandered around the cell touching the walls, disorientated. I thought the night would never end. I longed for some kind of comfort, a cigarette, a blanket to hide under, a glass of water. I got nothing.

★

If I thought they would now be satisfied, I soon discovered how wrong you can be. The next morning they had me up the stairs again.

'We want some more answers.'

'I've made a statement already. I've wrote a statement.'

'It's not enough. We want to know who else did the bombing.'

'The names Benny mentioned I put down. Look, I gave you your statement, but I didn't do the bombing. I don't know nothing.'

They raised their eyes to the ceiling.

'For fuck's sake let's not get back to that again.'

Questioning went on all morning and then they locked me up for an hour or so.

Somewhere else in the same police station Benny was still being questioned and still signing statements. The night before he had written a fourth confession, but the police still wanted more names. In the afternoon, this was the first question they asked.

'Who were the women, Conlon? Who were they?'

'I told you. Marion was one of them.'

'Who was she?'

'I don't know. I don't know her.'

'There was another woman, an older woman. Who was she?'

'I don't know. I never seen her.'

This went on and on, still in the same interview room, when there came a knock on the door and Grundy was called out. He was away for about fifteen minutes. When he came back at about half-four he said, 'Conlon, you know who the women are.'

'I don't, that's the truth.'

'You're lying again. You know very well.'

'Who then?'

'Hill has told us. He's made a statement. He says you were taught bomb-making by your aunt Ann.'

At first I couldn't take this in.

'My aunt Ann? Annie? Annie Maguire?'

'Yes.'

'You got to be fucking joking. Annie Maguire? She's more English than Irish. She votes Conservative, and talks with a London accent, she's a law-abiding woman. This has got to be absolutely fucking ridiculous.'

'I reckon Mr Simmons would be interested to hear you say that, Conlon. Mr Simmons believes Hill is telling us the truth. And you know what Mr Simmons is like.'

So the pressure, the heat, were on me again. They wanted another statement out of me, they wanted me to confirm the names of the women Benny had given them: my aunt Annie and Paddy's girl-friend. I shut my eyes. I had been deprived of sleep, food, smokes. I'd been stripped naked, spat at, jeered at, slammed in a freezing cell. I'd taken beatings. And now the lives of my mother and my sister were threatened. I was at the end of my tether but it would come all right in the end. It *had* to come all right.

But I agreed to make another statement.

They made it clear what they wanted me to write. The woman in the flat was really Annie Maguire, and she taught us the bomb-making. The girl I went in the pub with was Carole, Paddy Armstrong's girl-friend. Then they suggested certain other details of the bombing for me to write down, like where I was standing in the pub. At this stage I was agreeing to anything they wanted. If they'd said put down the Queen, or the Duke of Edinburgh, or the Pope I would have put their names.

It was a much shorter statement than my first but when I had finished they were well pleased.

Just before I began to write this statement I saw for the first time a man who I later found out was Superintendent Peter Imbert of the Bomb Squad. I thought he was probably Special Branch. He didn't introduce himself, he just came quietly into the room and stood by himself for about ten minutes, looking at me. Jermey and Grundy started on a new line of questions while he was there, questions about other IRA men in England, questions about explosives and bomb factories. I knew nothing about any of this, and I told them nothing.

Once I'd finished the second statement I was locked in a cell for about three-quarters of an hour, then pulled out of it again. By now it was evening, but I had little idea of the time any more. I was told I was to see a visitor, an army bloke in his twenties – a lieutenant in military intelligence is how he introduced himself. He was formal but polite. The lieutenant fired a whole lot of questions at me about my friends in London and the people I knocked around with in Belfast. He gave me a string of names and asked whether I knew them, with me just saying yes or no. The ones I recognized were all from the Lower Falls, well-known names most of them. The majority of names I'd never heard before. This man has since disappeared from the records of my arrest. I was probably not with him very long – somewhere between thirty and sixty minutes – before they returned me to my cell. He must have seen my state, and realized I wasn't going to be much help to him. By now the questioning didn't mean a lot. Time didn't mean a lot. I was utterly confused by exhaustion.

I passed another night in the concrete box. The next day they still hadn't finished with me. I was pulled out at nine-thirty in the morning, had handcuffs put on me and told: 'Come on, we're going for a drive in the country.'

They threw a blanket over my head and pushed me out through a door into the fresh air. We walked a few paces and then I was inside a car, accelerating away. A few minutes later they pulled the blanket off my head. There must have been press or television crews hanging round the police station, though they said nothing about them. As we started out they were crisp and businesslike.

'We want you to show us where you primed the bombs, Conlon.'

I looked around. We were driving through the Surrey countryside, small country roads that I had never seen before. I noticed that the driver of the car had a gun. One of the others indicated it to me, and started laughing.

'Say your prayers, son.'

The others all sniggered too. It was their idea of a joke.

We drove up a narrow lane and pulled up beside a monument, a stone cross which stood on the grass verge. Now, when I was arrested I had had a cross – a Celtic cross – on a chain around my neck. They said, 'This is like the thing you had on the chain.'

'Yes,' I said. 'It's a Celtic cross.'

'Is this where you primed the bombs, then?'

I looked at them, their faces were expectant. I said the easy thing.

'Yes. It is.'

Then they were driving me back. After a smile or two they said, 'Look around, Conlon. Is there anything you recognize? Any landmarks you've seen before?'

I looked. Nothing. There was nothing anywhere that I recognized.

'For Christ's sake, you must know somewhere, because this is the way you drove to Guildford. This was your route.'

By now I was going along with anything they suggested, going with the flow. So we passed a pub with the sign of an anchor or a ship outside the door.

'That looks familiar,' I said.

It didn't, I just said it to please them. They drove me back to Godalming and slung me into the cell.

In my cell I could suddenly see myself and what I was doing, maybe for the first time. I wanted to please the police just so I wouldn't be beaten any more, screamed at, abused with dirty names. I actually wanted to please these bastards. I was in a terrible state of confusion and fear. I was crying. I was breaking down and falling apart. And all I wanted to do was please these policemen – to please them and get away from them.

12

Charged with Murder

I think the Surrey police needed to believe I was guilty, and there was certainly pressure on them to get a result. In London the bombing campaign didn't stop, and meanwhile there had been two IRA pub bombs in Birmingham which killed twenty-one people. The Birmingham police had made arrests within a few hours of the explosions, and yet here was the Surrey Constabulary running around two months after Guildford with no face in the frame.

The British parliament had helped them a lot by rushing through the Prevention of Terrorism Act three days before I was pulled in. It was a panic measure after Birmingham, which lengthened the time they could hold a suspect without charge or access to a lawyer or magistrate. Benny Hill had been the first prisoner taken under it. The new law gave the police up to a week to get enough evidence to bring charges. If the old two-day maximum had still applied they would have been forced to put me before a court on the previous Monday, after which my story might have been very different. Instead the police had plenty of time to terrorize me into submission and shape the case against me well enough to convince a magistrate.

So now, in the afternoon after I went for the drive in the country they came and opened me up again.

'Right, you. You're going to Guildford to be charged.'

On the way in the police car they had a surprise for me.

'You'll be seeing a solicitor. So don't you say a dicky-bird about what's been happening to you down here. You'll be back with us after he's gone, so you know what to expect.'

At Guildford there was the usual routine, me taken from the car with the blanket over my head, up the stairs and into a cell. After half an hour they had me out and along to the charge-room. Jermey and Grundy were joined by a uniformed policeman who looked like a very senior officer, with a lot of pips and braid and ribbons about him. And standing very meekly behind them was a pale, thin, gangly young man, probably in his mid-twenties, with a candy-floss of ginger hair on his head. He was wearing a jacket too small for him – the cuffs seemed to be half-way up to his elbows – and a green tie, and he was holding a cardboard folder. I thought he looked scruffy, almost like someone I might have seen back in Kilburn, one of Carole and Paddy's squatter friends.

'Here's your solicitor, Conlon. You can have a couple of minutes with him.'

The young guy came forward nervously.

'Hello, I'm David Walsh from Simon, Muirhead & Allen in London. We've been engaged on your behalf.'

He looked at the policemen.

'Where might I speak to him, please?'

'Right over there, sir.'

They were indicating a little table in the corner of the charge-room. We went over to it and David Walsh opened his folder and took out a pen.

Of course I knew nothing about him. I didn't know how he fitted in, who got him for me, nothing. I looked back at the policemen. Jermey and Grundy were standing together, listening for whatever was said. I was half-hysterical. This was my first chance in five days to speak to anyone who wasn't a police officer, and I didn't know what to say. The policemen were no more than five or six yards away from us, staring. It was a very short meeting, a few minutes would be about right. I told Walsh I had made false confessions because my family were threatened, but I was not guilty. He asked me how I was feeling, how I'd been treated, which gave me my chance to tell him about the beatings. But Jermey and Grundy had given me a warning about this, so how could I talk about being beaten and abused in their hearing? So I tried to mark David Walsh's card, I pointed to Grundy and Jermey and said quite loud, 'These two policemen here have been very nice to me, they haven't pulled my hair, kicked me, punched me or beaten me up.'

I thought, that should put him on the right track. But at this moment, suddenly, Simmons came into the room. When I saw him I couldn't contain myself. It was Simmons who had threatened my mother. I pointed a finger at him and shouted out, 'But *this* one doesn't believe anything I said and I've tried to tell them the truth.'

There was a silence. The police officers began moving down the room towards us and that was it, the meeting was over. The senior uniformed officer read out the charge against me, a single charge that I had murdered Caroline Slater in the Horse and Groom public house in Guildford on October the fifth. I just said, 'I'm not guilty.'

Just before he left David Walsh remembered a couple more things he had to say to me. First, I'd only be one more night in police custody, after which I'd be appearing in court. The second thing he said was, in his timid voice: 'You should know that they are no longer allowed to question you. You don't have to say anything more to them.'

Then he left.

I can remember the door closing behind him, a solid hardwood door with a brass handle to it. I knew I had gone too far in what I said about Simmons, and now that door was closing I was at the mercy of the police again. Grundy and Jermey bounded over to me like two lions pouncing.

'What did you say? *What* did you say to that man?'

They had my arms up behind my back so far that my body was arched backwards. They pushed me out into the corridor, down past some cells, calling me all the filthy names they could think of and ramming my wrists up to the nape of my neck. One of the cell doors was open and someone came to the door and called out.

'Hey!'

I managed to get a look at the man. They were half-carrying me or I would probably have dropped to the ground from surprise. It was my uncle Hughie standing there, shouting out angrily, 'Hey! Leave him alone.'

They didn't stop, they just hurried me along while one of them shouted at Hughie, 'Get your head back in that door.'

I tried to twist in their grip to see him again but I couldn't. I yelled out, 'That's my uncle and he's got a very bad leg. He should be at home.'

We had reached the end of the row of cells, where there was a small room like an American-style prison cell, with an iron grille instead of a door, the bars painted sky-blue. They seemed to have mattresses stored there. I noticed two or three stacked by the wall. They turned me round and started pushing me back. 'We told you not to say anything to that solicitor! We told you to keep your fucking trap shut.'

My head flopped backwards, banging the wall.

'Just because you've seen a brief, Conlon, it makes no difference. You're still in our custody, got it?'

The next thing they grabbed me and pulled me out into the corridor again. Hughie's cell door was closed now. I was trailed past it, up a flight of stairs and into another corridor above. There was a row of interview rooms along it.

'We're taking you in to your aunt Annie Maguire. You're to tell her what you told us.'

'What was that?'

'That she done the bombing with you.'

'But she didn't. She never done the bombing.'

I tried to twist away as they opened one of the doors, to stop them pulling me in there. They got me by the hair, one on each side, and dragged me in through the door.

My aunt Annie was sitting beside a table. She looked as if she was in shock. There was a policeman with her and a woman officer. Annie and I were just staring at each other when Simmons came in behind me and broke the silence.

Even now, Annie Maguire and I remember things differently. I know I was still crying, I couldn't stop. I know I said, 'I'm sorry, I'm sorry.'

I was yanked by the hair out into the corridor again. The door slammed behind us and they hit me a lot of slaps across the face with the backs of their hands, saying, 'Why didn't you tell her she done the bombing?'

I felt desolate and confused. I had confessed to something I hadn't done and now I'd seen two innocent members of my family in police custody. As I was taken back through the police station, and into a car to go back to Godalming I was like a sleep-walker.

I didn't know it but the abuse of my family had started a week earlier, before even I was arrested. In the event over forty people were pulled in for questioning, scattered around various police stations. Benny had mentioned the names of Hugh and Kate Maguire in his first statement. I was horrified when I saw my uncle Hughie in a cell. He is a lovely man, and the thought that he suffered so much because of someone I had taken to him was hard to come to terms with.

Hughie and Kate's flat had been raided at half-four on the previous Saturday morning, an hour before the RUC had come for me. A number of armed police came in with dogs, tore the flat apart and dragged Kate and Maureen, her niece, off to a police station. Then Hughie was taken away to a different one. He ended up thrown into a cell in Guildford, with no bedding for the first three nights, no dressing for the ulcer on his leg, no doctor when he asked for one, no exercise. He was just left. They weren't really interested in him, they must have known he couldn't have had anything to do with the Guildford bombs. They interviewed him just one time at Guildford, yet they used the new Act to keep him detained in solitary confinement for the full seven days. By the end of the time his ulcerated leg was stinking.

Many years later, I learned that they treated Kate as badly, or worse. Hughie asked about my aunt as soon as he got to Guildford and they lied to him: they told him Kate had gone home. In fact – unknown to me – she was being held where I was, at Godalming. She had her period at the time but they gave her nothing. She had to wash her panties in the toilet bowl, she had bare feet the whole time. They questioned her very harshly, wanting to know if she had bombed Guildford, asking her what she knew about explosives, the IRA, things she knew nothing about, could never have known about, as must have been obvious after the first ten minutes.

Kate took her detention and interrogation very hard. When they let her go home at the end of the week without any charge – or apology – she was in a very bad way. Ever since her seven days in police custody, my aunt has not been able to eat any solid food and has existed on a diet of Complan and milk, even fifteen years later. She attempted suicide after her release because of the treatment she'd had. She used to be a very bubbly, cheerful woman. Now she is terrified of the police.

I was oblivious to any of this at the time. I was a zombie,

exhausted, yet I was afraid to go to sleep. I didn't think I dared sleep until I got away from these policemen, I thought they might come in and kill me. All capacity for logical thought had gone from me.

When they came to my cell in the morning the atmosphere had changed, very slightly. First they offered me food for the first time, a greasy bacon sandwich. I looked at it without interest and asked for a glass of water and one of my cigarettes. These I got.

I was going to court this morning, and the overwhelming atmosphere of hostility, which by now I had come to expect, had begun to fade away. The place still vibrated with a feeling of hatred towards me. The looks of contempt were still all around me, so were the heavily armed policemen. But we were going to court, and from there no doubt on remand to one of the prisons. The police had got all they were going to get from me, and they knew it. They had squeezed me dry.

So, again with a blanket over my head, I was planted in a car and our convoy set off back to Guildford. Even from quite a distance I could hear the crowd's shouts. I never really saw them because I was put back under the blanket as the car slowed down, but my impression was of mainly women's voices, screaming out their hatred, 'Hang the bastard! String him up!'

There were fists hammering on the roof of the car, and voices closer now, close to the car window, baying for my blood. Then the handcuff tugged at my wrist, the blanket was adjusted and someone said, 'Keep looking down. Look at the ground, or you'll trip over the steps.'

A minute later we were out of the car and inside the court.

I don't remember much about what was said. The magistrate was there, and I saw David Walsh and someone from the Director of Public Prosecutions. I had the feeling that everyone there gawping at me was hostile: news reporters, lawyers, court officials, policemen. They all wanted to believe we were the bombers, the vicious, mindless terrorists portrayed in the tabloid press, and so they did believe it. The court-room was a whole circus of hate and Benny and me were the star attractions.

Benny was put into the dock beside me. I looked at him I think blankly, as if unsure who he was any more, as if I didn't know what to say to him, even if I had the chance. I was crying again. The two of us weren't Gerry and Benny any more. We were Gerard Patrick Conlon and Paul Michael Hill, the alleged terrorists.

His face was very serious, but he winked and mouthed the words, 'It'll be all right.'

I couldn't, for the life of me, understand how.

The magistrate said we were remanded to prison for a week, and I heard the words with incredible relief. I was out of the hands of the police.

So now the whole process was played out in reverse, with the cuffs, the blanket, the shrieking and the abuse around the car, the car accelerating away and the voices fading away behind us. I was on my way to Winchester Prison.

After we had driven for maybe forty minutes the car slowed almost to a standstill and then picked up speed. As it did so I heard gates slamming behind us. As the car pulled up I made out a voice shouting from somewhere, 'Here they come.'

When we got out I couldn't understand why they kept the blanket over my head, as now we must be inside prison walls. Now I realize it was to shield me from the eyes of hundreds of prisoners, peering out from the overlooking windows to see the Guildford bombers coming in. I was guided up some steps and inside what I guessed to be a reception area. Here the blanket was slid from my head. Paul Hill had arrived in the same convoy and like me he was blinking and looking round.

A score of screws were standing there, twenty pairs of eyes fixed on us, glaring. The policemen took off the handcuffs.

'There you are, chaps. They're all yours.'

They said nothing to us before they left, which suited me fine. Just so long as they left.

13

In Prison on Remand

They shut Paul Hill and me into two tiny cubicles just off the reception area, and as I'm standing in the confined space there my relief at the departure of the police evaporates. I'm thinking I've no idea what prison life will be like. Just a week ago I was a free man who thought only of betting and boozing, and now I'm a prisoner. How will I be treated? Who will I be with? How will I survive?

Now I can hear Paul Hill being opened up and marched a short distance. I can hear his voice, and the aggression of the screws as they begin to process him. I sit waiting for my turn.

I'm opened up and called over to a desk.

'Strip off your clothes.'

I think for a brief moment of Addlestone, and I hurriedly do it. As I stand there the screw starts filling in a form.

'Name? Date of birth? Home address? Occupation? Religion? Next of kin? Diet?'

This one has me stumped. The only diet I'd ever heard of was people losing weight.

'I'm not on a diet.'

He looks up at me.

'Are you trying to be fucking funny?'

'No, I'm not on any diet. I don't know what you're talking about.'

'It means, what sort of food do you eat?'

I shrug.

'I don't know. Just ordinary food.'

He looks at the other one beside him.

'Christ Almighty, have we got a right prat here or what?'

They then itemize my clothes, measure me, weigh me, take my fingerprints. Still I'm naked, still the screws are all there, staring at me in sullen hostility. After about twenty minutes they throw me a pair of underpants that must have been used in the 1924 Cup Final. I put them on and they come down to my knees. I put on a shirt that's two sizes too big and a pair of woollen ankle socks so shrunk they hardly cover my ankles. Then a pair of brown trousers with a yellow stripe down the side. All Category A prisoners had this stripe down the side of their trousers so they could be noticeable at all times, and a matching jacket affair, and prison slip-on shoes. I stand there dressed and feeling completely ludicrous, like a performing monkey.

They pull out a roll, a shapeless lump of blankets which I gathered to be bedding. They thrust it into my arms, followed by a chamber pot, a large jug, a spoon, a fork, a basin. Now I am fully loaded.

The reception screw signs the form and rips it off the pad.

'Now get him out of my fucking sight.'

I was marched away by four of them down a long corridor. Any confidence I had that I'd be safer here than with the police had gone. The screws kept turning to look at me, and I felt the eyes of the two walking behind me boring into the back of my head. Not a word was spoken to me, but I felt so small and frightened in this immense and intimidating place.

The screws opened a gate and we went through into the main prison, where the wings were. And prisoners were milling about the landings looking down from the balconies as we passed. They must have been curious about me, because I had four screws in attendance. I was hurried through that wing and into a second. There as a big black square, with a yellow 'C' in the middle of it, painted on the wall there.

We passed through C Wing, down a small flight of steps and into an area with a few cells lined up on their own. I found Paul had got there just ahead of me. Four screws were waiting for us.

Paul was pushed into a cell, and me into another three doors beyond. I put down my load and stood there, still watched by my escort of screws. From the corridor I heard a voice, somewhere outside Paul's cell, snapping, 'Get water.'

I heard a tap running, footsteps, and a door banging shut. Then the same voice outside my cell, 'You! Get water!'

I hesitated, not sure how to carry out the order. Then I saw the white plastic jug and picked it up. I went out and saw the recess, a niche in the middle of the wall opposite the line of twelve cells. I filled the jug from the tap and took it back to my cell. With a thunderous bang the door shut me in.

From the way the screws had been looking at me I was sure they were planning to come back and attack me. That was the only way I could understand the evil eye I got from them; I didn't realize this is the way they always look at prisoners, day in, day out. So I immediately swept the bedding roll on to the bed, turned the upright wooden chair and pulled it to the corner. I sat down, with my back to the wall. The high window was behind and above me, the cell door was opposite. I waited.

I didn't know it yet, but I was in the punishment block, in a cell eight foot by ten, stinking of piss and stale sweat. The walls, the ceiling, the floor were filthy, and there was only this chair, a tiny wooden table and a low bed, a few inches off the floor and without a mattress.

After a while nothing had happened. I climbed on to the chair and looked out the window. I could only see high wire-mesh fencing with barbed wire on top. I got up the courage and called out of the window, 'Benny! Benny!'

Then I heard his voice coming back.

'Gerry?'

'Yes, it's me. What's going on? How the fuck did we get in here? What happened?'

'Not now. I'll tell you when we get exercise.'

I had to be satisfied with that. At least I'd heard a voice that wasn't hostile.

It was dinner time. The screws came and opened me up. I took my plate out and was served some sort of slop made out of mince, a brown-grey coloured slop. I looked at it without hunger. I thought it might have poison in it, screws' spit, anything. It smelt absolutely foul. But they had given me a bread roll, which I did eat. I left the rest, opened up the bed-roll, laid the blankets down where a mattress should have been, and lay down. For a long time I had been beyond exhaustion, doing everything stupidly and automatically. But now my eyes closed and I fell asleep.

The screws must have crept back after their lunch and looked through the spy-hole. I didn't even hear them opening up the door, but suddenly there was somebody kicking me on the sole of my foot.

'Get up! Get up, you bastard.'

I looked up blearily at two screws, who stood over me.

'No sleeping during the day. It's not allowed. The bed is only to be used at night.'

'All right.'

I rolled off the bed and got stiffly up.

'OK, slop out.'

'What?'

'Slop out.'

'What's that?'

They looked at each other with that look of disgust and contempt, as if to say Christ, what a prat.

'Take your tray out, put what you haven't eaten in that dustbin, wash your knife and fork.'

I hadn't used a knife or fork, so I emptied the plate.

'Can I use the toilet?'

'No, back in the cell.'

Inside again I could hear Paul Hill slopping out, so I waited till they banged him up and got up on the chair again.

'Hey, Benny! It's me! I'm doing my nut here. I'm going to kill one of those bastards soon.'

Paul's voice came back from three windows along.

'Take it easy. Don't be letting them wind you up.'

'Jesus, never mind them winding me up. What are we doing in here? Tell me what went on. What happened?'

'I'll tell you when we get exercise. It's no good talking at the window, you never know who's listening.'

Suddenly behind me the door was flung open. I turned. The screw stood there yelling at me, 'NO talking at the window. NO standing on the chair. If I ever catch you up there again I'll have that chair and that table OUT. Got it?'

That day the worst thing was the silence. I broke it by walking up and down the cell, pacing out my cage, with my thoughts spinning round. I was on a murder charge. What was my mother thinking? My father? What were they all saying about me back home? Would they believe I was guilty or innocent? All around me was a wall of silence.

About three o'clock the silence was broken by some noises outside and in spite of the screw's warning I couldn't stop myself. As quietly as I could I crept on to the chair and looked out. I could see now that the area my cell overlooked was an exercise yard and here were all these prisoners – a couple of hundred – walking around in a ring inside this cage of wire mesh. I stood and looked, fascinated, thinking I would be out there soon enough. They were strolling in little groups and I spent my time trying to imagine myself amongst them, trying to figure out what sort of blokes they were and which ones I would end up talking to.

It took me a little while to realize I could make out what some of them – the ones passing nearest my window – were saying: bits of conversation, mostly stuff I couldn't understand because there was a lot of prison slang mixed into it, words that made as much sense to me as a foreign language. But suddenly something came through quite clearly, something which made me go hot and cold. They were talking about me!

'You heard the news? We got some of the bombers here.'

'Yeah, came in this morning.'

They were casually talking about me as a bomber, me as a killer. I stepped from the chair, I sat down and put my head on the table. I realized in full how I was going to be seen in this place. The police had me convicted, the screws had me convicted and now I was hearing even the prisoners had me convicted. In their eyes I was a bomber, a murderer. Tonight all my friends would be going out for a drink, probably touching for a girl, getting on with normal life, things I should be doing. But instead I was stuck in this stinking filthy cell, surrounded by hatred. The thought overwhelmed me with self-pity and I started to cry. I cried myself to sleep, sitting forward with my head on the table-top.

I heard a loud noise and I woke up aware that the door behind me was wide open. I jumped up. The screw was there scowling at me.

'Come on, you. Tea time.'

I was terrified of these men, they seemed so powerful and wicked. I was too terrified even to speak to them, I just did what they said.

I went out and looked at the food. It seemed to be boiled fish and potatoes. There was also a strange little cake, three rounds of bread and a knob of margarine. I felt a slight hollowness in my stomach and knew I was beginning to feel hungry for the first time in a week. I took the tray back into the cell and ate it all except the fish. I wasn't too sure about that.

After my tea I began to pace the cell again, up and down, and I now noticed for the first time the names on the walls. One of the reasons the cells looked so dirty was that they were covered in tiny graffiti, name after name of the different generations who'd been here before me, as far up as a hand could reach. I found myself trying to read all the names, hunting around for new ones in obscure corners, anything to keep my mind distracted.

I had to slop out and collect a mattress. It was filthy. There were sweat stains on it, urine, vomit and blood stains, congealed semen and snot. They might have raked it to get the lumps away, but it obviously hadn't been washed for years. I turned it over and the other side was just as bad.

About five minutes later a screw opened up and threw in a pillow which hit me on the head. It was the same as the mattress, covered in snot and spew. I thanked God I had a pillowcase in my bedding roll to put over it.

I made up the bed, wanting to climb into it then and there, overcome by tiredness. But I was so petrified by now, so scared it was the wrong time, that I sat terrified on the bed watching the dark sky. I wondered what I would see from the window now, so I climbed up and could see the chain of lights on top of the roof opposite, and below it the fenced-in exercise yard. I was staring out into the night when I heard Paul's voice calling to me softly, 'Gerry! You at the window?'

'Yes.'

'Don't be worrying. Everything will be all right. See you tomorrow.'

I got down and I started trudging round the tiny cell again, exploring the graffiti, until I was opened up and confronted by a prisoner with a large can of tea. The screw behind him said, 'Tea? Want some tea?'

'No. But can I go out and get some water?'

The screw hesitated for a second, and then rapped out, 'Certainly you can get some water. Get it in the fucking morning.'

He slammed the door in my face.

A few minutes later the light went out. I stood there for a moment feeling strange and unable to work out why. The darkness felt good to me, almost comforting. Then I remembered I hadn't been in darkness, not for a whole week. I took off my clothes and crept into bed.

My sleep was deep and dreamless and lasted all night. I woke only when the lights came on and the screws hammered on the door, shouting, 'Come on, get up, get up.'

It was morning, but not yet light. I didn't know the time. When I swung my feet out of the bed the concrete floor was freezing so I put the socks on first, then the rest of my badly fitting clothes. The door opened, a screw glared at me.

'Slop out.'

I didn't react. I thought slop out was after meals, but I'd not had breakfast. The screw looked down at my piss-pot.

'Come on, slop *out*.'

I picked up the piss-pot, took it out and emptied it. I collected a breakfast tray and on my way back plucked up my courage.

'Will we be getting exercise today, Mister?'

'Hey! Don't call me that. Call me sir. When you talk to a prison officer, it's always sir.'

He banged the door and I turned to my plastic jug. I poured some water into the bowl and splashed my face. I wouldn't use the White Windsor soap, because it stank, a foul smell. I ate a piece of cold toast, a couple of bits of bread, and drank some more water. The door opened, 'Slop out.'

I moved out of the cell with my tray.

'Mister, when are we going to get exercise?'

The nearest screw spun round and grabbed me by the shirt, pulling my face almost up against his.

'We've told you before, you Irish bastard. When you speak to us you call us sir.'

He was snarling at me, the saliva spattering on my face. He dragged me back to the open door of my cell and slung me in. I don't know what happened for the next hour and a half. The time just passed, and then there was more activity outside, which climaxed in my door being pulled open.

'Get to your feet for the governor, Conlon. Name and number.'

I didn't know I was supposed to have a number, so I just said, 'My name's Gerry Conlon, I shouldn't be here, I haven't done nothing wrong.'

The governor was walking around escorted by a senior uniformed screw. He looked at me dismissively.

'Well we hear that all the time, Conlon, all the time. How have you been treated? Any complaints?'

'I don't know, I've nothing to go by, have I, governor? All I've asked for is exercise and every time I ask these two start yelling at me.'

The governor turned round to them.

'See that this man gets his exercise.'

But I hadn't finished, a new thing occurred to me.

'What are the chances of getting my own clothes?'

The governor raised an eyebrow.

'Have you got clothes?'

'Yes, but they took them off me when I come in here, and gave me these.'

'I'll make inquiries.'

Then he moved on and they banged the door.

Eleven o'clock was dinner time in the block, and by the time it came round I discovered I was starving. I ate it all – bowl of soup, piece of white meat, cake covered in yellow custard. I sat back, beginning to feel some of my strength returning. But then a new problem started. I needed to go to the toilet. I looked at the pot, but no. I rejected the idea and made a decision then, which I have kept to without once breaking it, never to use the pot for crapping. It was a mark of dignity and of self-respect, a line that I would not go across.

So I started trying to distract myself, walking up and down, longing for them to open me up and tell me to slop out so I could get to the toilet. At last I heard them coming back. But instead of opening me up first they went to Paul Hill's cell. I heard them barking, 'Slop out.'

And then: 'Right, Hill. Exercise. Get your jacket on.'

They were opening and closing a series of doors and there was silence again. But when were they going to come for me?

At last my door was unlocked.

'Slop out.'

I was out like a greyhound. Leaving my bowls and plate on the little table by the slop-out bin, I went straight into the toilet. Within thirty seconds a screw came in.

'Who gave you permission to come into this toilet?'

'No one, but I had to go.'

'What do you think you've got one of those fucking pots in your cell for, Conlon? They're for pissing and shitting in.'

'I just wanted to use the toilet.'

'Well, next time use your pot.'

When I came out again I tried to spin out my time at the sink, washing my plates and cutlery over and over again until I began to be afraid the screws would object. Going back to my cell as slowly as I could I asked, 'Am I going on exercise?'

At which the screw grabbed me and pushed me into the wall.

'How many times have you got to be told, you Irish bastard? When you talk to us, say *Sir*. And no, you're not getting no exercise yet.'

'But Paul Hill's on exercise.'

'We know he's on fucking exercise, we took him on exercise. You get yours when he finishes.'

He slammed the door.

I went to the window and looked out. There he was, walking round and round on his own. He would be in my view for forty yards or so and then out of sight for about the same. When he came near my window I tried to attract his attention.

'Psst!'

He didn't hear, just walked on. There were two screws inside the yard with him, lounging against the chain-mesh fence, and more screws with alsatian dogs patrolling the perimeter outside. He came round again.

'Psst!'

Paul looked up, saw my face at the window. I waved.

'Hey!'

Paul just shook his head fractionally and walked on. Then they brought him back in. I put my jacket on and sat waiting. I was longing to be taken out there, like a child waiting for playtime. Ten minutes went by, fifteen, and nothing happened. I thought I must call them, remind them. There was a button which rings in the screws' office and lets down the spy-hole flap on the outside of the door. Several times my finger was about to press the bell, and several times my courage failed. Then, after about half an hour, I could wait no longer and pressed. I heard the flap fall. I waited.

Five minutes went by, then footsteps. The screw strolled past my cell and as he went he slammed the flap back into position. Another five minutes went by and I worked up the courage to do it again. Again the screw came slowly up to my cell door, and this time he spoke.

'What do you want?'

'My exercise. I've been told I'm getting exercise.'

'Not today, you're not.'

'Why not? Paul Hill's had exercise. Why can't I have it?'

'Inclement weather.'

I was taken aback. I didn't know what this meant. I'd never heard the word inclement before.

'Sorry, what does that mean, what you said?'

'It's fucking raining. So tough luck, no exercise today.'

I went straight to the window and looked out. It wasn't raining.

Tea was salad with cheese, but I ate nothing. Despair and tension had taken my appetite again, and I could eat only the bread and drink only a cup of water. I was dreading what they would say and do to me at slop-out.

At last the key hit the lock.

'Slop out.'

And I was looking up into the face of a different, unknown screw. A new shift had come on.

I went out nervously to the recess aware of the eyes of one of these new screws looking at me. Then, quite unexpectedly, he said, 'Do you want a shower?'

I must have looked startled, it was the last thing I suspected.

'Yes please, Mister.'

'Well slop out and get your soap and towel and have your shower, then.'

I got in there fast in case he changed his mind. There was warm water and even though the soap stank it was better than the dirt, the accumulated dirt of the last eight days. I came out feeling the confidence rising in me again.

'Any chance of getting my cigarettes from reception? They took them off me when I came in.'

The screw who'd let me in the shower said, 'Sorry, I can't do anything about that now, but you'll be getting paid in the morning. Here you are, here's a cigarette.'

Then he locked me in.

I stood there astonished, inside the door. It was as if the unthinkable had happened. Someone had been kind to me, the first kindness I'd known since I was arrested. And it came from a screw. There was only one problem, I had no light. I was too terrified to get back on the bell, so I sat there for an hour and half cupping this unlit Player's cigarette in my hand, smelling it, trying to inhale the aroma of the tobacco. When the door opened the screw said, 'Want tea?'

'No. But could I have a cup of water and a light?'

The screw laughed.

'You sat there all that time? Why didn't you ring the bell?'

So I got my light and – probably – the best smoke of my life.

The next day I was told my pay: £1.29 in credit which I could spend in the prison canteen. I was given a printed list where I could mark what I needed – Old Holborn tobacco, papers and matches took up most of it, but I had enough to order a Mars bar as well. The screw took it away and I heard him opening up Paul. Then he called out to one of the others, 'Right, I'm off to get these two kids their canteen.'

He was gone about fifteen minutes. I was sitting on the edge of my chair with incredible excitement rising in my chest. It was the same screw who had given me the Player's the night before and, when he opened me up and handed me this brown paper bag, honest to God he looked to me like Father Christmas.

14

My Father behind Bars

All that Sunday the sky was heavy with cloud and I kept looking out, hoping for the rain to stay off just long enough to give me a few minutes in the exercise yard. I spent the time clumsily rolling cigarettes that turned out either too tight or too loose – until at last the screws opened me up.

It had been my door they came to first. I was taken out by the regulation escort, two screws plus a dog handler. The dog was let run around the perimeter as I walked alone in the open air up the middle of the exercise yard. It was the first time since I'd been at home in Belfast, eight days earlier, that I'd been able to breathe fresh air. Gratefully I took deep lungfuls of it.

I was not alone for long. I heard the perimeter gate squeak behind me and I swung round. They were bringing Paul to join me. I hurried back and we met half-way.

'What's going on? What are we doing in here? How did this happen, Benny?'

Paul turned me round and we began walking away from where his pair of screws stood talking to mine. He spoke in a low voice.

'This is not the time to talk about it. We don't want the screws hearing us.'

'Never mind that, what the fuck are we doing in gaol? I never killed nobody in my life? What am I doing on a murder charge? It all started with you, Benny. Tell me what's going on!'

But he wouldn't tell me. He kept shutting me up and going on about the screws overhearing us. He did say, though, that they'd threatened to charge his girl-friend, Gina.

'Don't worry, Gerry. It'll be all right, OK?'

'OK, but I only wish I knew what the fuck's been going on.'

Exercise came to an end with me none the wiser. I went back in, half thinking maybe it would be all right, and when I got to the cell I saw a prison letter-form on the table. My heart jumped. It meant I could write a letter, write to my mum and dad, tell them I was innocent. I sat down ready and eager to write, and immediately jumped up again. I rang the bell.

'I haven't got a pen.'

The screw brought me a prison pen and I sat down again. I wrote on the printed lines at the top, as instructed, *To Mr and Mrs Patrick Conlon, 32 Cyprus Street, Belfast 12.* Then I moved the pen into the blank space underneath. *Dear Mum and Dad.*

I sat looking at the letter, one sheet of paper. How could I explain what had happened to me on one sheet of paper? I couldn't even explain it to myself. How could I explain my innocence? It was such an enormous charge against me and I only had one small piece of paper.

Defeated, I left it lying there on the table.

It must have been half past six, after we'd slopped out, that it started to rain. Then I heard Paul calling me out the window and I got up to talk to him. The arc lights mounted on the roof of the hospital wing on the other side of the exercise yard shone down and illuminated the rain bouncing off the concrete.

Paul was calling out through the rain. 'Don't be worrying, Gerry. Everything will be all right. I'll explain first opportunity I get, but don't be worrying. I haven't done this bombing either.'

It was the first time he'd said it to me, that he was innocent. Up till then I hadn't known what to think. I knew neither of us bombed Guildford. So now I thought, this is going to sort itself out. How will they ever prove we did it? That thought came from my ignorance. I was so ignorant of the English courts and the English police. In Ireland it was simple: a policeman either shot you dead, beat you up or had you interned. But this, I thought, was England, home of *Dixon of Dock Green* and *Z Cars*. The RUC and the Ulster courts were perfectly capable of corruption, but even after Addlestone and Godalming, I still had this belief in English justice and decency. Wasn't it on the TV all through my childhood? So to me innocence equalled Not Guilty in an English court. That was how naïve I was.

Prisoners, even remand prisoners, can never afford to be naïve for long, and I was beginning to wise up, at least about what it took to survive in there. I had already worked out a few of my own ground-rules, making important decisions about keeping my dignity and self-respect – I wouldn't shit in that pot, I wouldn't call those bastards sir. Something new was taking me over, I was becoming a different person in Winchester, because the full weight of my position was on me. I had to stand up for myself, there was no running home to ma and dad, no refuge with uncles and aunts.

When I was first remanded to Winchester I saw David Walsh and told him I had excruciating pain in my kidneys and was getting nothing to ease the pain. I saw the prison doctor, but he prescribed me absolutely nothing – I didn't trust the prison doctor at all. I also wrote to my family about it. When they got my letter, they wrote to David Walsh as well, asking him if he could do anything. He wrote back to say that if they wanted an independent doctor they would have to pay for him to come and see me. Of course, they couldn't afford it. After a month, the pain passed but I was in absolute agony. Even today, I have problems with my kidneys.

The rest of the week wasn't as bad as the first two days. I started to feel less frightened and intimidated. Still they tried to get me to call them Sir, and I wouldn't. Paul was calling them Boss, like you do on a building site. I called them Mister or nothing at all.

After seven days it was time for our remand to be renewed. It had dragged past like a year, but we were beginning to understand how we could survive the long wait until we came to trial. Back in court, suddenly there were more of us: Paddy Armstrong, Carole Richardson, and Annie Maguire stood up with us in the dock to be re-manded once more, this time for a couple of days.

Annie looked in a bad state, though we never had the chance to talk. After it was over Paddy came back with us in the van, the women went to Brixton. Paddy had been arrested on the 3rd of December. He'd been held at Guildford and questioned all the next day. The police had frightened him into admitting his guilt, just as they had with Paul and me. Like us, Paddy was sure none of the statements would stand up in court.

Two days later we were back in court and there were more of us again: John McGuinness, Paul Colman and Brian Anderson, all from

Kilburn, were up for remand with us, all charged with Guildford, all remanded for another seven days. The block at Winchester was beginning to fill up.

The first time we were on exercise together was like a free-for-all, we were all at each other trying to get information.

'What the fuck is all this?'

'How am I in here?'

'The worst I ever done is smoke a bit of weed.'

'The worst I ever done is steal a few quid.'

We were all going from one person to another asking the same questions and saying the same things: we were innocent. Gradually there was a common understanding between all of us. We're not in the IRA, because the IRA would never have people like us. So we must be acquitted because they can never make a case against the whole lot of us. They would check out our backgrounds, see they had drop-outs, dope smokers, thieves, and say Jesus Christ, we've picked up the wrong people.

That night I went to bed feeling a lot better, got up the next morning with this great feeling of solidarity. We all had showers and now that there were six of us the screws had their work cut out. They could no longer have it their own way. One or two of us had visitors and things were brought in. So during slop-out John or Brian would leave a present at my door, a packet of crisps, bar of chocolate, can of coke. These were the first welcome contacts with the outside.

My mother sent me in some money, but I had no visits and I was wondering why not. My father was ill, but I was convinced he would go through hell to get me out of trouble. I couldn't know how horribly right that was.

I had been in the exercise yard about ten minutes on the Sunday, walking apart for a moment, thinking about football and yesterday's results, and how good it would be to have a ball with us and be able to play. Then I heard it.

'Gerry!'

It was a voice that I knew. I looked around, it wasn't any of the others calling me.

'Gerry! Gerry!'

There was a hammering and rattling noise.

'Hey! Gerry!'

More banging, a dull noise like on window glass, and I did know the voice – it sounded like my *father*. But how could it be him? That was the one impossible thing. I looked at the others, but nobody else seemed to hear anything. I walked on.

I came round to the same spot again and, I don't know why, I looked up towards the hospital block. Standing there in one of the windows, with his hands gripping the bars, was my father.

'Gerry! Gerry!'

My heart stopped. For a moment I could not comprehend, and then I gripped the fence and shook it. I'd have climbed it if that had been possible, I'd have been up there to him.

'What are *you* doing here? What are you in here for?'

And I thought of Annie Maguire and Hughie Maguire, and how both of them had been arrested. But they were in England. What had my father to do with this? What's he doing behind bars?

I heard his muffled voice calling down.

'They put stuff on my hands.'

Then I knew what had happened. He'd come over for me. He'd come over, as he always had before, to get his son out of a hole. And they'd pulled him in on top of me.

When he knew I'd been taken to England my father first tried to arrange legal representation for me and then, sick as he had been for years with T.B., booked himself on the first boat to Heysham. A Belfast solicitor named Ted Jones was supposed to go along with him, but he didn't turn up and Dad sailed alone.

When he got to London he tried to contact Hughie, but with no result, because unknown to anyone except the police Hughie, Kate and their lodger Maureen were all arrested. So my father went to Paddy Maguire's house in Third Avenue to see if he could stay there. By the evening they had still not contacted Hughie, though my father did talk to David Walsh at the solicitors. About seven, he and Paddy went for a drink with Sean Smyth, Annie's brother, and Pat O'Neill, a friend of the Maguires who was there to leave his children in Annie's care as his wife was in hospital and he was about to go to work on the night shift. My father had an appointment with David Walsh in the morning, and was planning to move heaven and earth to see me as soon as he could. No one had realized the effect of the Prevention of Terrorism Act, and they all thought he'd be able to. But while they were there, in the pub, the bomb squad raided the house. They were looking for Aunt Annie's bomb factory. They found the Maguire Seven.

Everyone was arrested. The four men were arrested as soon as they got back from the pub. Annie was arrested with my cousins Vincent, aged fifteen and Patrick, aged thirteen. All seven of them were questioned about explosives, and all had swab tests done on their hands to see if they'd handled nitro-glycerine. All the swab tests came out positive, except for Annie Maguire's. Subsequently, swab tests were held on gloves that were thought to be hers, which came out positive.

When I got back to my cell there was another prison letter waiting for me and I found the shock of seeing my father had removed the block I had about writing letters. I sat down and wrote to my mother, crying my heart out to her, saying I'd seen my father, how bad I felt, and saying please believe I didn't do what I'd been accused of. But I felt enormous guilt, because I knew my father could only have come to England because of me. It was my fault he was in here.

Next morning the governor came round and I told him I wanted to see my father. He said, 'But he's in the prison hospital.'

'Yes, I know. I want to see my father.'

'That's for me to decide, Conlon. You must make a formal application and I'll consider it.'

That afternoon I got a call from the prison psychiatrist, wanting to see me in the hospital to make a report for the magistrates' court about my sanity. I tried to get this shrink to come in on my side about my father, but he wouldn't. Next thing I knew, the following day, was that my application to see him had been refused on medical grounds.

In the middle of that week the screws opened me up and said, 'Visit.'

It was unexpected. I'd seen David Walsh earlier in the week – he hadn't been able to help me see my father either – so I thought it might be him coming back. It wasn't. As I testified at the trial, I walked into the room and found Rowe and Simmons from the Surrey police, waiting for me.

When I saw Simmons I went mad, I went across the table for him.

'Youse bastards. What sort of people would put stuff on a sick man's hands? That's what my father's says was done.'

I never found out what they wanted because the interview more or less ended there. I yelled and shouted at them, saying I was innocent and my father was innocent, and they backed off. Then the screws took me back to my cell.

I didn't see my father until we all went back to court for the remand hearing on the Friday. He was there looking pale and ill, and breathing with difficulty.

'Is there anything in this, son?'

'I haven't done this. I'm innocent, dad. I'm as innocent as you.'

My dad knew me, he knew me as a baby, a little boy, a teenager. He knew when I was lying and when I was telling the truth. And he believed me.

15
Transferred to Brixton

When I saw him at court my father told me the story of what had happened to him and the Maguires. Unknown to those of us in C Wing punishment block – me and Paul Colman – four of those who had been charged along with my father were being held in a different wing at Winchester. These were Paddy Maguire (my uncle), Sean Smyth (Annie Maguire's brother), and Pat O'Neill (a family friend) and Sean Mullin (a flat-mate of John McGuinness and Brian Anderson). These men were all being held in Winchester's other punishment block on A Wing. So here were ten innocent men being held in the worst possible conditions, while my father was in the prison hospital, more or less in quarantine. I could only get to see him when we went to court for our weekly remand hearings. Even then, sometimes he'd be too sick to go.

None of us could explain why this disaster had fallen on us. It utterly devastated the Maguire family, it played havoc with the lives of McGuinness, Anderson, Colman, Sean Mullin, and it entirely took away the youth of Paul, Carole, Paddy and myself. And in the end it even brought about a tragic and innocent death. But that was still in the unknown future.

The charade of weekly remand hearings went on while the police prepared their case for the committal proceedings. Meanwhile, every time we went to Guildford for remand appearances, they'd be waiting for us outside the court, the mob of men but mostly women. They'd have nooses and placards reading HANG THE MURDERING BASTARDS and STRING THEM UP, and they'd be screaming at us raw hatred as we passed in the prison van. We were all still frightened, but were

114

Top: Me as a child with my father
Bottom: My father, Guiseppe Conlon

Top: Sir Michael Havers, QC, MP, leading counsel for the prosecution
Bottom: Sir John Donaldson, Guildford trial judge

Top: Detective
Inspector Tim Blake, an
investigating officer
of the Guildford
pub bombing
Bottom: Detective
Superintendent
Peter Imbert

Top: This picture of me was taken by a prison warder in Gartree Prison, 1988. It was the first photograph taken of me for fourteen years.
Bottom: Vincent Maguire

probably beginning to overcome our fears as we were all together on these two blocks. There seemed to be a strength in numbers, which probably gave us more confidence in dealing with the situation, and the screws. It made it harder for the screws to intimidate and take liberties as they had been doing in the beginning.

But the hostile atmosphere wherever we were, in prison or out, generated a growing hatred and bitterness in us, as the weeks dragged by. I felt it all the more because of my father, who I would see most weeks at the court struggling to breathe, going slowly up and down the stairs. He seemed so frail that it seemed unbelievable he was being put through this. But he and I weren't alone. There were fourteen people remanded to prison for these offences at that time, all innocent and all victims of the Surrey Constabulary and the Metropolitan Police's desperate need to find scapegoats. Patrick and Vincent, the young Maguires, were charged later, on 24 February 1975.

I felt the anger growing inside myself, overcoming the intimidation of the law, and I'd make outbursts in court. I'd shout out, 'I'm an innocent man, I shouldn't be here.' Also I'd abuse the police if they came near me, calling them bastard torturers and telling them they'd fitted me up along with my father.

They were probably trying hard to get more evidence against us before the committal, but there was none. All they had were the swab tests on the Maguire Seven and the confessions extracted from Paul, Paddy, Carole and me. No one else had confessed, although Brian Anderson told me he'd been on the verge of it, at Guildford. He was feeling like saying that he had taken part in the Guildford bombing and making a statement, when the copper interrogating him was called out to the phone. During this phone call Brian had a chance to recover his composure and call on whatever strength he had left to resist. If it wasn't for that telephone call it would probably have been the Guildford Five – and Brian Anderson was a Protestant.

In the end, murder and conspiracy charges were dropped against Anderson, Mullin, Colman and McGuinness, and one by one they were let go. Also the police gave up trying to frame my Aunt Annie for murder at Guildford, though they continued to press the case against her and the other six for handling explosives.

I had had a few meetings with my solicitor in the meantime, and one very positive thing had come out of them. David Walsh told me that, if I was not at Guildford on the day of the bombing, then I must have been somewhere else. In the interests of my own defence I *must* remember where, and what I was doing. So I said, very confidently, 'No problem. I was at the Carousel Ballroom. That was the night the Wolfhounds played, and I went there with Paul Hill and met my aunt Annie and Hughie and Kate.'

Looking rather pleased David Walsh went away to check it out. But next time he came, he had a long face on him again.

'I've got bad news, I'm afraid. The dance at the Carousel was on Friday the 11th of October and the Guildford bombing was on Saturday the 5th. So your alibi is in a mess unless you can establish what you did on that day.'

I was desperately disappointed. What a wonderful alibi it had seemed, because it included Kate Maguire and Paul Hill, and there would have been scores of witnesses to back it up. When I first thought that was the night of the bombing I reckoned I was going home and it was just a matter of time.

Walsh tried again. He asked me to try and remember everything, but when I came to the day in question, I was stuck. All I knew at first was, it was a Saturday. What had happened on Saturdays? For a start Paul Hill went down to Southampton to see Gina Clarke. He did that several Saturdays. What else did I do on Saturdays? Went to the pub, went to the bookies . . . The bookies! In a flash I thought of something. I asked David Walsh, 'Get me a newspaper for October the 5th, any paper as long as it has sports coverage.'

I was thinking, this is a stroke of luck, because the one thing I can always remember is the name of a horse I've backed. So he returned next time with the newspaper and I turned straight to the racing page, running my finger down the runners of the day. My finger stopped at a horse in the two-fifteen race at Newmarket. His name was John Cherry. It had been a two-mile flat race, a stayer's handicap, and I'd had four quid on him at 17–2. He'd won.

Suddenly the whole day came back to me as fresh as yesterday: October the 5th, the day John Cherry won for me.

It starts with Paul Hill getting up before me, and bringing in some breakfast, a bun and some milk which we eat sitting on our beds. Then we take our washing down to the basement of the hostel where there are two washing-machines and a spin-drier. I probably sit there studying the racing and noting down a few horses – including this

John Cherry – while Paul goes to the dry-cleaners. When our washing's done we go down to Woolworths in Kilburn High Road and get some shaving gear. Then we go back to the hostel, have a wash and shave and sit around waiting for the pubs to open.

We're in the Memphis Belle by eleven, having our first pint of the day. Suddenly I spot Paddy Carey going past in the street with his bird, and knock on the window to invite them in. Paddy has a lager and his bird a coke, and we play a few records on the jukebox.

After about twenty minutes Paul sees Danny Wilson passing by, and jumps up to go and see him. Danny is a ginger-haired guy who comes from a big family in the Lower Falls. His older brother Barney is an ex-boxer, now a referee. But Danny is barred from the Memphis Belle so he says he'll see us across the way in the Olde Bell later on.

Paddy Carey leaves with his girl to go on some sightseeing bus tour, so Paul and I cross the street to the Olde Bell. Paddy Armstrong is in there, along with a fellow called Ninty who's stoned out of his head and raving about being Jesus.

Then Danny Wilson comes strolling in with two mates, a Belfast man and a Jock. It's the first time Danny and I have bumped into each other in England, but of course I know him back home. They sit down with us, but the barman comes over and says Danny's mates are both barred because of the fight they'd started the night before. So they leave. Then Ninty sits down with us, but keeps falling off his stool. We haul him over to a bench-seat by the wall and prop him up on that. We next see two fellows putting up posters for the concert by the Wolfhounds at the Carousel Ballroom the next weekend. This is a Belfast group which we all know, and Paul buys a couple of tickets from the two men.

After Paul has left to catch his train for Southampton, Paddy and I start shuttling back and forth between the pub and the betting shop. My selection wins the two-fifteen race ridden by Geoff Lewis, but I can't get another touch that day. By four o'clock, I leave Paddy in the bookie's and go back to the café beside the Memphis Belle and then go back to the hostel. I've had at least six or seven pints by this time, so I just collapse on my bed and fall asleep.

At some point Paddy Carey comes in and hands me a bag of cassette tapes and a player that belong to his bird. Around the same time Paul the Greengrocer comes in from work in his trilby hat. I'm still half pissed from the afternoon. Later, I go into the TV room, where I see Paddy Carey's friend Joe O'Brien, with a black eye he got in a pub fight the night before. About nine I go to the phone in the hostel and dial the number of the Engineers' Club in Belfast, where I hope my father will be with my aunt Bridget. I've worked out this scheme of getting a pound's worth of free phone call by telling the operator that when I put my money in it hasn't worked. But the pound isn't enough, because when I get through my father is at the bar and with his lungs he can't get down to the telephone fast enough.

I go back into the TV room until about half past ten, and then to bed. Nothing about the Guildford bombing sticks in my memory until the next day, when Paul comes back to say his train was diverted through the town.

I was pleased to have finally remembered the events of that day. I remembered the doubts I'd had back in Godalming police station, writing those statements, saying those things I'd been doing in Guildford and not being able to remember what I'd *really* been doing on that day. Now I knew what I'd been doing, and all thanks to a horse called John Cherry.

We, the Guildford Four, went for our committal hearing on St Patrick's Day, 1975. It was held in the impressive surroundings of the Guildford Guildhall and now for the first time I saw the prosecution's junior barrister, Michael Hill. He scared the daylights out of me. He looked like Al Pacino in *The Godfather*, another Michael, and he was very impressive, very compelling. Here, I thought, is a man who can really make a cock-and-bull story sound like gospel. He had the court enrapt with the tale he was telling about us – we were cast as arch plotters, bombers, murderers, the works.

Our side said very little, their only interest was in getting the trial held out of Guildford, where they didn't think we could get a fair trial. In the end it was set for the Old Bailey, on a date to be fixed. Paddy Maguire was delighted it was the Bailey.

'Don't you be worrying, boys,' he'd say. 'The Old Bailey is the fairest court in Britain, and British courts are the fairest in the world. We'll be home safe and sound.'

A couple of days later we were moved to Brixton.

It wasn't until I was at Brixton that I really understood what everyday existence for a Category A prisoner is supposed to be. At Winchester there were no special facilities, so the punishment block had been set aside for us, which meant we were living according to a regime of punishment rather than high security. We had no indoor association on the block and we met no other prisoners.

At Brixton, A Wing is for remand prisoners, but those who are thought to be security risks go into a special unit within it known as A Segregation. This is annexed from a part of the wing, a little Fort Knox but built for men instead of gold. To enter A Seg you are taken through the normal wing and up to the third floor and a small door. A screen is pulled back and you're checked out by the screw, who then opens up. Inside there are two landings, the ones and the twos, with sixteen cells to each landing and one man to each cell.

We were shown our cells, put down our kit, and the first thing we noticed was they didn't lock the doors immediately behind us, as they would have done on the block in Winchester. We went out and got water together instead of one by one, and the screws were wandering around the same as we were wandering around. We stood there looking at each other, scratching our heads and thinking should we go back into our cells or what. But we didn't, we started talking together outside the cells on the landing there, standing in little groups. The screws didn't say anything because we were on association, except we didn't know it.

Everything in A Seg is done by landings – slop-out, exercise, association – and on that first day, when we arrived, our landing was on association. When we looked down over the landing rail we saw the other prisoners sitting at the tables, playing cards, talking among themselves. It wasn't until the next day, though, that we went down amongst them. We understood the routine by then, and we trooped down the stairs together. Suddenly everything froze, there was a deadly silence. The other prisoners looked at us and we looked at them, and then after a few seconds they resumed their card games and chatted as if nothing happened, as if we weren't there.

But gradually we got to know them, and the atmosphere relaxed. These were all men awaiting trial for serious crimes, armed robbery, murder, fraud. Some of them like us would say they were innocent, while others were real hard men who'd been through this before. But they weren't outwardly hostile to any of us, and we found that we could get along with them perfectly well.

So we settled in at Brixton and it was an improvement. I was on association with my father and the others for two and a half hours every day, the regime was much more relaxed, the place was cleaner. The prisoners were quite friendly to us, but I still had some problems with some of the screws.

One incident springs to mind, and this was the first time I rebelled. My mother couldn't afford to come and see me and my da, but she would send us parcels every week of cigarettes, biscuits, Irish newspapers and sweets. We used to look forward to these parcels, which my mum would wrap up really carefully; we also knew that she couldn't really afford this.

Anyway, one day I was in the showers and the parcel had arrived. A screw who was particularly nasty came down to my father who was playing cards with the others. This screw put the parcel on the table and then put his fingers in his ears and ran a short distance to hide behind another table as if it was a bomb. My father – understandably – became very upset and turned on him, swearing at him. As I've said, my father was a very mild-mannered character, but all the frustration he'd been feeling for months just came out. He told this screw he was an innocent man who knew nothing about bombs.

I came out of the showers a bit later, not knowing what had happened. As I was getting dressed, a London prisoner on remand for robbery (for which he was later acquitted) who'd become a friend of my father's came into my cell and told me what had happened. Another friendly prisoner had just given me half a grapefruit. Just like my father, all the anger inside me came bursting out. I went looking for this screw.

I found him in the office sitting behind his desk. I started to give him loads of abuse and he made some flippant remark about the Irish and bombs. That was it. I stuck the grapefruit straight in his face, and went behind the desk to attack him. He tried to take refuge in the little kneehole under the desk, and I just starting kicking him until the other screws came out and threw me into the punishment. The next day I was given twenty-eight days' punishment; no cigarettes, no radio and in solitary.

After three months, they came and collected Paul Hill. It was not until after Paul was gone, that I had for the first time a copy of all the statements made in the police station. By then it was too late to find out answers to questions I then had. He was flown immediately back to Ireland, to face a charge of murdering an Englishman, an ex-soldier, in Belfast – a charge quite separate from the Guildford bombing. The murder had happened in July the previous year. The IRA had apparently found the man drinking in a pub in the middle of the Divis flats, taken him away and executed him as an Army spy. Now Paul Hill was taken away to stand trial before one of Northern Ireland's jury-less Diplock courts, accused of the killing.

We knew little of the allegations. When in July we heard of his conviction, and that he had got a life sentence, it was a terrible setback to all of us. We all felt terribly sorry for him as we knew he was convicted of something he didn't do. The feeling returned that it could happen to us here in London, a feeling which even Paddy Maguire, with all his enthusiasm for the Old Bailey, couldn't erase.

David Walsh continued to visit me from time to time as he prepared my defence. I am sure he was doing his best, but I could tell he found it overwhelming.

The legal team assembled for me seemed impressive at the beginning. The Queen's Counsel they briefed was Lord Wigoder. Having a Lord, a member of the British Establishment, taking my side seemed a genuine bonus, but a terrible shock was in store for me.

I'll never forget the first time I was taken in to see him. It was a hot August night in Brixton and we'd had that warm summer rain, making the air feel cleansing as I walked across the exercise yard towards the meeting. It was late, about half past six, and the whole of Brixton was banged up except me. I was on my way to see the people who were going to defend me and put right this stinking injustice once and for all. I felt good about it. They would be my knights in shining armour, or the US cavalry charging over the hill just before the Indians scalp me.

I was taken down a little underground corridor, sky-blue walls it had, like being in a submarine, and off it was a small room. David Walsh was there, and my junior counsel Gordon Ward, who I liked the look of straight away. I can't say the same for Wigoder, though. He was very aristocratic, very haughty, as remote from me as you can be. We shook hands and it was as if I'd made his hand dirty, as if he might catch something. Then somebody started us off, talking about my chances in the trial, and when I asked Wigoder what he thought, he replied in his clipped, Oxford tones, 'Do you want me to be honest with you?'

'I do.'

'It's a very difficult case. You must understand that it will be tremendously difficult to secure your release in the face of this mass of evidence against you.'

I could hardly believe what I was hearing.

'What do you mean? Do you mean I'm going to prison or what? Because I'm innocent, I've done nothing wrong.'

I don't think I will ever forget his next words because they shook me to the core.

'That may very well be the case, Mr Conlon. But the evidence suggests otherwise.'

I tried to swallow. My mouth must have been parched dry.

'And you think I'll be found guilty?'

'On the evidence presented, I think you will.'

'So how long am I going to prison for?'

'Well, a life sentence would be mandatory, and I would presume that there would be a very long recommendation.'

'A recommendation? What do you mean?'

'The judge will recommend that you spend a certain minimum length of time in prison.'

'How long?'

'I would say it will probably be at least thirty years.'

That was my first meeting with the man briefed to argue for my innocence.

16
Trial Over

On Tuesday, 16 September, Paddy Armstrong and me were taken to reception as it was the day our trial started. We were both shitting ourselves but trying to put on a brave face. In reception, we saw a screw reading the *Sun* and another reading the *Mirror* and both had headlines like 'Snipers Guard the Old Bailey as Bombers Go On Trial'. According to the newspapers, we were already guilty before we'd even got to the Old Bailey.

We were then handcuffed and placed in an armoured vehicle and as the gates of Brixton opened there were police cars everywhere. Paul Hill was already handcuffed in the van. It was the first we'd seen of him since he'd left Brixton to go and face the other charge in Belfast. Each of us was locked into an individual cubicle within the van. All the way from Brixton, the police sirens were going and our convoy was going through red lights. People in the street were stopping and staring. As we neared the Old Bailey we could see crowds of photographers. We drove in by the back entrance, down a long slope on to a metal turntable which turned the van completely around. The screws unlocked our cubicles one at a time. Paul first, then me and Paddy third. We were taken up by the bridge, the chain linking our handcuffs, and checked off against a list as we went into the Old Bailey and taken up fifteen or twenty flights of stairs to the top landing and locked into separate cells.

I was hoping beyond hope that we would get a fair trial, that what we had to say wouldn't be rejected out of hand. Here I was, somebody from the Falls Road about to do verbal battle with some of the best legal brains in the country – I prayed the jury would see us as we really were. I was terrified.

I was there for about half an hour and then I was visited by Gordon Ward, my junior counsel, and David Walsh. They told me they would try their best. I remember saying, 'I'm innocent. Do you believe I'm innocent?' And they both said, yes. This was a comfort.

Ten minutes before the court was to sit, we were all taken down a little corridor, turned left and saw Carole sitting on a little bench guarded by two screwesses. Carole was putting on a brave face as well. We all tried to comfort each other by saying everything would be all right. But I think we all knew we stood very little chance.

When the four of us were sent up the stairs in Court Number Two at the Old Bailey I remember my hand gripping the cold metal handrail. It had the same feeling as the scaffolding I used to work on with my Uncle Hughie. My legs were shaking and I wanted to piss my trousers, I was so scared.

We stood together in the dock, looking out over the well of the court. But everyone was looking at us. The public gallery was full, the press gallery was full, the well of the court was crammed with all these robed lawyers wearing wigs, and all these court officials. Only the jury box was empty and the judge's seat.

Lily Hill was there, but not my mother. She couldn't afford to come, she'd have lost her job. No one from my family was there. There was none of Paddy's family either. So we didn't have that feeling of much support out there, just the weight of the English Establishment gathering itself together to make sure it crushed us once and for all.

The judge made his entrance looking fearsome in his long wig and red robes. This was Mr Justice (now Lord) Donaldson. I later found out he had never before conducted a criminal trial at the Old Bailey, having had most of his experience in industrial relations and commercial cases. So it was a first time for all of us.

The clerk of the court read out the charges against us, in language I only half understood: 'You are charged in an indictment containing eleven counts. In the first count you are all four charged that on days between the 1st of November, 1973, and the 4th of December 1974, whilst within Her Majesty's dominions, you unlawfully and maliciously conspired together and with other persons unknown to cause by explosive substances explosions in the United Kingdom . . .'

There were three pages of this, and we had to plead guilty or not guilty to each charge. I could hardly do more than whisper 'Not guilty' each time. Carole and Paddy were equally frightened, but Paul was different. He'd come back from Northern Ireland already convicted of the other murder, and he'd gone to Wandsworth, where they were giving him a very hard time. We had got together tobacco to give him when we saw him, and it really cheered him, he was very defiant, unlike the rest of us. So he stood up and they asked him, How do you plead to the first charge? He flicked back his hair and said, 'I refuse to take part in this. Your justice stinks.'

He refused to say anything to the other charges, though his brief put up a not guilty plea for him. He must have been very nervous inside to come out with anything like that, because it was a stereotype of a Republican response, not recognizing the court. So it couldn't have been a much worse start for us.

Then the jury was sworn in. It was all male, and there was nothing much else to read into them except that there were two black guys among them. I saw this as a wee gee, a tiny sign of hope, because in prison the blacks and Irish have good relations and you could be sure, at least, they wouldn't be best friends with the police. Then the trial began. It lasted altogether for five weeks.

The man leading for the Crown was Sir Michael Havers QC, the Conservative MP. As he made his opening speech, so elegantly and fluently, I was already beginning to feel the unreality of it, as if I had taken up a position outside myself and was looking down from somewhere near the ceiling at a court-room drama instead of a real trial, *my* trial. Havers spent two days spelling out the prosecution's case, the same tale which I'd heard from Michael Hill, the prosecution's junior counsel, at the committal but in much more detail.

Then he started calling witnesses, people who had been mutilated in the Horse and Groom, who'd lost limbs, who'd been scarred and traumatized by it. You could hear the audible gasps from the gallery as they came one by one into the witness-box, where Havers would take them through the events of that night nearly a year ago.

At times I tried to get these witnesses to look at me, so that I could convey to them somehow with my eyes that we didn't do this. Something terrible has happened to you, but we're not the ones who did it.

None of these witnesses actually picked us out in court, they were never even asked. There was evidence heard that a man and a woman had planted one of the bombs, a courting couple. The couple was seen by several witnesses, but none of us three men were ever put on identity parades. Carole, who was supposed to have been the girl in this bombing pair, had actually been put on identity parades in front of several of the witnesses and no one had picked her out.

Then into the box came the police, telling how the four of us confessed to the bombings. I would watch these policemen intently, catching all their idiosyncrasies, the shaking of a wrist, the touching of the watch, the twiddling of a ring on the finger. They came over very impressively, very calm and dignified in their uniforms, suits, blazers, club ties, hands resting on the sides of the witness-box, chests out, shoulders back, faces looking as if butter wouldn't melt in their mouths. They were very professional in the witness-box, and they denied everything we had said about their treatment of us. Asked did they lean on us, beat us, ill-treat us, they said, 'Certainly not.' If it was Wigoder cross-examining they'd remember his title, and it would be, 'No, My Lord.' Compared with that, what sort of sorry figure was I going to cut in the box – twenty years old, thick accent, long hair, denims?

After a while it gets very difficult to sit and listen to what I knew were lies. In the dock we used to whisper jokes to each other, or we'd just switch off for long periods, playing pencil-and-paper games. We even played hangman.

There were a few wee gees from the cross-examinations, though. When Detective Inspector Blake was in the witness-box Wigoder put it to him he'd battered me. Blake denied it, saying he'd never even set eyes on me until our committal. But I'd seen his tattoos at Godalming, when he rolled up his sleeves to do the business on me, and I'd told Wigoder about them. So Wigoder made Blake roll up his sleeves. He showed the tattoos and the court could see how accurately I had described them. Blake's explanation – that I might have caught sight of him in shirtsleeves in the police station – sounded very limp.

There was another time I remember where Wigoder did well with Jermey. On top of the signed statements, Jermey had produced twenty pages of verbals, the record of my interrogation at Godalming, the questions and answers. All of it was incriminatory, and none of it, naturally, showed the smallest wee hint of police brutality. Wigoder asked him when he wrote these notes, and he said it was done seven hours later. Wigoder said something like, 'You must have a phenomenal memory to get everything in there in sequence.'

In reply Jermey was talking about how there was more to a policeman's job than meets the eye, and one of the skills was an accurate memory, when Wigoder suddenly interrupted him with – 'What was the first question I put to you in the witness-box?'

Jermey couldn't remember. He had just claimed to be able to remember a thirteen-hour interrogation session word for word seven hours after it finished, but he couldn't repeat a question put to him just a few minutes earlier.

It was good to have these moments, because I was going back to Seg A in Brixton each night, and my father would rush up to me to say, 'Gerry! How's it going?'

'Oh, it's going well, dad. Looking good. Jermey looked a right prat in the witness-box today.'

I was telling white lies. The truth was, I felt more and more convinced that Wigoder had been only too right when he'd given me his gloomy prediction. Without the intervention of Jesus Christ in this trial, we were going down.

But I still had to go into the witness-box. Paul had again got our defence off on the wrong foot by being flippant when he gave his evidence, refusing to answer questions, answering sarcastically or with other questions. Paddy didn't seem to improve things. He stuck to his guns all right, but he sat there in the box almost in coma, mumbling and bumbling along in the thickest Lower Falls accent you can imagine. Then it was my turn.

It felt almost like going to sit in the electric chair, they opened the little door in the dock and I had to walk down past the jury, up into the witness-box, trembling in every limb, knowing that my accent would be hard for them to understand, knowing I was wearing jeans. I was totally intimidated. Every time I looked up at the judge I could see the enormous sword behind him and to me it represented the terrible death I was going to die here in the Old Bailey, giving my evidence.

Wigoder asked me about growing up in Belfast, coming to England, who I'd been with, what my jobs were. He asked me to detail what I'd been doing on the day of the Guildford bombings and I did so, trying to speak up and make myself believable. He asked me for my account of my arrest and questioning by the police. That part was hard, I had to speak publicly about how I'd been abused and threatened, how I'd cried and then cracked. Wigoder was efficient and patient. But I could still sense that detachment in him. When Paddy's QC had questioned him there was the feeling of sympathy between them. From Wigoder for me I felt none.

But I thought I was beginning to do better when, suddenly, I was pulled out of the box because two of Paul's witnesses, who had been deferred from the day before, turned up. So just as I was getting used to the ordeal, I had to go back to the dock and listen to a lot of evidence that was irrelevant to me, knowing I was going back an hour or more later to pick up the threads.

When I did it was Sir Michael Havers's turn. Of him, at least, I wasn't really afraid – in fact I preferred the thought of being cross-examined by him than by his junior Michael Hill. I had noticed Havers had a twitch in his eye, which made him seem to be winking when he got excited. Sitting in the dock a few times earlier in the trial I'd be doing it back at him, and at least once I know he saw because he flushed and looked hurriedly away. It was a tiny wee sign of weakness which made it possible for me to face up to him.

Even so I was having great difficulty controlling my nerves. There was a moment when he didn't catch something I said and asked me to repeat myself. I felt like snapping back, 'Are you deaf or something?' I just managed to suppress it.

At one point I told Havers, 'Look, it doesn't matter if I'm innocent or guilty. At the end of the day you people need someone to send to prison and you're doing it to me.'

He ended by trying to say that I had deliberately made my confession riddled with inconsistencies because I wanted to pull the wool over a jury's eyes.

'I have no need to pull the wool over a jury's eyes,' I said. 'I am telling the truth.'

'Did you enjoy leading the gang which blew up these people in Guildford?'

'I'd never been in Guildford till the police took me there. If they'd told me to put down the Pope's name as one of the bombers, I would have done it. I'd have put down anybody's name to save my ma.'

As I got down, I could see Lily Hill in the public gallery starting to cry, and I thought of my mother. It would have killed her to be there, to have heard me describe all the things that had happened to me. I was glad she wasn't. I had been describing how they had beaten and humiliated me, things I would be prevented from saying normally in front of my mother – or in front of any woman. I have never told her even to this day what actually happened to me in Springfield Road and Godalming police stations, because I am too deeply ashamed and embarrassed for what they did to me.

I left the box and my defence was over. We produced no alibi witness – we thought we had Paddy Carey, but the court was told he failed to turn up – there are no other witnesses, and that was it. Gerry Conlon's defence and alibi over in the blink of an eye, just a couple of hours at the end of a five-week trial. My brief sat down.

The summing-up was typical of my feelings about the whole trial. Donaldson went on about our backgrounds in Belfast. He told the jury they had to decide who they believed, the policemen with twenty years' service or us.

'It's for you to decide,' he kept saying, over and over again for two days.

I thought it was like Pontius Pilate, washing his hands. The judge should have realized we were innocent. Instead he put the onus on twelve people who must in the end have been overawed by the police and bamboozled by a lot of big words and court-room mumbo-jumbo. When you read the summing-up now it seems fair. But when you were there, in court, listening to it – to the way he put emphasis and weight on different words, to the way he leaned forward or sat back in his chair, or looked over his half-moon glasses at certain points in a certain way – then it wasn't fair. It was weighted, surely and fatally, against us.

The jury could not agree in the time left to them that day and were sent to sleep in a hotel. We went back to Brixton where my father was already banged up. So I got the screws to let me into his cell, and they allowed me to be with him for a good twenty minutes. So there I was telling him it would be all right, and him saying the same, but I had an awful feeling of dread that night. I couldn't sleep very much, I was thinking myself into the heads of those jurors and wondering how well they were sleeping that night.

Next morning it was the usual routine; we went out, got our breakfast, had a wash. When they came for me with the handcuffs to go out to the Category A van, I asked a screw could I see my dad. He gave us about two minutes together. My father just put his arms around me and gave me a kiss on the top of my forehead, and said, 'Good luck, Gerry. Come up and see me when you get out.'

But I think he knew. He was too intelligent not to know.

The jury were out most of the morning, until Donaldson brought them back to tell them he would accept a majority verdict. They went away again, and we sat in these little cells below the court waiting to hear our fate. I thought about all the photographers I'd glimpsed on the street through the window of the A van, and the headlines there would be about us the next day. So far all the popular press had us convicted. There had been a lot of coverage of the prosecution case and almost none of our defence. Headlines like 'BOMBERS' IN COURT said a lot about press fairness. Otherwise a lot of column inches were used up revelling in all the high-security measures by the police against an IRA rescue attempt. There were marksmen on all the surrounding roofs, spotter helicopters, flak-jacketed armed guards. The jury too had been carted around under armed guard. It was laughable, all effort and money down the drain.

But at seven minutes past two the jury came back. They had agreed on their verdicts. The foreman got to his feet and the first charge was read out. His answer came back: 'Guilty.'

The foreman had spoken the word another thirty-two times before all the charges against each of us were dealt with. But after the first, I hardly heard him. I had known all along that it was either all of us walking free or none of us.

17

What Went Wrong

Suddenly the lawyers were talking about mitigation. Carole's QC was saying he wanted to enter a plea for no recommendation, on grounds that she was still only seventeen. The judge agreed to that and immediately the other briefs took the cue, and started getting ready to say something or other. I was horrified. Mitigation to me means getting leniency for something you've admitted, something you've done. Well, I'd maintained my innocence all through my remand, committal, and trial. I wasn't going to have Wigoder get up and throw it all away now. So I beckoned the junior barrister over to me.

'Tell him to sit down. He's making no pleas in mitigation on my behalf.'

'But he's got to, the sentence –'

'I don't care about the sentence. I've been found guilty of something I haven't done, and you're not going to get up and be begging for me and making it sound as if I have.'

So when the turn of Wigoder came round he got up and said, 'I do not think it would be appropriate or helpful to address the court on behalf of Conlon.'

The judge sent us back down while he thought about the sentences. I don't know why he hadn't done this already, as he'd had plenty of time while the jury was out. But for some reason he now needed more time, either to decide on the penalty he would inflict, or on the choice words he would use to describe them.

When he came back the seemingly reasonable tones we heard

during his summing-up now changed to hostility. First he wanted us to know that only ten years earlier we would certainly have hanged. He also wondered aloud why we hadn't been charged with treason. This still, of course, carries the death penalty. Then he dealt with us one by one. To Paddy he gave life imprisonment, and a minimum of thirty-five years; to Carole life imprisonment with no recommendation; and to Paul, he said he should be released only 'on grounds of old age or infirmity'.

I was the last. He fixed his eyes on me and I swear he was enjoying himself.

'Life imprisonment, with a recommendation that you serve not less than thirty years.'

I felt a terribly strong desire to jump up and scream, 'For nothing!' But I stopped myself. If I'd struggled successfully to keep my dignity and self-respect on the block at Winchester, I could do it here. I think a year earlier I *would* have screamed or become hysterical, but ten months on remand had changed and hardened me. So I was able to 'remain impassive' as the newspaper trial reports had it. But it was still a very thin thread that was keeping me down.

I don't remember much about the next few minutes. The court, which had been hushed as it listened to the judge's sentence, now erupted into whispers and bustle. Papers were sorted and stacked, brief-cases stuffed, and we were taken back down for the last time to the cells.

We were kept hanging around for I don't know how long; we spoke to each other, but I don't know what we said. Carole was nearly unconscious in her despair and horror at what had happened. Paddy was shaking, like he had a violent fever, and was white as a ghost. Paul held himself together incredibly for a man who, at twenty, had just received the longest sentence ever imposed under the existing Murder Act. I don't know what I looked like myself, I know what I felt like. I felt like shitting myself.

What had gone wrong for us? It might be better to ask, what went right?

It should have been so difficult for the prosectuion to convict us when you think what little they had to connect us with any IRA active service unit. In relation to us, they had no explosives, no detonators, no guns, no ammunition. They had no maps of London, no maps of the south-east of England, no lists of targets, no lists of prominent people. They had no usable intelligence information, no touts, no grasses, no identification, no safe houses, no cars. What they did have, however, was evidence of all these things in relation to bombings that they knew were linked with Guildford and Woolwich. These proved beyond doubt that the people who did all those other bombings must have also gone to Guildford and Woolwich. The only people who didn't know were the four of us and our lawyers. This only began to emerge outside of the prosecution ranks when four of the men responsible were arrested two months after our trial was finished.

They had nothing except our signed statements. Those signed statements were utter rubbish. When you look at them, you see they contradict each other on all the important points. They don't agree on who planted which bombs, on who drove which cars, on where the explosives were stored, on where the bombs were made, on where they were primed. The police had frightened us into admissions which were – or should have been – completely worthless.

The court couldn't see beyond the fact that we *had* confessed; it couldn't understand how we could have been made to confess to something we didn't do. So it would have been good to have shown them Brian Anderson, the Protestant whose father was at one time a top man in the Orange Order in Comber. Brian would have told the court what he told me on remand, that he very nearly confessed to the Guildford bombings, if only the copper interviewing him hadn't been called away to the phone. He wasn't guilty any more than I was. But if he had put up his hands that day he would probably have got himself a minimum thirty-year sentence like mine.

We could have heard of an even more strange case. Years later, shortly before my release, we found out that at the same time I was arrested the police also raided a refuge in Arlington Road (the place, according to one of Paul Hill's statements, where nitro-glycerine was stored). A down-and-out made statements confessing to both the Guildford *and* the Birmingham bombings, and yet the police let him go.

Although there was available evidence at the time of my trial that I was ill-treated, it was never properly highlighted. A doctor in Belfast said I was suffering from a kidney condition at Springfield Road and was probably in pain. He had prescribed medicines which I had never been given. Also available to be called could have been my uncle Hughie, who saw me being frog-marched through Guildford police station after I'd first seen David Walsh, calling out from his cell, 'Leave him alone.' Even better than this could have been my Aunt Kate who was at Godalming at the same time as I was, although I didn't know it. Kate heard me calling out.

She says now: 'I did not know Gerry was in Godalming. I was in a cell at the time and I am as certain as I can be that I heard the sound of him calling out in pain. I heard him cry, "Mammy! Mammy!"'

None of these witnesses were called to support the idea that the confessions came from ill-treatment.

My defence would also have looked better if my alibi had been supported. In his final statement, Havers taunted me with having no alibi, at which Donaldson in his summing-up was forced to point out wasn't true. I *did* have an alibi – I just didn't have anyone to back it up.

So what happened to Paddy Carey, who I knew saw me in the hostel at a time when I should have been in Guildford planting the bombs? He had left Quex Road not long after me and gone back to his wife in West Belfast. In the end it was my mother who found him, and found a solicitor to take his statement. So Paddy was due to fly over on legal aid to appear in my defence. He arrives on the day he was asked and is sitting in the hall at the Old Bailey. At this time I'm in the witness-box, but the Clarkes – Paul Hill's witnesses – are put in in the middle of my evidence and probably this puts everything back. So one of my defence team says to Paddy, 'Look, you're not going to be called today after all. You'll probably be called tomorrow.'

Paddy says, 'Where am I going to stay?'

'Oh, you'll have to make your own arrangements,' he is told and left to get on with it.

'Well bollocks to this,' thinks Paddy, 'I got no money, I only got this return plane ticket. I'm going to use it now.'

So he goes straight back to Heathrow and back home. Next thing the court was told was: 'Mr Carey has not turned up.'

Another question was what happened to Paul the Greengrocer. He too had gone. In fact he had left the hostel the same night on which I wanted to prove my alibi, which would have made him very likely to remember the occasion. The trouble was, he had seemingly gone without a trace. If I could have had him in the witness-box as well as Paddy Carey things might have been very different. No one apparently knew where he was.

Danny Wilson was another witness who could have been produced. He was drinking with me on the day of the Guildford bombings and saw me put away six or seven pints. He was also one of the many people arrested at the same time as me under the Prevention of Terrorism Act, and would have told vividly of his ill-treatment by the Surrey police. Danny was taken handcuffed and naked to Guildford in a police van. He was questioned and threatened for seven sleepless days and nights and then released without a charge. If Danny had been a weaker person, he might also have found himself serving thirty years.

There is another thing I wish my defence had been able to do. I wish it had convinced the jury that the IRA would never have wanted an idiot like me in its ranks, and certainly not running around planting bombs. Ironically, this would have meant getting me a set of *bad* character references, but there were plenty of people to do the job – people like Father Carolan and Father Ryan, the priests at Quex Road who thought I was a crazy dope-smoker. Most people who ran into me at that time recognized me as an unreliable, unstable type of character. And anyone who knew anything about the IRA could have told the court such a person could no more have become the quarter-master of a Provisional IRA company – as the police wanted to believe I was – than jump to the moon.

I had plenty of time over the years to pick through what was lacking in my defence. I think, in the end, it boiled down to the fact that the lawyers were terrified of dealing with terrorist offences, uncertain about the new Act, ignorant about the IRA and how it operates and overwhelmed by the blind determination of the police to get us convicted at any cost.

In the final analysis, the defence had none of the forensic evidence available to the prosecution (which would have formed one of the strongest arguments of my appeal fifteen years later). The defence would have been able to prove with absolute certainty that the people responsible for bombing Guildford and Woolwich were not us.

18
Wandsworth

The Category A van crossed London Bridge and drove south-west through Elephant and Castle. We didn't know where we were going because that's the policy: Category A prisoners on the move are never told their destination. I prayed it would be Brixton. I accepted I would never again sit in the comparative comfort of a remand wing, but at least in Brixton I would be near to my father.

The prison convoy trundled down Kennington Park Road until it reached the Oval cricket ground. So far so good. But now, instead of branching left down Brixton Road, we kept straight on towards Clapham and that was it – it wasn't Brixton. I saw Paul mouth the name the same moment I thought it: Wandsworth. Anybody who'd even done a day's remand knew that the two hardest prisons in the system were Manchester's Strangeways and London's Wandsworth. Both were militant strongholds of the Prison Officers' Association, and in both the POA had the final say in everything that happened. It was in these places the system preferred to incarcerate all the toughest cons.

We arrived in the courtyard and Paul and I were taken out, The A van did not stay long, but immediately drove away with Paddy still inside. I later found out he went to the Scrubs.

I was apprehensive as two screws marched me into the reception area. As an already convicted man, Paul had been kept here all through the trial, so for him there was no formality. He picked up his box with his prison clothes, changed and was whisked off within a matter of minutes. I was left standing at the desk.

There were cons sitting around on benches, probably waiting to be processed, but they made a nice little audience for the pantomime the screws now put on. Your man handed over my Category A book to the reception screw, who was sitting behind a sort of lectern, like you might read a text from in chapel. He never looked up, he just said, 'Empty your pockets, Irish bastard.'

I was frightened and just froze. So now he did look at me, a look of loathing.

'I said empty your fucking pockets.'

I took out a two-ounce tin of tobacco, two packets of cigarettes and a box of matches and put them on the desk. He picked up the tin and, holding it far from his face like it contained excrement, prized it open. Then he poured its contents into the waste-paper basket beside him and replaced the tin on the table. Next he picked up the cigarettes and very deliberately crushed them, wringing the packets between his hands. These, too, he dropped into the bin.

'Get your clothes off.'

I undressed and he made me stand there in front of him while he wrote down all my details very slowly. After a while his nostrils started flaring. He yelled out of the side of his mouth: 'Fill a bath for this bastard. He needs a wash.'

One of the cons started giggling and I could hear water rushing into a bath somewhere near as they took my fingerprints. Then a towel was slung at me and four screws marched me through to the bathroom. It was a big old enamel bathtub, full almost up to the brim.

'There's your bath, get in.'

I put my foot over the side and into the water. It did not just feel cold, it felt somewhere close to freezing. I snatched out my foot and looked at them. But they snapped, 'Get in that fucking bath and wash yourself.'

I set my teeth, eased my body into the cold water and started rubbing my skin miserably with a bar of disgusting prison soap. The four screws stood over me laughing and joking about it. By the time they let me out my teeth were chattering.

The clothing scene was reminiscent of Winchester, but far worse. The underpants were like a pair of Stanley Matthews's old football shorts, and there was a long cream-coloured vest and a shirt. The shirt was obviously built for the Incredible Hulk, it had at least a size 19 collar. If the wind had caught me inside it I'd have been blown over the wall. I wrapped myself in this tent and reached for the trousers.

I had at the time a slim waist of only twenty-eight inches. These trousers were thirty-eights. I rolled up the bottoms and stuffed the huge excess of shirt-tails into the top, but it made no difference. I rolled the waistband over until it looked like I had a punctured lifebelt round my waist. But the trousers still hung loosely round my hips. If I took a few steps they began to slide towards the floor.

Finally I was given shoes two sizes too big and a denim jacket and returned to the desk. There was no question of me marching now, I shuffled along. The cons and the screws thought it was hilarious. I got my cell card (a red card, as I was a Catholic, which I had to hang on my door) and was loaded up with the kit: bedding roll, basin, plates, plastic knife, fork and spoon, jug and cup, pot.

'Come on.'

As always, it was one screw in front and one behind. I followed the one in front as best I could, but after twenty yards I had to stop, put down the bundle and hitch up the trousers. Then I went on, trying to hold on to the trousers as well as the kit. So I started dropping things. We made another twenty yards like this until the leading screw unlocked a gate and we were inside a wing.

There were cons milling around everywhere on the floor of the wing, and we had to weave our way through them. At first they were laughing and pointing at this Charlie Chaplin character as I tried to balance my bundle and keep my trousers up at the same time. But then it turned nasty: one of them recognized me.

'That's that murdering IRA bastard.'

There was pandemonium. They were shrieking insults at me, dancing in front of me and yelling abuse, and I was shuffling along in this ridiculous way. Somehow I got down that wing, literally having to hold myself together.

There's a spot in Wandsworth known as the Centre, a circular hall acting like a hub from which the wings radiate. I didn't know it, but the floor of this Centre is kept shined up at all times for visitors and it's an absolute taboo to walk into the middle of this polished floor. So now we were in the Centre and the screw just said, 'Straight on.'

So I wandered straight across the middle, hardly able to see where I was going with this bundle in front of me, and the screw just screamed at me, 'GET OFF THE CENTRE, YOU FUCKING BASTARD!'

I didn't know what he meant. He'd said 'straight on'. So I stood there, revolving stupidly, trying to see what the trouble was. The screw leaped across and yanked me towards the edge of the floor.

'You never, ever, EVER walk across the floor, stupid git. That floor is sacred. You walk round the edge, always round the edge, got it?'

I just nodded my head, wishing this sacred floor would open up and I could disappear into it. I didn't dare speak in case I burst into tears.

'OK. Now go on, that way.'

Then I was taken straight into the punishment block on E Wing.

I shouldn't have been on the block at Wandsworth at all if two Irish prisoners, Gerry Hunter of the Birmingham Six and another called Mick Sheehan, hadn't been attacked in one of the workshops by another prisoner. The governor then decided it wasn't safe for prisoners convicted of IRA offences to mix with other men on the Category A block. So he simply put us in solitary confinement on the punishment block.

I was put in the cell about five o'clock. I dumped my kit and looked around. There wasn't much to see, just another dirty, dingy, stinking cell, the same filthy grime in the corners, the same graffiti, the same spilled food on the floor, the same smears of blood on the walls.

I was tired and drained, but not sleepy. Slowly I made up my bed and got out my radio and listened to what they were saying about us on the news. We were the headline story, the longest sentences ever handed out for murder, all that. They brought me some kind of watery stew which I couldn't eat. I only had a piece of bread and jam. Then I returned the radio to a football commentary, Real Madrid against Derby County. I lay down and tried to concentrate on the match, anything to distract me.

Then they put my lights out, and it was only seven o'clock. I shivered, still cold from the bath but also from delayed shock. I was listening, trying to listen, to the commentator's voice, but it was so unreal. I got to bed and lay there with the radio on trying not to think.

I was woken by the heavy toe of a screw's boot kicking the door.

'Get out of bed, you Irish bastard. And make sure you make the bed after you.'

It was still dark outside and the floor was cold as ice. I was making the bed when the screw opened me up.

'Slop out, one trip.'

This meant I had to carry everything together, pot, basin, water-jug. I did it clumsily under the eyes of the screw, spilling water on the floor.

After breakfast they came in and made me rip the bedclothes off my bed. I was handed a sheet of paper with a diagram on it, showing exactly how to fold them and how to place them on the mattress: sheet, blanket, sheet, blanket, pillowcase, bedspread. It had to be done in that precise way and I spent the next half hour all thumbs, struggling to fold each sheet and blanket correctly.

Then I used up some time looking out the window, a view with nothing much to see – grey prison buildings and a grey sky – but a view I would soon know in every minute detail, brick by brick, slate by slate. Suddenly the door came flying open and a new voice barked at me.

'Name and number to the Governor.'

It was the chief prison officer, on governor's rounds, and I stepped down and started towards the door to meet him. Suddenly the governor himself swept around the corner and into the cell. The only thing I had time to register was his belly. It stuck out in front of him, as if artificially inflated, and now he came in so quickly I couldn't get out of the way. So I cannoned off this hard, massive stomach and was knocked backwards into the cell. He glowered down at me.

'You little bastard, Conlon. You didn't get the right sentence yesterday, You should have hanged, you know that?'

I shrank back. This enormous figure frightened the daylights out of me, otherwise I might have laughed. If you could have found the plug in him and pulled it out I swear he'd have gone up – 'zzzzzz' – away into the sky like a punctured balloon. Instead he swivelled on his heel and marched out.

I had already been wondering which cell Paul Hill was in, but by dinner time it already made no difference. I was told he'd gone that morning, moved to another prison. I didn't see him again for two years. I did see Gerry Hunter, though. He was collecting his dinner and he looked terribly nervous, like a rabbit that had a car's headlights shone in its eyes. He seemed half frozen by fear. We just nodded heads to each other and went back in with our dinners.

I saw Gerry Hunter again on exercise, though that afternoon I went out first on my own. I must try to describe this ordeal. The exercise yard was a small triangular space bounded by the block the Catholic chapel, and D Wing where all the other long-term prisoners were. It was probably only about ten yards from one end to the other, with a small ditch or dry moat running around the edge at the foot of the buildings, then grass within that and a circle of paving stones in the middle. It was claustrophobic to be in there, like I was walking around at the bottom of a well, so terribly aware of these clown's clothes I was wearing, and all these windows above with men's faces peering down.

Ten minutes later they brought out Mick Sheehan and Gerry Hunter, looking as nervous as I felt. The screws on exercise appeared completely terrifying, quite deliberately hoping to look something like the Waffen SS. The highly polished peaks of their caps came down at a steep angle over their eyes, they wore black leather gloves and would watch us in silence, never moving, never speaking except to bark an order. They made us walk in a circle five yards apart, and wouldn't let us talk.

Suddenly I heard a voice calling down from one of the windows.

'Irish scumbags.'

Then another: 'You should have been hung.'

Something fell and bounced off the grass into the little moat. I saw it was a PP9 battery and it hadn't fallen, it was thrown.

'Hey, Conlon! Only twenty-nine years, three hundred and sixty-four days to go.'

Another missile came down. It was a jam jar. It smashed in the moat and when I looked I saw they had filled it with shit. Loads of batteries, bottles, jars filled with shit and urine, rained down on us.

I turned to the screws.

'Hey! Can't you see what's happening?'

But they stood motionless staring straight ahead, smirking a little. We had to keep walking.

This was exercise. It normally lasted an hour, every day.

In the next fifteen years, I was to spend a total of just over three years in solitary confinement. Unless you have experienced it, it is a difficult thing to explain or describe – the loneliness, isolation and vulnerability. Your cell is a bubble of silence, where the only noises are the ones you make yourself. If you have a radio it soon shrinks into a background buzz, because you spend so much time listening to the beat of your own thoughts. It's like being walled in a tomb.

You pace the cell, walk up and down quickly at first, then more slowly, measuring out the steps. Seventeen and a half feet from window to door, nine and a half feet from wall to wall. You read and read the tiny names scribbled on the walls, you talk to those names, have dialogues with them, give them faces and imagine the crimes they must have committed to get themselves in here. Some of them, though, must have been innocent like you . . . Emotionally, I was in an absolute muddle. It was probably the hardest jigsaw puzzle that anybody could ever put together. I didn't understand the emotional state I was in, that I was in trauma. Confusion, an identity crisis – everything. Profound guilt was the hardest to come to terms with because I knew I had played a major part in my own downfall by signing statements and accepting total responsibility for what happened to my father. Trying to come to terms with those things at my age was too great to handle. And always self-pity is lying in wait, to descend on you without warning, making you cry to yourself, 'Why me?'

Self-pity and silence are the two enemies. You go to the window because it's a source of sounds. You can hear prisoners talking dimly, distantly, over in D Wing. You strain to catch what they're saying, as if you could take part in the chat. But you can't, it's too far. In the morning there's the sound of the sparrows, and prisoners throwing stale bread out to them. They chirp to each other and even from that you're feeling excluded.

If you're not at the window you're at the door, ear pressed to the crack, trying to eavesdrop, to catch the sound of what people are saying, to catch what's happening and remind yourself you're part of a larger system. There are other people in other cells going through the same thing you're going through. You try to hang on to that. They haven't just locked *you*, 462779 Gerry Conlon, up in this box, dropped the key down a grating somewhere and forgotten you. They haven't kept this place as a living burial chamber just for you.

And then, for long periods, your brain shuts down and you just sit looking at the wall. Then you stop noticing time go by, which can be the most frightening thing of all.

That night after tea at seven, just like the night before, my light went off. I looked out the window and saw other lights still blazing in D Wing, so I knew this was special treatment: longer hours of darkness for the Irish bastards on the block. I put myself to bed and tried to sleep.

I lay there thinking about our trial — what went wrong, whether, how and when it could ever be put right. I wondered if Paddy Maguire's belief in British justice had been dented at all by the verdict. And I thought of my father, who came over to England to help me and got caught up in this foul, shameful mess. He was coming up for his own trial in three months' time but, after what happened to us, what hope could he have?

These were the thoughts dragging miserably through my head when, suddenly, the cell door swung open. A screw stood there framed by the light.

'Get up, Conlon. Visitors.'

19
More Questions

'What do you mean, a visit? At this time of night?' I sat up in bed and rubbed my eyes.

'That's my instructions. Visit for Conlon. So get dressed.'

I pulled on my outsize clothes and followed the screw. We went down to one of the visiting rooms. I found waiting for me two policemen.

I didn't recognize one of them. He introduced himself as Detective Sergeant Lewis of the Bomb Squad. The other I remembered very well, because he had given my defence the chance of a rare wee gee during the trial. He was Chief Superintendent Peter Imbert, the Bomb Squad chief.

In court Imbert had first given evidence about the Woolwich bombing, for which Paul and Paddy were indicted, but not me. Imbert had gone on, though, to tell the court that he had visited me at Winchester a few days after I went there on remand, and that I had at that time admitted involvement in Guildford. In court we denied that this visit ever took place, because it hadn't. It was Simmons and Rowe, we said, who had visited me – and without my solicitor being present. That was the time I'd had a go across the table at Simmons.

Imbert had insisted it was him, but when I told Wigoder to get hold of the Winchester gate book, we were able to prove our point – Imbert's name wasn't there. That was the wee gee.

Apart from seeing him in court, I also remembered Imbert coming for a minute into the interview room in Godalming when Jermey and

Grundy had been working on me to give them a second statement, the one about the supposed bomb-making of Annie Maguire. He hadn't spoken to me then, so this was the first time I'd ever actually met the man.

Now Imbert sat me down and said, 'We want information regarding the bombings.'

He was very low-key, very clinical. I knew what he was talking about because I'd heard the news on my radio. Only that morning a bomb had been put under the parked car of a Tory MP, Sir Hugh Fraser, outside his house in Holland Park. It was noticed by a neighbour walking his dog, the cancer specialist Professor Hamilton Fairley. He had activated the detonator and blown himself up. It was a terrible thing and also exactly the kind of atrocity which put maximum Establishment pressure on the Bomb Squad. Bombs had been going off all year at Army bases. Now there were attacks on eminent people outside their homes, and Imbert needed a result badly.

He wanted any information I could give that might help. He understood that I probably didn't feel like helping at this moment in time, but really I had nothing to lose.

I let him do most of the talking because I didn't know what I could reply. I just sat there and listened, nodding my head to tell him I understood what he was saying.

By the time he had finished it was clear to me that, if I *could* help them with information that they thought significant, I could also help my father.

As far as I was concerned, there was only one response I could make, even though it was a terrible thing to have to do. If there was any way I could help my father – however bad it made me look – then I would do it and justify it later. I already had lied and incriminated myself to save my mother, at a time when I didn't even know my father was arrested. If the police and courts could have believed the rubbish in Godalming, I thought at this point anything I said they were capable of believing. I was prepared to do the same again for my father.

I asked, 'What sort of things do you want to know?'

They wanted the names of all the IRA people in England. They also wanted the safe houses, arms and explosives dumps and supply routes. Basically, nothing I could tell them. They mentioned a few

names just for openers, saying he'd want confirmation of their IRA
connections. I knew I couldn't do anything for them, not of any
value. But I nodded my head and played them along. Then they got
up and said, 'Right, that's all for now. We'll be back to see you in a
few days. Think about what we've told you.'

I was taken out of the interview room and back to my cell.

I lay in the dark clutching at straws. If I did this it couldn't be for any
personal gain. I was serving five life sentences, and, looking on the
bright side – I wasn't getting out till I was fifty – part of me feared
there was nothing that could change that, although I kept trying to
convince myself I'd be out in a few years. The other side was, if it
ever got known that I'd been brussel-sprouting, it could be very
dangerous for me amongst the other prisoners. So no one could say I
was doing it for myself.

But if it could help my father, even though there was only a slim
chance, I knew I had to give it a try. I'd always blamed myself for
what happened to my father, because it was me he'd come over to
England to save. Now his salvation could rest in my hands. I knew
that I had no choice at all. Of course, I would have to put up a
convincing show. There would have to be a lot of names scattered
around, a lot of confident chit-chat about IRA activity. Would I be
able to do it convincingly? I went to sleep feeling very vulnerable but
deciding that, if they honestly thought I was an IRA bomber, then
there was no garbage I couldn't make them swallow.

When the two of them came back a week later, Lewis had a
concealed tape recorder. I didn't know about this until much later,
but I have now been able to read the transcript of what I said that
day, and to hear the original tape.

From the start I had to make out I did Guildford and was an IRA
man, otherwise nothing I said would be credible.

I threw everything at them I could think of – first of all names.
There were names from Kilburn, names from Southampton, names
out of West Belfast, names out of the newspapers and names out of
nowhere but my own imagination. Then there were addresses. I gave
them streets without numbers, house numbers without streets, vague
locations, exact addresses, squats, flats, pubs, clubs – whatever they
wanted. I also tried to give them what they could think was 'inside'
information. I drew on any stuff I'd gleaned over the years from idle

talk in pubs, on building sites, in betting shops, in Irish clubs – anywhere that the Irish congregate. Chats with remand prisoners in Brixton were another source. I would even go back to the stories I'd listened to in the Lower Falls during the first days of the barricades, when I was a lad of fifteen hanging about for the crack.

At times the results were hilarious. Lewis had all these photographs and photofits, each one numbered off, and he wanted me to put names to as many as I could. At one point the conversation went like this:

LEWIS: Now 23, 24, 25 are photofits so, you know, they're not pictures, but do they remind you of anyone?
PRISONER: Kenny EVERETT, first one, definitely.
IMBERT; Who?
LEWIS: Kenny EVERETT?
PRISONER: Aye.
LEWIS: What's that, 25?
PRISONER: Kenny EVERETT, on televison! On radio!
LEWIS (*laughs*): Oh!
IMBERT: Kenny who?

The stuff was absolute cock and bull, completely useless. Either it was invented or it was common knowledge. They could do nothing with it in the short term or the long run, because I knew nothing worthwhile to tell them, But I hoped it would be enough to help my Dad.

At the end Imbert said, 'See you, Gerry.' But he didn't come back for more.

I did get a visit from some more policemen about six weeks afterwards, Munday and Doyle. Munday, a police inspector attached to the Bomb Squad, gave evidence in my trial and my father's. Doyle was introduced as a sergeant. Again I put on an act, but again they got nothing worth having.

I was not thinking straight. When these conversations became known about two years later they caused enormous problems for me in my relations with other prisoners. Also, what reason could I have had – after what happened to me – to think I could put my trust in police goodwill? So with hindsight, talking to the police in the reckless way I did was a very silly, naïve thing to have done. It has caused me nothing but grief since.

As one last perspective on what I was like at this time, I'll quote from a governor's report made out shortly after I had these conversations. The Assistant Governor who wrote it obviously saw me as a convicted terrorist. But his little thumb-nail sketch of my personality is interesting to read.

Conlon impresses as a most confused young man. In spite of the seriousness of the offences his commitment to the IRA appears somewhat superficial and one has the impression that he planted the bombs more out of bravado than for any deep political belief. He seems far less ruthless than some of his colleagues have come across and I think that when he planted the bombs he did not realize the full implications of what he was doing. Even now I get the impression that he does not allow himself to think about what he has done and is trying to keep the incident out of his mind. Similarly I do not think he has grasped the implications of his sentence because again he has pushed them to the back of his mind and bolsters up his spirit by talk of being released in a few years . . .

Some people may find this hard to believe, but at times, and especially at the beginning, I found my innocence a very heavy burden in prison. More exactly I found it an embarrassment, very hard to express without blushing, very difficult to just up and say, 'I shouldn't be here, I'm innocent of what they claim I've done.'

But there was a beautiful relief in being able to say it, if only I could find the right person to say it to. One of the only moments I can remember feeling any kind of happiness in Wandsworth was one Sunday on exercise, soon after I got there, and I was walking with Gerry Hunter. By this time they had started allowing us to talk, and I remember there was a screw there who'd been on attachment to the Crumlin Road or somewhere over in Northern Ireland. So there he was in his SS cap and black gloves, and he started whistling a Loyalist party song – 'No Surrender' or 'The Sash' – which obviously intimidated us as it was intended to do. And suddenly, just as we were under the wall of the chapel walking our tight little circle, Gerry turned round to me and said,

'You know Gerry, I'm innocent. I didn't do the Birmingham bombings. All of us were innocent.'

And he looked so sheepish as he said it, so embarrassed about it, that I immediately recognized how he was feeling, and, of course, I immediately believed him. I just said, 'I didn't either. I didn't do any bombings either.'

It was wonderful to know, not just that he was innocent, but that he had the same feeling of embarrassment about it as I had. And after that Gerry Hunter and I became friends. Prison has taught me that real, lifetime friendship is a very rare thing. But, starting there on the block in Wandsworth, I made a real friend of Gerry Hunter.

But he and Mick Sheehan were moved out of the block not very long after that, which increased my isolation, because there had literally been no one else for me to talk to. I became very withdrawn. I tried to keep my head and body together in various ways. I did press-ups and sit-ups in the cell, I got a daily newspaper in and used to pore over every single bit of it. No newspapers are ever so avidly and carefully read and re-read as they are in prison. Then, when I'd read the paper, I'd pick out the longest word I could find and try to make other words out of it – anything to keep my mind going.

Then there was the library. The first time I went to the library was a fiasco. It was just after I arrived. Nazi-type screws opened me up saying, 'Library.'

So off I went, still dressed like a prat in these enormous trousers, walking between two screws and up to the library.

'You got two minutes in this library. Choose six books. Go.'

I started hunting around the shelves, looking nervously at the other prisoners in there, and them looking at me. The way they looked at me – they were the dogs and I was the meat. Then one of them muttered, 'IRA bastard.'

At that ripples of anger against me started going round the room. One of the cons spat at me and I took this as a sign I should get out. I thought I was going to be attacked for sure. I edged backwards towards the desk, trying to keep my eyes towards the other cons, some of them looking like they could have done me serious damage. And as I went I just swept a pile of six books up and dropped them on the check-out place, still facing the main part of the library. The con who was librarian gave me a funny look as he stamped the books, while I willed him to hurry so I could get out of the library and back to the punishment block with my books.

When we got there it took me a quarter of an hour to stop shaking. At last I came round to picking up one of the books, opening it. I couldn't understand a word of it. It was in German. I opened the next one, also in German. They were all in German – my one chance to get something to read and I'd emptied the German section of the library.

When they brought me tea I said, 'Excuse me.'

And he barked, 'SIR.'

I said, 'I went to the library today and unfortunately came back with a load of books in German.'

Screws are normally very slow-witted, and this one was no exception. He just looked at me warily. I said, 'I can't understand German.'

Still nothing from the screw. He thought I must be laying some trap for him.

'Any chance of getting them changed, please?'

At last the screw relaxed. With a request to deal with the bastard had his cue.

'Certainly you can get them changed,' he said. 'You can get them changed in two fucking weeks.'

And he slammed the cell door.

It was at that point that I began to realize how important books would become to me. Throughout my fifteen years I would scour the libraries in the hope of finding a good book. Some weeks, I could find nothing. When I did get a good book out I would ration it – read it so slowly to make it last as long as possible. The first book that made a real impression on me was *The Ragged Trousered Philanthropists*. I just picked it up in Brixton library – I had never heard of it before. This book, and *Strumpet City*, told of human suffering and ordinary people and I really related to them.

On top of the problems I had at Wandsworth coping with the block, I soon had to suffer the opening of my father's trial on charges of handling explosives. It began at the end of January 1976, and I found it terribly difficult to get information from day to day about what was happening. There seemed to be a lot of wrangling about the scientific tests from their hand-swabs which, according to the prosecution, proved that the Maguire Seven had handled nitro-glycerine whilst getting rid of the evidence of a bomb factory in my aunt's house.

The results of these tests were the only evidence of any kind against the Seven. But to my mind the argument distracted the court from the main point – how did the nitro-glycerine get on their hands in the first place? The defence tried to show that the tests were mistaken, and that the Seven were an innocent bunch of people being made to look guilty by mistake. I knew the truth, and so did my father – they were an innocent bunch of people being made to look guilty on *purpose*.

Then in February 1976, with the Maguire Seven's trial still dragging on, and me at the end of four months' solitary, the screws opened me and told me, 'Get your things together, Conlon. You're on the move.'

20
Wakefield

The gate lodge of my new prison had an electronically operated door and the reception area was ultra-modern, with pleasant lighting and neutral screws who, when they processed you, didn't look like they wanted to chew your ears off and spit them back in your face. I was given some clothes that fitted me, shown into a little room with a table and chair and, after five minutes, given food. Even today, after long years of prison cuisine, I can't work out what this dish was. It was shaped like meat loaf but it was all the wrong colour, and it smelt disgusting.

I sat looking at this until they came back and took me off to movement control. From here you could see all four wings radiating outwards from A to D and, after the modern, hi-tech entrance, this was a shock. It was just another massive, grey, Victorian prison. It was Wakefield.

The wings at Wakefield are very large, four landings high. I was taken down A Wing and put in a cell on the threes, 'The first night you're here you miss association.'

Then I was banged up, but I didn't have much time to be sitting there feeling sorry for myself, because I soon heard a knock on my door.

'Hey! Do you need anything? Do you need tobacco?'

I heard someone calling to the screw, who came and opened my door. Two prisoners were there, both Irishmen.

'Hi. I'm John Foley, this is Bobby Cunningham. We've brought you some stuff.'

They handed me tobacco, biscuits and a bottle of orange squash. I thanked them.

'That's OK. See you tomorrow.'

The warm human contact, the thoughtfulness, gave me a huge boost. I'd known nothing like it for months. I went to bed that night, turned on Radio One and was sitting there listening to the music, eating biscuits and drinking squash, like a kid on his birthday.

Next morning everyone was opened up together and I slopped out, having a look around. There was a couple of men on the landing, another couple walking past, but they hardly looked at me. That itself was new and welcome – I was used to being a target, an object of attention, whenever I was with other prisoners.

Bobby Cunningham came up.

'Coming down to get your breakfast?'

'Oh, don't they bring it up?'

'Not here. It's self-service. Come on.'

I went down with him to B Wing where we queued up, got our food, and came back up. I had breakfast in Bobby Cunningham's cell and he filled me in about Wakefield.

There were something like seven hundred and forty prisoners here, of which seventy per cent were sex cases – nonces. In the eyes of the rest of us, the nonces skewed the balance of the place, it was they who made it such an evil-feeling prison. The nonces were weak and inadequate, most of them, which made the screws a lot of lax, idle bastards because three-quarters of the prisoners never stood up to them. That's why the food was terrible. That's why the place had such a sick atmosphere.

On the evening of my first day, during association, this wee man came along to my door all dressed in white and saying, 'Hello, do you want a corned-beef sandwich? A pint of milk?'

I'd hardly eaten in Wandsworth and the fellow looked completely harmless, as if he wouldn't have dared step on a beetle. So I said, 'Oh, thanks very much.'

So the wee guy was just about to come into my cell with the sandwich when Bobby Cunningham spotted him and just roared at him, 'GET THE FUCK OUT OF HIS CELL!'

He chased him off, and then came back and said, 'Don't ever go near that guy. He's a nonce, a rampant poof, OK?'

Some of the sex cases were appalling. At twenty-one I had still had almost no experience of life outside the circles I grew up in and I found it shocking to be in amongst these people, and especially to be in a *minority* amongst them. Some of the things they'd done were so appalling it would make you want to spew, and many of them were also very odd characters. There was a fellow there I remember who wanted to be a woman, and he was growing breasts. You'd hear him singing to himself in a high voice, trying to sing like a woman. To me, at that time, it was almost impossible to take being in there with all these freaks and inadequates. I was a sane man locked in a lunatic asylum.

The trial of the Maguires was still going on when I came to Wakefield. I found quite a number of Irish prisoners here, so I was getting plenty of good support from the likes of Bobby Cunningham and Jerry Mealey. But when the jury stayed out for two and a half days I was in a very bad way, my mood swinging from depression to hope and then back again hour by hour.

The verdicts came through at last and I heard them on the radio. It was the lunchtime news. In spite of the long debates they must have had in the jury room they found the Maguire Seven guilty on all charges: Annie Maguire guilty, my father guilty, guilty right down to my cousin Patrick, who had been thirteen when the police originally arrested him. One juror stuck out to the end to acquit young Patrick, but on all the other decisions they were unanimous.

The judge again was Donaldson and the prosecuting counsel, again, was Havers. Donaldson gave my aunt Annie and uncle Paddy the maximum fourteen years apiece. Vincent and Patrick were sentenced to five years and four years, and Pat O'Neill, Sean Smyth and Guiseppe Conlon each had twelve years. In my father's case this became a life sentence.

My response was anger, a wave of determination to fight back. Up until now I had dreamed of amnesties, of reductions in my sentence – perhaps even, in my wildest moments, of escape. Now none of those would do any more. We were going to win our freedom by proving our innocence, and by no other way.

I had tremendous difficulties in controlling myself in Wakefield because I was so frustrated. One of the things that caused me to go crazy at times was the food, because it was filthy, like pulp. There's one incident that sticks in my mind. Every Thursday the menu would be rice and beef curry or corned-beef fritters. Usually I would have the curry, but they'd just run out, so I had the fritters. The guy I was with, who was two cells down from me, decided to wait on the curry. So I'm in my cell eating the fritters when he passes by with the curry. Thirty seconds later, I hear a scream. So I go out on the landing and see what's up. My mate with the curry is screaming, 'Look what's in the curry.' So I have a look. Guess what's in the curry? A mouse's head.

That was some con's idea of a joke. The cons who worked in the kitchens used to put soap in the custard. They were always screwing the food up, which they didn't have to eat because they could eat whatever they liked in the kitchen. Malicously, they used to destroy any decent food, a rarity in itself, which the rest of us were going to eat. One day they served fish up – nearly everyone rejected it – they threw it on the centre as a form of protest. It was like in Aberdeen when all the fish is lying on the quay. Only this fish was stinking. Yet you had some prisoners coming out and picking it up and taking it away to cook later on. Some prisoners had absolutely no principles. There was no general solidarity there in that prison – the only people who had solidarity were the Irish and the Cockneys.

On several occasions I ended up throwing my food over the screws. When this happened, they'd pounce upon me like lions and tigers. Alarm bells would go off and they'd get me in a headlock, force my arms up my back and frog-march me from the main prison to the punishment block.

The punishment block was segregated from the main prison, surrounded by a high wall with wire on top. When they took you in, you had to cross a steel bridge that was caged in. It was like going inside a submarine – pipes run along the sides of it, painted a cold blue, a very long and narrow room. Very claustrophobic, the thing that really reminded me of a submarine.

The block was formerly a control unit. In the early 1970s the Home Office introduced control units to contain 'disruptive prisoners'. It was based on the idea that ninety days' punishment here would keep you in order. But, if after forty-five days or so, you insulted a screw, you went back to day one. So you could spend a year in these places. Eventually a guy called Micky Williams sued the Home Office over the way he was being treated and the control units were officially closed down. The ninety-day rule went, but the units were made into punishment blocks.

So these blocks were used for solitary confinement and punishment. Every offence under the heading 'discipline' came under Rule 47A of the prison code. Rule 47A was the rule that brought you into this block. It had a whole load of sub-sections, which covered everything, a type of Catch 22.

The first thing they did was place you in a cell and tell you to strip. You'd be surrounded by at least four screws while this was happening. After being stripped, you'd be thrown an old blue hospital robe and told to go to the shower, down two flights of stairs into the cellar. You would turn right into a shower area – about 8-foot wide and 4-foot deep, tiled through with white just like public baths. The tiles were broken – the first thing that would catch your eye was the blood, embedded in the tiles on the ceiling and the wall. The screws would watch you showering. It was oppressive, degrading – wherever your eyes went, you could see the blood. I couldn't help looking at the screws, thinking am I going to add to this blood. You *knew* the reputation of the block and how brutal the screws were. Fortunately, I never got beaten up in the shower.

After you'd finished having your shower they'd take you back up to your cell and the clothes you'd been wearing would be gone. People used to insert bits of demin from old trousers into their jeans to make flares. You'd always try to get a decent jacket, but now it would be taken along with your other clothes. You'd be left with ill-fitting clothes again, looking like Coco the Clown. Everything in prison was designed to stamp out individuality. The well-scrubbed jeans would be gone (with the flares in them) and you'd be left a pair with a size 36 waist, 34 leg and turn-ups you could carry water in.

Then would come the adjudication, and you'd be standing there in these clothes looking like something out of a circus. The adjudication was an absolute farce. Your punishment, for throwing food for example, was usually twenty-one days in solitary confinement. They would say, 'Give your name and number to the governor,' which I never did. They would proceed to tell what happened. '462779 Conlon threw his dinner at such and such a screw.' You'd be found guilty and given twenty-one days.

No one would get a result at Wakefield, they would always be found guilty no matter how innocent they were. It seemed to me that everything the screw said was gospel and accepted. The punishment would be savage at Wakefield in comparison with other prisons.

In Wakefield I was up and down the block like a yo-yo at times. I was there for about ten months in total. The punishment would range from five to twenty-eight days, and in Wakefield's punishment block you couldn't see the sky. The windows had a double layer of thick perspex with little holes drilled in for ventilation, and in the summer it would be like being in a sweat box. You had nothing, absolutely nothing, in the cell; they even took the mat off the floor. If you wanted to go to the toilet you could only go at breakfast, tea or dinner. The screws used to congregate round the toilet when you were trying to use it. Absolutely horrible, there is nothing more humiliating than this.

The exercise yard of the punishment block was at a forty-five degrees slope. There were wavy lines that went up and down the wall of the yard. These were different colours waving like a snake's back. If you spent any length of time looking at them, you tended to become disorientated. You also had screws at each end of the exercise yard, standing in encased bridges. They would stare down on you like zoo keepers. You'd be the animals.

Exercise was really important: it's the only time you're in the fresh air. But the exercise yard on the punishment block at Wakefield was something else. For example, if you spoke, your exercise was immediately terminated. You'd be taken back to the cells. Exercise was the only chance you got to see anyone else on the punishment, so it was difficult not to speak, especially if you hadn't spoken to anyone for two weeks.

There was a screw who I'll call Smith and he had an intense hatred of Tony, an Irish prisoner with red hair who was *very* shy. Smith used to bait him all the time. One day I had a terrible headache, and while Smith was harassing Tony I said, 'Why don't you fuck off and leave him alone?' He told me to mind my own business or he'd nick me. At this I just lost my head. I pushed him against a pillar – the alarm bell went, the screws came along and nicked me. I thought, if he verbals me up I'm not going to let him get away with it. Next morning, on adjudication, Smith came and starts giving his evidence. It was lies, exaggerating what I'd done. He said I'd grabbed him by the throat and tried to bite him. I thought, you horrible bastard and so when it came to my turn to plead to the offence, I said, 'I plead guilty but he hasn't told you what really happened.' I said he came over and made homosexual advances to me and tried to touch me up. That's why I attacked him. He started screaming, 'I'm a married man.' The governor told me to leave the room. When I came back, he told me I'd got ten days, which was unusual because this type of offence was usually brought before the board of visitors to hear and you could get between fifty-six and 112 days' punishment. I think the Governor only gave me ten days so that the offence wouldn't come before the board of visitors, who would then have heard me give my reason for 'attacking' Smith.

When it got round the prison and everyone heard what I'd said, they started calling Smith 'Duckie' and blowing him kisses and generally making his life an absolute misery. Gradually he lost his arrogance and left people alone. That was one small victory I had in Wakefield.

The presence of the Irish republican prisoners, here at Wakefield and in most of the twenty other prisons where I've been, affected my entire prison life. But, because I was not IRA and never became IRA, I want to explain why these men had such a strong and lasting effect on me.

I mixed with them first and foremost because they were Irish and so was I. Some of them, like Roy Walsh, I grew up beside in West Belfast, and our shared background made it inevitable we would knock around together in prison. Others, like Shane Docherty and Joe O'Connell, were in a position to know for sure I was innocent and because of this they felt a sense of responsibility for me. So there was always going to be, to a greater or lesser degree, a natural sympathy amongst all Irish prisoners.

But there were other reasons. The first is that the Irish were constantly singled out by the screws, and by the whole prison system, as a special group deserving special treatment. The Irish were subjected to very particular forms of discrimination, especially in relation to visits. The Irish were constantly hassled and harassed and confronted and challenged to assert their identity as Irish. It was paradoxical, because one of the reasons the screws did it was through fear of terrorist-type offenders, fear that they would mix with other prisoners and infect them in some way. Until now there hadn't been significant numbers of republican Irish in English gaols. In Wakefield I began to see how scared the system was of them and how it tried to contain.

them by isolating them from other inmates. The more important result was that their solidarity with each other was increased.

This situation would have forced solidarity on any group, even if it hadn't already existed naturally and, in fact, there were quite a few Category A Irish who were not convicted of IRA offences – John Foley in Wakefield was one – but who became, like me, part of the Irish group in prison.

The last reason is the most difficult to explain, especially if you are talking to people whose ideas about the IRA come from the English tabloids. Republican prisoners are different from other prisoners, because they are not there for personal gain and they are not freaks. That sets them apart from everyone else. They are generally very disciplined. They don't involve themselves in the pettiness of much of prison life, such as setting up complicated attacks on the nonces, and grudge attacks on screws or other prisoners. They also look after their own. If, for some reason, somebody gets in a sum of money, the first thing he does is buy food for the Irish table. If anyone begins to become depressed – as I did very often – they would try to help you, talk you through it, coax you out of it.

Every day in prison is like walking through a minefield. It's full of danger, full of people who can be set off into acts of unbelievable violence by any trivial thing – by not saying good-morning, or by saying good-morning, or by just looking at them. So the attitude of the Irish – sticking together at all costs, taking no shit from anybody but not looking for trouble either – meant that they were a strong influence for good over me, offering the protection and sense of belonging which I so badly needed. They were like an extended family. That will sound strange only to those who have the 'IRA Monsters' stereotype in their heads.

When I first arrived at Wakefield the feeling among the Irish prisoners was particularly strong, because one tragic act of unselfish solidarity by an Irish prisoner had just reached its end. Frank Stagg had died on hunger strike. Frank Stagg and Jerry Mealey began the hunger strike to protest against the iniquitous system for visits, and to campaign for transfer to prisons in Northern Ireland where families could visit more often.

'Irish' visits, as they were called, were unique. No other prisoners' families were treated so badly by the system. When my mother came over to see us she had to save all year – money and accumulated visiting days – and then use her annual holiday for the purpose. She could get her travel paid, but only at the cheapest rates, which meant overnight ferries and coach fares. There would be no assistance for accommodation even when the prison is in a remote place, such as Parkhurst. With my father and me in different prisons, as we were for a lot of the time, my mother's problems were made worse. But finding the time and affording the trip was only the beginning of it.

Everything was done that could be done to make the families feel they, too, were criminals to be punished. First there was the vetting. Anyone who wants to visit a Category A prisoner has to be interviewed by the police, which is an ordeal in itself, because they're persistently saying, 'And why do you want to see these bombers?' as if it was something suspicious, something to be guilty about. Photographs then had to be sent to the prison and to the Home Office, and application had to be made in writing.

My mother, when she came over, would stay several days and see me morning and afternoon until she'd used up her annual entitlement of visits. But first she had to find somewhere to stay, a bed-and-breakfast near by. Even this was a trial, because some of the people in the boarding houses, as soon as they caught the Irish accent, would slam the door in her face. The prejudice of the screws towards 'bombers'' families spread easily into the local area. My mother would be forced to trudge with her suitcase from one place to the next till she found somewhere willing to take her.

Then, when she came to the prison, she could never be certain I was still there. Category A prisoners can be moved at a moment's notice, and if a visit is due – so what? This happened after my father joined me at Wakefield. The very morning my mother got there to see us, after eighteen months in the same place, I was moved to Canterbury without warning. Her plans for the week were then in ruins. She stayed on for three days to visit my father, and then travelled all the way to Canterbury, where she visited me for a couple of days more.

But it's when you look at what happened in the visits themselves that you wonder how she had the strength to keep coming back. Inside the prison the screws spoke to her rudely, treated her like dirt. There would be a policewoman on hand to search her. A metal detector would be used, her bags were searched, her purse and pockets emptied, she would be told to take off certain items of clothing. Years later, when my little niece Sarah was born and my sister Ann brought her to see me, the screws ripped that child's nappy off to see if it was being used to bring anything illegal in to me.

Then there was the hanging around, the deliberate time-wasting. The visits would start from 1.40 onwards and by 1 o'clock my mother would be there, first in the queue outside the prison gate, without fail and whatever the weather. I'd be in movement control on time, waiting for her to be announced, and nothing would happen for ten, fifteen minutes.

'What's the hold-up on my visit?'

'Your family's not arrived yet.'

It would be bollocks. I knew my mother was sitting in that room waiting for me, watching the clock, knowing the visit would end, come what may, at 3.30. Another ten minutes would go by and there would be nothing I could do. But I'd feel the anger and frustration rising in me about the way my ma was being treated. Then a screw would wander in, stop to talk to the senior officer there, chatting away for another five minutes. Then he'd turn around as if it had just occurred to him and say, 'Oh, Conlon, you've got a visit.'

When I went down to the visit there was an alsatian dog and its handler with me, and two other screws, one carrying my Category A book. When I got to the area set aside for closed Category A visits – that means the closely supervised ones – I would be strip-searched in case I had any stiffs, or illegal letters, on me to pass over. And then, at last, the visit would begin.

The room is very confined, six foot by ten, with three wooden chairs and two small tables. The tables are pushed together but separated by a high hardboard screen. I sit on one side and my mother sits opposite me, and over the screen I can see only her head. We are not allowed to touch each other except to shake hands at the start. You can't hug or kiss or anything else, just touch hands before you sit down. After that, nothing can be exchanged between the two of you except words. Behind my mother's head I can see the screw standing a couple of feet back, and behind mine she sees the second screw in the same position, looming over us, watching every move. If she is with my sister Ann, then there are two screws at their backs. If my father is with me, *we* have two screws. And, in between us, sitting like a tennis umpire, is another screw. He has a notebook open and his pen out. His job is to write down everything that we say.

No prisoner's visitor from Belfast is ever happy talking about things back home, especially giving the gossip or talking about people. These things are the most natural kind of everyday chat, but when you know they think your son is a bomber, and they're writing down everything you both say, you worry they'll start reading stuff into it that isn't there. So that's one line of conversation ruled out.

But then, how can you talk about anything personal either? Nothing in prison is a secret. Everything is spread around, by screws and by prisoners, because gossip is the disease of boredom. So if anything personal is ever said during a visit you can be sure it will go the rounds, be quoted back at you, laughed about. So what *can* you say?

'How are you keeping?'

'Oh, fine, fine.'

'You said you had a cold.'

'Did I?'

'In your last letter.'

'Oh that. No, it's gone now.'

'Oh good.'

I'm sitting so uncomfortably. I've been living for this moment for weeks, I've been anticipating it, thinking about seeing her, wondering how she'll look, knowing I'll be able to tell her I'm all right. And now here I am, suffering through this wooden conversation, looking sideways at a screw who I despise, who hasn't got the brains to be a bus conductor, writing down every word we say, and writing down a little commentary about us, what he thinks about us, what he reads between the lines. And here I am wishing it would get to 3.30 so this torture can end, so I can go back to my cell and cry, because of what this is doing to my ma.

And she would come back day after day until her holiday and accumulated visits were used up.

It was to stop this that Frank Stagg died, and Jerry Mealey almost died. I remember seeing Jerry when I first got to Wakefield, after he'd got out of the hospital. He was in his early thirties, but he looked like an old man dragging himself along the landings, shuffling down the stairs. They did it because they wanted the right, which is every prisoner's right, to petition to be imprisoned near their families.

The difference it would make for families would be enormous. It would take away this terrible artificial occasion of the annual visit, day after day sitting opposite each other with nothing to say. It would mean a single visit every week at the end of a simple bus ride. It would keep up the contacts with the rest of the family. It would give something fresh to say each time. By consistently refusing to grant my appeals to be put in a prison in Belfast, they put my mother through fifteen years of unnecessary and undeserved punishment. And it wasn't only her. They did it to scores of Irish prisoners' families, and still do.

21
Appeal

When I was first talking to Bobby Cunningham and Jerry Mealey there on A Wing, Bobby dug me in the ribs with his elbow and said, 'So, you bombed Guildford, hey?'

Bobby was an Irish man who had just started a twenty-year sentence for conspiracy to cause explosions. He looked at me with a teasing smile on his face.

'You did it, hey?'

I blushed from the top of my head down to my chest, my ears were lighting up like neon signs, I was so overwhelmed by embarrassment. Here was I, who in court had been made out to be a crack IRA officer, the leader of the bombers and the most murderous Provo in England, having to say to Bobby and the others, 'No, all that stuff in the press about me was horse-shit. I didn't do it. I'm innocent.'

And they looked at me and said, 'Well, what the fuck are you doing in prison?'

Now that my father was convicted and it was brutally clear that my insane attempt to con the police into helping him had been useless, there was no reason to make out I was a bomber, except that I still had this irrational desire not to talk about my innocence.

At Wakefield I had seen a man going about the prison named Michael Luvaglio, who had been convicted for a fruit-machine murder years earlier in Newcastle. Luvaglio was well known in the prison as an unjustly convicted man who'd never had his name cleared, though he'd taken his case – with new evidence – all the way to the House of Lords. That decision became a precedent for allowing judges to substitute themselves for juries, when assessing fresh evidence. It was Luvaglio's case that the court of appeal relied on a year later when dramatic new evidence came to light for me.

So now, in his ninth year inside, Luvaglio used to do the flowers in the prison church, and every day I used to watch him going back and forth with the flowers in little vases, bowed down by sadness. You could see it from his movements, his way of holding himself, the way the clothes hung from him, like shrouds. And everywhere Luvaglio went in prison people would be saying, 'There goes Luvaglio, he's innocent.'

Luvaglio's innocence had become public property, everybody was coming up to him with useless advice, useless information, because everybody knew he was innocent and the House of Lords had still knocked him back. I didn't want to be a Luvaglio. I wanted my pain and my sorrow to be mine, and not the property of the whole prison. So although I had made a private vow to fight for my and my father's release, I didn't want to spend my energies fighting for it within the prison. I felt better saying nothing.

My father had no such problems. He was tireless. Wherever he went, whoever he saw – doctors, priests, lawyers, screws, fellow prisoners, fellow prisoners' *visitors*, van drivers coming into the prison, anyone – he'd be going up and buttonholing them saying, 'My name's Joe Conlon, I'm innocent and I shouldn't be here.'

At the very beginning of 1977 my father joined me at Wakefield, which was a great joy to me. He was the same as ever, never losing a chance to insist we were guiltless, an attitude so infectious, I found it gradually became easier for me to assert my innocence for myself. But by now the plot had taken another turn – Guildford was suddenly back in the news. A new IRA trial had opened at the Old Bailey with dramatic references to 'our' bombings.

The men in the dock openly admitted doing what they were accused of – a series of attacks all dating from a time after our own arrests. They were the Balcombe Street group, the most successful IRA active-service unit to have operated in England. They had kept going for a year and a half and done almost fifty attacks, getting caught in December 1975 after a siege in Balcombe Street. Now the leader of the gang, Joe O'Connell, stood up and said he refused to plead because the offences were political. But, he added one thing. He had a second reason for refusing to answer the charges, which was that 'the indictment does not include two charges concerning the Guildford and Woolwich pub bombings. I took part in both, for which innocent people have been convicted.'

At the trial O'Connell and the others decided to use the occasion not to defend themselves but to publicize our innocence. Every day embarrassing forensic details were coming out, linking the type of bomb used in Guildford with bombs set off by the Balcombe Street group after we had been arrested. Even worse for the police, it was said that a government forensic scientist had placed Woolwich first in a series of bombings done by the gang, but had later deleted it from his report at the request of a Sergeant Doyle of the Bomb Squad. I recognized the name. At Winchester, just after my conviction, I had been visited by a Sergeant Doyle, in the company of Chief Inspector Munday.

Now solicitors were coming to see us as they started preparing an appeal on the grounds of fresh evidence. I saw Alastair Logan – Paddy's solicitor – and he agreed to represent me.

It was around this time that the campaign for the release of the cockney prisoner George Davis was successful. It was a maximum-publicity campaign, with people digging up cricket pitches and daubing the notorious graffiti GEORGE DAVIS IS INNOCENT OK all over the country. I remember one day in the shop I was with a guy called Johnny Massey, a Londoner, and he was saying, 'You got to be going home now, Gerry. George Davis got out, and you got more evidence than he ever had.'

But first my father's and the Maguires' application for leave to appeal, which they had lodged straight after conviction, was heard. The main appeal was on Donaldson's summing-up, arguing that he hadn't properly dealt with the defence case. By this time, with the high we were on over the Balcombe Street admissions, we were all convinced they would get a result. It didn't happen. Lord Chief Justice Roskill was the main judge hearing it, and he knocked it back, saying there had been nothing wrong with Donaldson's summing-up, and that was that. My father hadn't even been allowed to be at his own hearing.

He treated the result as just a set-back. As usual, he was thinking of me before himself. My appeal was the main event on his programme.

'Don't worry, son, you're going to be out,' he'd tell me. 'These people have admitted they did it and you didn't. And when you get out, you'll be able to tell the world what they've done to us. Then we'll get out.'

The appeal was set for October 1977, and we were still on a great high. We were certain to walk out of court free.

Then suddenly I was moved to Canterbury, just as my mother had come over for her annual visit. It would have been the first time she'd seen my father and me together for three years, since we were at Brixton on remand. So that year the visits were even more painful than usual. My mother was bearing up, she was very strong and she refused to be beaten down by all this. But what they did in moving me so suddenly, on the day she was expecting to see us together, was cruel.

Another hard knock came soon after. My conversations with the police at Wandsworth had come to light. I had forgotten all about the interviews and, of course, I never knew they were taped. Now, though, it looked as if Havers was going to try to use them against us at the appeal. It was a very bad moment. I explained to Brian Rose-Smith, my new appeal solicitor, how I'd been emotionally black-mailed into talking to the police and told him how all the things I'd said had come from innocent sources. But that didn't lessen the acute shame and embarrassment I felt about the whole subject.

In the end the appeal judges – we had Lord Roskill too – wouldn't allow the tapes to be produced in evidence, although I'd found it hard to believe that they were going to damage our case anyway. In the witness-box the Balcombe Street people were completely credible. They gave such profound detail about the planning and execution of the bombings we'd been tried for that it was obvious they had been there. They were able to tell the weight of the bombs, the type of mechanism and where they were placed. They described which cars were used, where they were parked, and where the bombs were primed – and one of them even mentioned two old men with their shopping bags who were known to have been customers in the Horse and Groom before the bombs went off.

The judges accepted all this. But when it came to letting us out of gaol they couldn't bring themselves to do it. So they said we'd done the bombing together.

There was absolutely nothing to link us with the Balcombe Street men. If we'd been associating with each other, you'd think some of our fingerprints or hairs, some trace of us would have turned up among the masses of evidence found in the active-service unit's safe houses. But nothing did. And there was no trace whatsoever of them in any of our various statements, or in the verbals the police had used against us. If I was ready to name my own family and my friends from Belfast, why wouldn't I jump to hand them these names, written in Day-glo ink and wrapped up in Christmas paper?

The judges never looked at the contrast between us. The active-service unit were all from the Republic. They were disciplined, quiet types who never drew attention to themselves, while we were drunken, drug-taking, thieving, gambling young vagabonds from Belfast. The judges didn't seem to ask themselves whether we could have all co-operated together in an operation so precise, dangerous and difficult. They just accepted that we must have.

But how could they not see that the evidence of the Balcombe Street men made utter nonsense of the original police case against us? An elaborate yarn had been spun around us about recces, bomb-factories, explosives dumps, cars. The whole thing was exposed as a fairy-tale once the concrete *facts* produced by those real IRA team were accepted as true. It was they who reconnoitred the pubs, made the bombs, stored the explosives, hired the cars. There was no need and no room for a bunch of weirdos like us to get in on the act.

It made no difference, and we were knocked back to gaol. It took about an hour to read out the judgement in that cold, hard way they do it. The last sentences of the judgement were: 'In the end we are all of the clear opinion that there are no possible grounds for doubting the justice of any of these four convictions or for ordering retrials. We therefore propose to dispose of all those applications for leave to appeal by refusing them.'

Carole was crying. Disbelief was written all over Paul's and Paddy's faces. But somehow we had to face it – the judges couldn't see the wood for the trees. Or, more likely, they couldn't admit – even to themselves – there might have been an almighty miscarriage of justice.

22

Strangeways

Down from the Category A cells at the Old Bailey there are five flights of narrow stairs. I was pushed down with my wrists cuffed together behind my back, so tight that they were already becoming chafed and, by the end of the day, were bleeding. The screws were gloating about us being knocked back, and they celebrated the fact by bouncing me a few times off the walls of that long steep stair-well as we went down.

Once inside the A van we headed north, up the M1 and M6. Two or three hours later I heard the driver radioing ahead, asking for police assistance at a fuel stop. Then we drew into a service station.

The whole place was secured, ringed by armed men in flak jackets, carrying pump-action shot-guns. The only cars at the petrol pumps were a little red car and a station-wagon with a family gawping out of it – mum, dad and two kids – like this was a Wild West show come to town. We swept up, two motorcycle outriders, two squad cars, six screws with me, all armed. And strutting around the pumps like Mr T, with this sidearm in a holster hanging from his belt, was a police sergeant. He had a huge RAF whacko moustache and was having the time of his life, thinking, 'Look at me, look how important I am.'

I didn't hear the words but when I saw the father leaning out of the estate car to ask him something, I could imagine what was being said.

'What's going on?'

'Prisoner on the move.'

'But Jesus, who've you got in there. The Incredible Hulk?'

'IRA bomber. Maximum-security prisoner. In case they try and spring him, see?'

And he flipped open the flap of his holster, just in case the man hadn't noticed he was wearing it.

You spend these journeys in the A van peering through the little one-way windows looking for road signs, looking for a clue. We came off the M6 at the East Lancs Road, which I'd once hitched along with Skee and Anthony. I'd been almost penniless and starving then, but I had been free. Now I was chained up in something like a bank vault on wheels, I was still almost penniless and I hadn't eaten properly for hours. But I didn't feel starving. All my appetite was taken away at the thought of where we were obviously going: Strangeways.

Strangeways for a long time has been regarded as the hardest, nastiest, most poisonous gaol in the system. I'm surprised that the recent protest didn't happen in 1980 instead of 1990. I'd already had four months in Wandsworth and eighteen months in Wakefield, ten of them on punishment. Now I was going to have a taste of something even worse.

The A van's suspension tilted and it accelerated through the gates of the prison. It circled the building, parking beside a tall old brick chimney. I was pulled out, my wrists still tightly handcuffed, the chain on my cuffs linked by another pair of cuffs to the wrist of a big fifteen-stone screw. He yanked me up to a small, secure door and suddenly we were in the block.

They left out the normal processing you'd get in reception, and took me directly into the punishment block. They were telling me, 'We don't fuck around here, we don't take any shit whatsoever in this place.'

It was a long, narrow, stone-flagged passage, no more than four feet wide, with two dozen cell doors on each side. Half way down was a wider part, an area tiled in linoleum, where the office and the recesses were. Over the doorway leading into this area I saw a sign in blood-red paint: DON'T COMPLAIN YOU BASTARDS. YOU'VE ALL VOLUNTEERED.

I was uncuffed and the block screw gave me a water-jug and basin.

'Get water.'

I got water. The screw reminded me of the bastards in Wandsworth; he wore the same specially adapted peak to his cap, but so that it came down close to his eyes to give this menacing effect. He marched me along the continuation of that cell passage, with more cells on each side. It was a massive punishment block by the standards I'd known in other prisons. And outside each cell was a little alcove containing table, chair, mattress, blankets, sheets. I could see then that it was a hard regime, and there would be nothing whatever in the cells. The screw opened a door and I was fired into it.

I remembered the smell of the cell at Winchester, the filth of Wandsworth, but this was the worst I'd ever known. The bed frame was four inches off the floor, but the springs were loose and sagged down, so when you sat on it your arse was on the concrete. There was a dirty chamber-pot, and that was it. Then they gave me a mattress, the usual type of mattress caked with vomit and everything else. A bit later I got a table and chair and it was time for my tea.

They gave me something on a plate It was obviously food and at some time had been hot. But it looked like a cow pat and smelt of pig swill. I ate the small cake that went with it and put the tray plate in the corner, as far away from me as I could until slop-out. I got up at the window.

Below and opposite was a big blue plastic dome which, I discovered, contained the prison gymnasium. To one side I could see the side of a wing, with faces at all the windows, and conversation going back and forth which I could hear in snatches.

'. . . and they're playing Man United tomorrow . . . well I told him, that screw's a nonce himself . . . got any bob? . . . he told me he got a joey yesterday, and guess what was in it? . . . that was real crap they gave us for tea. My Barbara's written to the Home Office about this food . . . Anyone got snout they can spare?'

And I saw prisoners slinging lines, long lengths of string with packages on the end, passing snout, cannabis, Mars bars, newspapers from cell to cell. And every now and then someone who wouldn't use his pot for a crap would sling a little 'mystery parcel' of newspaper out, and it would split and spill the excrement over the blue dome.

I spent a total of nine weeks on what they call Good Order and Discipline at Strangeways before they moved me back to London and the Scrubs. GOAD is not quite the same as punishment, because you have furniture and privileges, but you're in solitary confinement. It's seen as more of a preventive measure, taken by the governor if he suspects you might be going to do something against good order. That's how I suppose they felt about me after the appeal was knocked back.

But anyway it wasn't long before I discovered what the true punishment regime at Strangeways was like.

On my first morning, a Saturday, a screw called Shepherd, a grey-haired Yorkshireman, came down.

'Want exercise this morning, Conlon?'

'Yes, OK.'

So after breakfast he slung me in a pair of coarse grey prison trousers – greys – the kind I'd been excused from wearing at Wakefield because they gave me a rash. I said, 'I'm not wearing those.'

'Well, lad – no greys, no exercise.'

'No exercise then. I'm not wearing those.'

He went away, me sitting in my filthy cell with nothing to do and an hour or two went by. Suddenly the door opened again, 'Stand up, Conlon, name and number to the governor.'

I'd hardly got my arse off the chair when I saw a blur passing the open cell door, and heard a voice calling out, 'That man needs a haircut.'

I swear I wouldn't have known the man again, he was past me so quickly. The door banged shut and I sat there, nothing to do. Dinner came, some more of this slop which I tried to eat, gave up and lay on the bed. I was disturbed some time later by a rattle of keys and the screw is back.

'Haircut, Conlon.'

'I didn't ask for a haircut.'

'It doesn't matter, the governor says you're getting one, now get out here.'

I didn't move, so two of them came in after me, pulled me out, held me down in this chair. A sheet was tied around my neck almost garrotting me and there was this prisoner standing ready with a pair of scissors that looked like shears. I'd always worn my hair long, and it must have come down past my ears and a little way down my back. Shepherd stood back and considered me, then he said, 'Give him one of your specials.'

So this prisoner grabbed hold of my hair in lumps and just chopped it off all the way round, starting about an inch above my ears. A pudding-basin cut leaving me looking like Friar Tuck. The screws were standing there pissing themselves, as if this was the funniest joke of the week. They laughed even louder when the so-called barber reached for his electric clippers and mowed into the back of my neck. He drew blood in several places.

I was slung back in my cell almost in tears about my hair, and with trickles of blood running down my neck. I picked up the little prison-issue mirror and saw what he'd done. I turned and flung the little mirror against the wall smashing it to fragments.

The next day, the Sunday, I was again invited to wear the greys for exercise and I refused again. On the Monday the screws opened me up and handed me a nicking sheet: *Offences against the rule of the prison – refusing an order to wear regulation trousers on exercise, Saturday and again Sunday*.

It meant I had to go before the governor at 11 am for an adjudication, the normal process by which rule infringements are dealt with. It was held in a little office, where the governor, Brown, was sitting behind the desk. When I saw him I almost staggered back. His eyes stared at me, the only moving things in a face so badly disfigured that it looked like a mask of scarred, dead flesh. He had no lips, ears, eyebrows, eyelashes. I later learned his tank got a direct hit from a German shell during the war, and he'd been the only survivor.

'Name and number for the governor.'

My number was 462779 but I never supplied it, or my name, on principle. When they tried to force me to I said, 'He knows who I am, he's got my file in front of him, hasn't he?'

'Name and number for the governor.'

'He *knows* my name and number.'

In the end Brown put an end to this by saying, 'Well we know who, and *what*, he is. Read the charge, Mr Shepherd.'

'Refusing to wear greys on exercise, sir.'

'How do you plead, Conlon?'

'Not guilty.'

Then Shepherd read his evidence, and Brown said, 'Conlon?'

'Must be wrong, because I wasn't on exercise on either day. I haven't been on exercise since I came here.'

'Is this right, Mr Shepherd?'

'Yes sir, he refused to go on exercise wearing the trousers.'

'Then I suggest you amend the charge, Mr Shepherd.'

So then they read out the amended charge – *refusing to go on exercise wearing the trousers*.

So Brown said, 'How do you plead, Conlon?'

'Still not guilty.'

'Well, I find you guilty. But you're new here and I'll be lenient this time. Fourteen days close confinement, no privileges. You can go.'

No privileges meant no radio, no smokes, no newspaper, no library. Nothing. Your cell had no furniture, the bed was taken out for fourteen hours a day, there was no table or chair. You'd get your dinner and sit on the floor propped against the wall and eat it from the floor. It was as close as they could bring you to eating like a dog. If they denied you a spoon or a fork, that's how it would have been.

You're in your cell twenty-three hours a day, unless it rains. Then it is twenty-four, and in Manchester it can rain for a week at a time. If you're lucky you get a cell on the side of the block facing outwards, towards the gymnasium dome. That side you can see sky, and the windows of the nearby wing, so there is usually something interesting to look at. But if you get put the other side of the passage there is nothing but the rear wall of the boiler-house about two feet from the cell window rearing forty or fifty feet above you. I spent about five weeks of my time in Strangeways looking at that brick wall.

I remember the rain. Prisoners are never allowed out in it and after a while you begin to miss the feel of rain. So I'd be reaching my hand out trying to just *feel* it, to get back the lost sensation of falling rain. Prisoners spend a lot of time trying for small satisfactions like that.

Bigger satisfactions are usually to do with putting one over on the screws. When I went in for the governor's adjudication that first Monday, I knew I might get fourteen days CC because Brown's reputation had gone before him. So before going in I'd made a tight little parcel of tobacco, papers and matches wrapped up in a piece of paper and bound around with a strand of wool from my blanket, and I'd tucked it in between the cheeks of my arse. So when the screws came in and stripped my cell – the little there was to strip – and searched my clothes I at least had that. It didn't last fourteen days, but it was a small victory over the screws.

During my nine weeks on the block at Strangeways I think I only saw fourteen screws and they were all, to a man, incredibly stupid. They were ruled by the timetable, doing everything robotically because they are utterly incapable of initiative. Their minds are so feeble that, if you had any sympathy going to waste, you might almost feel sorry for them. Their childish cruelty and pathetic attempts at humiliation begin to seem after a while just that, and then they lost their power over you. You'd be in the showers and they'd be coming to the peephole and sniggering and passing remarks. They'd jostle you to make you spill your pot at slop-out. I just stopped feeling humiliated and ashamed in the end – the screws were the ones who should be ashamed. A lot of them were fanatics for the National Front, they used to wear insignia under or even on their uniforms. But that would be typical of the breed – they were hooked on authority and brutality of a very basic kind.

For most of the time the block at Strangeways was kept almost full, because Brown was such a disciplinarian, and completely behind the screws in everything they did. And nobody ever came down the block without getting a kicking. Once there was a kid who I'll call Mike, who was doing four years for burglary. He was probably about twenty-two, the same age as me at the time. He came to Manchester in transit from Lancaster to Leeds, and it was a Saturday. So he was in his cell up on the wing listening to the football commentary on his radio – probably his home team Leeds United – when they opened him up to go out and get his tea. He said, 'It's just two minutes to full-time, I'll come out then.'

'No you won't, son. You'll get your tea now.'

'Just fuckin' let me listen to another minute, won't you?'

The screw carried on down the landing opening everyone else for their tea, and this kid came out and got his tea, and then everybody was locked up again.

A few minutes later they were back in Mike's cell in force and dragged him down the block. I heard this scuffling coming from the passage, and then a kind of yelping, exactly like you'd get from standing hard on a dog's paw. I listened and I could hear the boots going in, as Mike was kicked all over the block, making this yelping sound. Then they threw him into the cell beside me.

I waited till they'd gone then I called out, 'You all right? What they done to you?'

'They battered me, they battered me.'

It was all he could say, but I could hear this sobbing coming from him. So later that night the Catholic priest came round as usual hearing confessions from anyone who wanted to go to mass the next morning. So he came into my cell and I said, 'Father, you've got to go in next door, there's a kid come in and he's taken a terrible beating from the screws. It sounds like he's in a bad way.'

So the priest went into this kid's cell, and about twenty minutes later he came back to me and said in this rather resigned voice, 'Yes, he's had a fair kicking all right. His eye's starting to close and his nose has been bleeding, and his mouth. They gave him a right going over, so they did.'

'Look, father, this sort of thing happens all the time. You've got to go out and tell the police, someone, what's going on in this block here.'

Well the priest looked down at the ground, and he looked out of the window, and he said, almost in a whisper, 'Well, Gerry, now. That would unfortunately be more than my job's worth, you know? I wish it were otherwise, but you see . . .'

I just stood there, absolutely astounded. I found myself shouting, 'So just who are you working for, father? God or the fucking Home Office?'

He just walked out of my cell.

Up until then I had been going to mass on Sunday at Strangeways, but this disillusioned me, I couldn't have respect for the priest any more, and when he came back down the block after that he just couldn't look me in the eye any more. I had already become disillusioned with the Catholic priests within the prisons, because of a bitter experience at Wandsworth.

When I was on the block there, I used to go to chapel regularly every Sunday with Gerry Hunter. We used to go in last as we were on the punishment block and because we were 'IRA terrorists'. We always had to sit at the very back of the chapel and were the first taken out at the end of the mass. The week that Gerry Hunter was moved from Wandsworth to Gartree, the Catholic priest came to see us in the block as he usually did once a week. Only, this time, he said he'd been having complaints from his congregation about us attending the mass. People were saying they weren't going to go if we were allowed to go. So he thought that – if we wanted to attend – we should sit in the vestry away from the congregation, so that nobody would know we were there. I was absolutely shocked – I couldn't believe it. A Catholic priest saying this to me? It seemed to go against everything he believed in.

I attended once, but felt so humiliated by the experience that I never went back again. I also started looking at Catholic priests in a different light after it.

For a prisoner to make a complaint against a screw for brutality was a very difficult and dangerous thing to do. The Board of Visitors deal with the complaint, and are heavily influenced by what the governor has to say. If they don't uphold it – which in general they almost never do – you're immediately on a charge of making false and malicious allegations. For this you receive an automatic 112 days on the block, plus loss of remission the same. If it should ever come about that a prisoner makes a *successful* complaint he's in even worse trouble, because then the screws are out for their revenge. So no prisoner in his right mind ever lodged complaints against screws, not at Strangeways anyway.

I met one decent man who came in to see us sometimes on the block, a little Dublin rabbi who used to come down and have a chat. He was very shrewd and he'd be very aware of what was going on. I remember him having some sharp words with the screws about things that were happening. He did his best for Mike, for example, though to no avail. But even he was probably intimidated by Strangeways, because that was the kind of place it was.

The screws loved to play domination games with the prisoners. They'd get them to perform little tricks. If you had a man who couldn't do without tobacco on the block and he was there with no privileges, then the screws had him eating out of their hands – he'd do anything, anything for a cigarette. The screws revelled in it. They'd get some hard man in, taking liberties, mouthing abuse at them for a week, but then his snout would run out. And suddenly he'd be at his door calling out to the screws, begging them, pleading with them for a cigarette.

'Give us a cigarette, boss. I'm dying for a smoke.'

It was horrible to see and hear how they'd be laughing at the screws' jokes, calling them by their first names, doing humiliating little tasks and tricks. They'd do a tap dance, they'd do things they could never admit in front of their wives and girl-friends and children. They'd be selling their dignity and self-respect for one Benson & Hedges.

There'd be some prisoners they'd never subdue. One was called Fred the Head.

Fred was doing four years for assault. He was about six foot tall and weighed about sixteen stone, mad as a hatter and couldn't give a fuck for man nor beast. Certainly not screws. They were petrified of him. He did nearly all his time on punishment.

One day the screws were giving him a hard time and when he got his razor the next morning, he shaved his head completely bald. When they opened his cell for breakfast, he emerged like a rhino with a lump of his own turd shaped like a cone on the top of his head. He grabbed the nearest screw and proceeded to rub his head all over his face. The screw screamed – Fred just got more punishment, but he never got a kicking. No screw wanted to be 'shitted up' by him – their little bit of power would be fatally undermined by this, and they'd lose face. They could never exert authority again over us prisoners. All we would have to do if they tried was sniff. No one can do you for sniffing, can they?

23

Wormwood Scrubs

The year 1977, which had begun so hopefully, ended for me in dejection. My appeal had failed, my father's appeal had failed, I had tasted the soul-destroying cruelty of the block in Manchester and now, as I returned to London, I found I would have to face the consequences of my foolish conversations with the Bomb Squad two years earlier.

Wormwood Scrubs, where I now found myself, was another huge old prison with tremendous variety among inmates. The Irish were very strong, but there was a large black population, and a big collection of cockney gangsters. The wings were so large that the prisoners formed themselves into smaller subgroups. You could see them at the tables, where everybody ate their meals. The tables were set out in the well below the landings, numbered 1 to 25, and the different clans had different tables. The Irish tables were 13 and 14. The up-and-coming young cockney villains were on 4, the old-style London gangsters were on 15 and 16.

It has always been possible for certain prisoners to get positions of power, like feudal barons. They used to talk of tobacco barons, but nowadays they are more likely to be drugs barons. But whatever it was, if they could control a valuable commodity within prison they could get to the top of the pecking order. In the D Wing at the Scrubs when I first went there a notable East End villain was top dog. We would call people like him 'The Face'. There are loads of 'faces' in prisons. Cockneys are all 'faces'. He was so powerful that when the screws had a problem, they'd say to The Face, 'Look, please could you sort this out, because I can't.'

The Face had run a club in Soho, and had a colourful background. For a gangster, he had very high principles and complete determination never to compromise. This meant there were a lot of things he would never deal in. The Face hated pornography, which is all round a prison like the Scrubs. He hated drugs, also all round the prison, and homosexuality, which was not unknown there. But The Face was the bookie as well as running various other smaller rackets, and he was a character, one of the many reasons why I found the Scrubs a more interesting prison than most. The Face wasn't the only character in the Scrubs. There was this black prisoner called Mackie, who had come from Jamaica in the late sixties, and you could hardly understand him because of the thick patois that he used.

Mackie was a terrible gambler, his whole life in prison revolved around gambling. He'd bet on two flies going up the wall and the first thing you noticed was his bald head and two rows of gold teeth. He felt he had suffered a serious miscarriage of justice. Without going into all the details, he felt his 'crime' would be regarded as taking justice into your own hands in Jamaica. He used to work with an Irish guy in the laundry and kept saying, 'If I'd been white, I wouldn't have got as long as I'd got.' The Irishman said: 'So what you're saying, Mackie, is that you want white man's justice. Is that it?' Mackie agrees, 'Yeah, man, white man's justice.' Mackie starts to drive the Irish guy nuts about his case, going on and on, driving him mad. So somehow or other the Irish guy gets hold of a bucket of whitewash and a paint brush, takes Mackie up to his cell and tells him, 'They'll take notice of you now.' He proceeded to paint Mackie with the whitewash and gets a placard saying 'Me wants white man's justice'.

He sends Mackie down to the governor's office where an important meeting is taking place and tells him to lie down outside the door. By this time, half the wing knows about it and have congregated looking at Mackie, covered in whitewash down on the floor, waiting to see what the governor's reaction's going to be when he sees Mackie suddenly a white man lying in his underpants. After about twenty minutes the door opens and the first one out is the chief governor who looks down at Mackie. He just says 'Hello Mackie' – just steps over him and walks away. The rest of the people in the meeting do the same. That was that. Mackie went off and found the Irish fella who told him, 'Don't worry Mackie. We'll think of something else, the next time.'

Mackie wasn't the only one who changed his appearance to make a point. There was a guy in there when I first arrived and the same Irish guy who had advised Mackie prompted him to get a response from the prison authorities, which again backfired. This guy, who I'll call Peter, was doing fifteen years and wanted to send a photograph to his family to remind them what he looked like, but the prison authorities wouldn't allow it. In prison, they take a photo of you every two years as an update for their records. When Peter was told by the screws that he was going to have his photo taken for this, this Irish adviser told him he had the perfect opportunity to make his point.

Peter had really long hair and a long beard, like a caveman. The Irish guy says: 'What you do is this. We get hold of the barber's kit and we shave half your beard off on the left-hand side of your face and we shave half your hair off on the right hand side. That'll teach them not to give you your photograph.' So that's what they do, and his head looks like a harlequin. He marches down the stairs – again, everyone's gathered to watch – to movement control where the screws are waiting to take his photograph. Peter says, 'Tell David Bailey I'm coming.' The screws take one look at him and nearly freak out, tell him he can't be taken for a photograph like that. The next morning he's nicked for changing his appearance, gets fourteen days' punishment and is moved to another prison.

Anything you wanted, bar a woman, was available in that prison, at a price. I've seen cells with cocktail bars in them. I've seen people maintain heroin habits there. But this atmosphere of wheeling and dealing and struggling for an edge, an advantage, meant that it was a bad place to be on your own, without allies. When I first arrived this was my fate. The reason was that the story of how the prosecution had tried to produce those conversations in Wandsworth at the Appeal had gone round the republican prisoners, and they didn't like the sound of it. It seemed to them that I had co-operated with the police. I had been talking about people as members of the IRA and making out I was a member of the IRA – a senior one at that. At the very least they thought I had been blundering around in an area I knew nothing of, and should have stayed well clear. At the worst I could have unwittingly put their own members in mortal danger.

There was a period on D Wing, when I first got there, of being treated with open hostility by the Irish. None of them would talk to me and there was no communication, no chance for me to account for myself. But soon there came two saving graces. The first was Shane Docherty. He had been convicted when still a teenager of sending a whole lot of parcel bombs to eminent English people, but though he was IRA he was really a law unto himself. Not long after all this he made a public statement renouncing violence and apologizing to his victims. At this time, though, Doc was a regular member of the republican group, but he could see I was in difficulties and he took it on himself to begin to acknowledge me.

The second saving grace was the arrival of my father, a month or so after me. I hadn't seen him for six months and though I found him changed – more ill and older-looking than I could have imagined – it was a big boost to be back with him, and on the same wing.

Shane was on very good terms with my father – who wasn't? – and he came into my dad's cell one day and referred to my problem with the other republicans.

'I think it's outrageous. These tapes weren't that significant. I think Gerry should come down with me, speak to some of the boys and tell them what really happened.'

I was relieved. What I'd said to the police had been about some of them – Doc himself is mentioned somewhere, as a name I'd picked up while on remand – and I felt I owed them an explanation. So I saw three of them, and they listened to me. I explained it was a desperate gamble, that my father was ill and that I was at my lowest ebb immediately after my conviction. They listened in silence and then said they'd have a talk with everyone else.

A couple of days later Doc came back to me and said, 'The situation is, we know now what was said on the tapes. We have access to a transcript.'

I couldn't imagine how they got one, and he didn't tell me. But he went on: 'I've read it and I can see that nothing you said could have helped the police at all. That is the general view. So it's been decided that anyone who wants to talk to you can talk to you.'

It was a great relief because, as I've already explained, the company of Irish prisoners was very important to me, particularly in a place like the Scrubs, which was such a clannish society. So gradually, over the next few months, the great majority of them started acknowledging me and then talking to me again.

The Scrubs was my home for the next eighteen months. Every day prison life went on, absorbing me in the normal business of keeping my head above water, keeping a watch on my back, and then looking for an edge.

But meanwhile, outside the walls, there were the first stirrings of support for our case. My mother is a great believer in the power of prayer, and for a year she had been going down to St Peter's Pro-Cathedral in the evenings, three times a week, to do the Stations of the Cross and pray for our release. Father McKinley, the priest, came out into the church one evening and saw her there, and saw the tears running down her face. So he went over to her and put his arm round her.

'What's wrong, Sarah?'

She said, very simply, 'My family's in gaol. My husband's in gaol, my son's in gaol, my brother's in gaol, my sister-in-law, two of my young nephews. And, father, they're innocent, and nobody will believe me when I tell them. Nobody wants to listen.'

The priest took her into the presbytery and made her a cup of tea and they talked. That night he couldn't sleep, he lay there thinking about what my mother had said. He knew my father, of course. He'd also known Paddy Armstrong very well as a boy, taught him to play snooker in the Boys' Club, all that. He'd known me a little too, when I was at school, and I think he knew of my later reputation for unreliability. But particularly when he thought of Paddy he thought of a timid young man, absolutely terrified of violence, and he knew he couldn't be a bomber. Well, if Paddy wasn't, then neither was I. And my father was the last man he would associate with bombings. So the next chance he got, Father McKinley said to my mother, 'Sarah, I don't know what I can do, but if I don't do anything, then I know I'll be making them right in the things they have done to your family.'

So he started a letter-writing campaign within Ireland, along with my mother and Lily Hill, trying to contact people who might help reopen the case.

Then, in England, there was this wee Irish nun, Sister Sarah Clarke, who is a kind of might atom. She looks like a saint but she has a withering tongue that would strip paint if she set her mind to it. There were also two priests, Father Faul and Father Murray, who had been interested in our case from the moment of our arrest. They'd also been writing letters, badgering people on our behalf.

*

Meanwhile my father's health had deteriorated sharply. He still tried to look after me. He'd tell me not to get into unsuitable games like gin-rummy and bridge where I was obviously a learner. Then later, when he thought I was good enough, he'd back me, give me the money and the tobacco and say, 'Go out there and make a few quid.'

My father was a very shrewd gambler, so I learned a lot from him about which were the players I could win from and which were the ones who'd always beat me, come what may. At one time I fancied myself at snooker, and there was a very good player called Dave Scott who regularly ran up breaks of seventy and eighty. So he gave me twenty up for a fiver one day and hammered me. It was a lot of money in prison terms – nearly two weeks' wages – and my father was furious.

'What sort of idiot are you, playing the likes of Scott? You rush into everything, you got to think about the game, the odds. You might as well give him the five pounds before you start.'

He loved to watch me playing the one game I could really shine at, football. He used to appear at the touchline before our Sunday morning games and whisper, 'I want you to score five, because I've got a wee bet on you.'

And sometimes he'd tell me to make a mug of some player who he thought fancied himself too much, and I'd try to score through the guy's legs or something. I enjoyed the game anyway, but twice as much when my father was watching.

I suppose his being with me on D Wing must have stopped me doing what I wanted from time to time, particularly stupid things. But we didn't fall out for long. He had always had this powerful need to protect me and, anyway, he talked sense. He helped me lose for ever the embarrassment I'd had about mentioning my innocence He said I must always mention it, and he hammered away at this topic over and over, as if he knew he hadn't much time.

'Never be ashamed that you are in prison, because you're here for nothing. Always walk around with your head up, you drop your head for no one. It's the judges and police, who done this to you, who should.'

I wasn't the only one he spoke to like this. People came and talked to him about all sorts of things, because he always talked sense.

There came a point when he decided not to go to work any more. The screws came and tried to make him, but he laughed at them, waving them away. They could see he wasn't fit. It took far too much out of him just getting down to the tailoring shop where he worked – he couldn't walk twenty-five yards without stopping for a rest. And through all this he went on radiating innocence, as even hard-bitten screws couldn't help noticing. The governor, Norman Honey, was increasingly concerned. He had my father taken off the block and got him open visits, and he even began lobbying the Home Office to get him parole. Within the prison system itself, then, he was increasingly being treated as a harmless, innocent man.

Then two Labour MPs, Phillip Whitehead and Andrew Bennett, took an interest. They had been coming to see Shane Docherty, because Doc was thinking of making this gesture of publicly leaving the IRA, and was petitioning for a transfer to Ireland. But Doc could see how fast my father was going downhill, and he kept saying to these two, 'You should be seeing Joe Conlon. The man's innocent and he's dying slowly on D Wing. If we could get him to Ireland we could maybe get him home to his wife on compassionate grounds.'

Bennett and Whitehead are both very good, honourable men. They began to see my father, and gradually the word got around about Joe Conlon and then, because I was his son, about the Guildford Four.

I was playing football one Sunday morning in 1979, completely lost in the game. I wasn't in prison when I was playing football, I was at Wembley or Parkhead or the Maricana, or I was back home in Peel Street playing with the Comanches – anywhere but here on the tarmac at Wormwood Scrubs. Then a screw came out, an absolute bastard but he was looking excited.

'Conlon, Conlon. Got to go to movement control right away.' I waved at him, and said, 'Yeah, yeah. When the game's over.'

'No, no. You're wanted now. You got to go now.'

I kept on playing and he kept on shouting at me, dancing around on the touchline, so I went over.

'What is it?'

'Can't tell you, just get over there.'

I was nervous of a wind-up, but I thought maybe my mother had sent something over like a pair of trainers, and I'd better get them now rather than have to wait until the morning.

So I trundled over to movement control in my football gear,

pouring sweat, and all of a sudden I saw this tall thin grey-haired figure waiting for me, wearing a black cape and a red skull-cap, and my first impression was, here was Batman come to see me. Then I heard this screw saying to him, 'Your Eminence, this is Conlon.'

And the caped figure came up to me and just put his arms around me and said, 'I'm Cardinal Hume. Will you take me to see your father?'

It's very unusual to get a visit in the cells, but we walked over to my father's cell, other prisoners gawping openly at us and me feeling very nervous and tongue-tied. We went into the cell and I said, 'Dad, Cardinal Hume's come to see you.'

Then I felt better, because I knew my father's quality. I knew there was now no way Cardinal Hume would not go away convinced that innocent people were in prison. I couldn't have done it (and in fact I didn't because I headed straight back to the football pitch), but I knew my father could. And he did, because when Cardinal Hume left he said to the screws, 'Make sure you treat these men well, because there may have been a miscarriage of justice.'

And he has continued to say ever since that this meeting was enough to convince him we were innocent, even before he'd seen the evidence.

The visit of Cardinal Hume gave us new hope and we were even thinking of a peaceful transition towards our release, after a few months, a year or two at most. But our sense of peace was shattered within a matter of days.

It all started because a number of prisoners had been transferred from Gartree to D Wing at the Scrubs. They built up a lot of discontent over the different regulations about money, namely private cash. Rightly so.

In all prisons there are two types of money that can be spent at the prison shop or canteen: your prison earnings and your private cash. No prisons allow tobacco to be bought with private cash. The same with tea and food. Only prison earnings will buy these things.

But at many prisons, Gartree being one, there's no such restriction on toiletries like shampoo, soap and toothpaste. You can buy these with your private cash, which leaves you more of your meagre earnings (£3 a week) to convert into tobacco and food. This was not so in 1979 at the Scrubs. There you had to use prison earnings to buy toiletries, which meant you probably had to go without tobacco every so often just to buy toothpaste or soap or razor-blades.

When an influx of Gartree people arrived there was a lot of resentment on D Wing, not surprisingly, because tobacco is much more than just a smoke in prison, it's a form of currency. Things are bought with it among prisoners, and it's used as a medium for gambling.

Somebody had the idea of a sit-down protest on the wing, a refusal to be banged up. It started one night after tea, in rather a carnival atmosphere – very peaceful, with the prisoners milling around among the tables, chatting and some of them singing, and some of them drinking prison hooch. The screws were there too, not trying to interfere, waiting for orders. As it passed nine-thirty I was with a couple of other men on the ground floor. We were talking to the assistant governor in charge of the wing, Gregory Smith, and he was commenting on how peaceful the protest was. We were speculating on how soon there would be some sort of negotiations.

About this time Shane Docherty went up to the Fours and looked out. He came flying down saying there was an army of screws in riot gear packed into C Wing exercise yard – the mufti squad. Well, we'd already heard rumours of screws being bussed in from Aylesbury, Wandsworth, Pentonville and Brixton, but we thought they'd be sure to try to negotiate us back into our cells before they used force.

But suddenly there was a terrifying noise, a hundred men all yelling together. The centre gate of the wing burst open and a battalion of Darth Vaders charged through. They were dressed in brown overalls and wearing riot helmets, riot shields and were beating the shields with pick-axe handles.

The three standing nearest the gate when it opened were a guy who'd had polio named Nick, a guy called John, and Fred, who'd lived in Holland and was a good bridge player. They just spun round and went down like skittles, knocked clean out of the way. After that it was a complete free-for-all. The screws waded in busting any head in sight, spattering blood everywhere. We just bolted for the iron stairs which led up to the landing, we thought the only safe place was a cell. There was panic and pandemonium, the handrails on the narrow stairs were bending under the weight of men trying to get out of the way. The screws had a battle-cry, 'Get the niggers! Get the Irish!' (Lord Mountbatten had been murdered three days earlier.)

I fought my way up to the twos, and looked down to the ground floor. The screws were laying about them viciously, beating people as they fell, groups of them standing over a man curled up on the floor, just beating him and kicking him until you could hear bones cracking like pistol shots. The air was full of horrible screams and shouts and groans.

Meanwhile screws had entered the wing by the top landing and were running along closing the cell doors to prevent prisoners taking refuge in the cells. I was on the threes by now and a man named Bob, a tall gangly fellow with a moustache, was with me and he spotted an open cell.

'Come on Gerry, in here.'

We got into the cell and shut the door and leaned against it listening to the massacre going on outside. I had just seen Billy Power, one of the Birmingham Six, being ambushed by a gang of mufti screws who by now had climbed the stairs and started to sweep the landings. Billy was just picked up and kicked like a football along the threes, howling and screaming at the pain.

It eventually became quieter. There was no longer the cacophony of howls and yells, screws grunting with effort, bones splintering, pick-axe handles bouncing off skulls, the thunder of boots along landings. Now we heard the groans of injured men being carted away, and then, one by one, the cell doors being opened up and the prisoners being pulled out, given a kick and a slap and dragged to their own rightful cells.

When at last they pulled me out – by the hair – I managed to get a look down at the ground floor just before a boot mashed into my ribs. There had been a bloodbath. The ground floor was awash with blood, thick, glistening slicks of it on the floor, splashes of it on the walls and door, wet dripping gouts of it on the handrail and the stairs. It was as if someone had taken bicycle pumps and filled them with blood and sprayed it in every direction.

And everywhere there were shocked and wounded prisoners – grey hair turned red, gaping head wounds, eyes staring with shock.

But the screws hadn't finished. They were laughing and giggling as they turned their staves on anything breakable – cups, cupboards, bottles of sauce. I saw one take a bag of rice, burst it open and pour the rice into a pool of blood on the floor, mixing it in with his boot. I saw them going into cells, smashing radios and record-players, ripping up photographs and books.

My own cell had been completely wrecked. They'd broken my battery-operated record-player, my records. All the photographs of my family torn up. A guitar my brother-in-law had sent me was smashed. I sat on the bed and found my arse in a puddle – one of them had pissed on the mattress. I moved to the floor, listening to the confused sounds from the wing. Prisoners started getting up to their windows, finding out what had happened. Stories flew around – that people had been killed. People were saying they'd seen people being brutally beaten with batons. The nurses' home of Hammersmith Hospital faced D Wing, my side of the wing. The nurses were shouting over 'What's been going on over there? What's been happening?' because they had heard it. Prisoners were shouting back to the nurses, telling them what had happened, asking them to call the police.

The screws came round, screaming abuse through the doors, telling the prisoners to get back down from the windows. I could hear the screws moving down the landings opening and banging the doors. I had no idea what was happening – whether people had been taken away. Eventually, a squat little PO opened my door. He was *covered* in blood – his face, his hair, his white shirt. To look at him, you'd think he had been attacked himself. He stared at me with wild eyes 'Any injuries?' I just shook my head quickly, although my face was all swollen up on one side and I'd had lumps of my hair pulled out.

It was a long time before, eventually, I heard a final door slam and a voice calling out, 'They're all back. Every prisoner's back in his cell. Roll count complete.'

24

My Father Dies

My father had survived the riot because he had gone into his cell to rest just before the mufti squad arrived, and when he heard the attack happening he had closed his door. If he'd been caught in the open floor like me I'm sure he would have been killed. He would never have been able to get away.

The D Wing was clamped down for weeks afterwards. Visits were cancelled, exercise was cancelled, association was cancelled. Work, chapel, library were all cancelled and we were locked up twenty-four hours, bar slop-out and meals. The only prisoners who spent any time outside on the wing were the cleaners, scrubbing away the blood. The entire wing had been sentenced to twenty-eight days' punishment and twenty-eight days' loss of remission – and the weather was sweltering. I knew this would play havoc with my father's breathing. He had reached a stage where he needed a flow of fresh air, and there wouldn't be too much of that in a closed cell in a heat wave. One prisoner, Roy Walsh, insisted on keeping my father's door open during the heatwave, as he could see the difficulties my father was having in the suffocating heat. Roy ended up getting punishment for this.

After about a month the weather and life on the wing gradually began to get back to normal. Some time in October I was sent back to work. I didn't do any work, I was just sat with the other guys I hadn't seen for so long talking, when two screws came in.

'Conlon. Cell search.'

So I went with them, I didn't know why they wanted to search my cell. But as it turned out the search had been a ruse. The screws didn't take me back on the wing, they took me into reception, handcuffed me to another screw and the next thing I knew I was in a Category A van. Ghosted.

They took me to Wandsworth, down the block, locked me in, and the next day I saw the governor.

'You've been sent here on a ten seventy-four, Good Order and Discipline. You'll be held here for twenty-eight days and then either returned to the place you've come from or transferred to another establishment. Take him away.'

I lived out my twenty-eight days on the block and hoped to be transferred straight back to the Scrubs. I found myself instead back in the A van heading towards the south-west of England. I was concerned it might be the Isle of Wight, where visits are much more difficult for prisoners' families, but it was once again Winchester.

At Winchester, with all its bad memories, I heard that my father had been turned down for parole. We wrote to each other, and I gathered he had been taken into the prison hospital on hunger strike. I was frantic with worry. I wrote home to my mother telling her to tell my father not to be silly and to come off it right away. My father had gone on hunger strike as he was at his wit's end at being turned down for parole again. I kept desperately trying to tell him to come off, that everything would be all right. Suddenly I lost my reason. I smashed up my cell, made a pile of everything burnable on the mattress and set fire to it. The screws smelt the smoke, opened up and I walked out in a cloud of smoke as they went in with fire extinguishers to put it out.

The governor didn't even put me on punishment, he just said, 'You'll only be here a couple more days, you'll be seeing him soon.'

I was back in the Scrubs, walking into D Wing towards my father's cell, within the wing. By this time I knew he'd come off hunger strike. The cell was empty. I looked at the identification card on the outside and found it was turned back to front with 'HOSP' scrawled on it.

Back at movement control I asked about him and a screw named Curren was standing around. He said, 'He's where he should be down in the hospital, Irish bastard.'

I was carrying this Roberts radio, and I just smashed it down on his head, shaking with anger and grief, because no one had told me anything about my father since I'd got back to the Scrubs. I was dragged down the block and charged with assault. The governor came down next morning but he only gave me a suspended sentence. He said I could see my father in the evening.

I hadn't seen him for nearly two months and was shocked at how he looked, eyes sunk in his face, gasping for breath and so small-looking in that hospital bed.

He perked up a little when he saw me, and seemed to make some progress after that. He started eating a little, and then we had some cheering Christmas visits. Ann came with her new baby, Sarah, who we'd never seen in the flesh. My father was cheered at seeing his granddaughter but after they'd gone he took another turn for the worse. I remember seeing him on New Year's Eve. I went into the hospital with a packet of biscuits sent from Billy Power on the wing and a newspaper, and as soon as I went in there I knew something was wrong. He was lying there completely on his own, his face blue and a terrible rasping noise coming from him. He somehow got out the words to tell me he needed the inhaler, so I tore into the dispensary and found the two hospital screws playing draughts.

'Will you come and take a look at him!'

'In a minute, in a minute.'

I kicked the draughts board up in the air and got hold of one of the screws by his ear.

'Look at my father. Give him something, you bastard, give him something.'

Then I started wrecking the dispensary, smashing chairs into cupboards, breaking glass. Next thing alarm bells were going off, screws were running in from every direction, and the doctor was looking at my father. He was taken at once to Hammersmith Hospital, which is about three hundred yards from the Scrubs. I was taken back to the wing to await adjudication. When I saw the governor I said, 'If I hadn't done that he'd probably be dead.'

The governor again treated me leniently, telling me my father was in a serious condition and he was going to inform my mother. I'd be allowed down to the Hammersmith to see him myself.

My mother came over with my Aunt Bridget. Hughie and Kate were in to see him too, and Sister Sarah Clarke went in every day. And then, after a few days, I myself was taken out, handcuffed and put into a car, the first car I'd been in since 1974. When we drove round the corner to the Hammersmith, the whole place was swarming with armed police, in the grounds, around the doorway, in corridors.

My father was in a room on the ground floor. He had a drip plugged into his arm and I don't know what other treatment he'd been getting, but he looked about fifty per cent better than I'd seen him for months. He was sitting up and the nurses were there clucking over him and saying he'd been a good boy, eating up his tea and all that. I went away feeling that so long as he stayed where he was and they kept up the treatment he was capable of getting back on his feet.

But a few days later a screw said he'd seen someone looking in at the window of my father's hospital room. So some bright spark decided it might be an IRA reconnaissance, and that any time now they'd be trying to spring Joe Conlon from hospital – Joe Conlon who couldn't walk twenty yards. So in a panic they bundled him in his pyjamas into a taxi and whisked him back to the prison hospital.

Then my mother could no longer stay, she was terrified of losing her job. So she flew back to Belfast. And it was like being at square one again, my mother back across the water, my father back being looked after by these screws who've had the bare minimum of paramedical training and now thought they were brain surgeons.

By the 18th of the month he'd gone back downhill again, lost all the ground he'd made up in the Hammersmith, and was developing pneumonia. He went back to the Hammersmith and I was sitting in my cell listening to the radio late one night – around ten o'clock – when a screw came and told me I was going down to see him now, in the middle of the night. The hospital was again full of policemen armed to the teeth, I was taken up the stairs past a policeman holding a pump-action shot-gun and into his room.

I couldn't understand why it was so full of people, Catholic priests, Home Office people, screws, police, doctors. The room was crowded, with everyone standing round muttering or just standing quietly, as if they were there to witness something.

My father had an oxygen mask on, drips stuck in his veins. He was awake. I went near the bed, still handcuffed to the screw, and saw that even with the oxygen he was labouring for breath. I began to cry. My father moved, twitched his hand up and pulled away the oxygen mask.

'I'm going to die.'

'No you're not. You're not going to die.'

'Yes I am. Don't be worrying. I want you to promise me something.'

'Yes, OK.'

'I mean it.'

'Yes, I promise you.'

Speech was taking it out of him, but it was so important that he raised his voice.

'When I die I don't want you attacking no screws. I want you to start clearing your name. My death's going to clear your name and when you get your name cleared, you clear mine.'

I was crying. I leaned forward to touch him with both my hands, but one wrist was still handcuffed. And then he looked past me at all these people and said loud enough for them all to hear, 'If any of youse people think I'm guilty, look me straight in the face.'

They all dropped their heads forward on their shoulders and he said, 'How does it feel to be murdering an innocent man?'

Then a screw came forward and said to me, 'The visit's over.'

And I was led out.

I sat in my cell just buried in grief. I knew I was never going to see him again.

I must have gone around the next day and the day after that in a fog, not knowing what was around me. The priest would come in and see me each night, just to say he'd seen Joe and he was talking a bit today, things like that. Then, some time after eight on the Wednesday night, the 23rd of January, he appeared at my door with this strange look on his face, sad and sympathetic.

'It's the news you've been waiting for.'

I looked up, 'What's that, Father?'

I couldn't think what news he was talking about. He said, 'Your father passed away peacefully.'

I sat in silence, trying to grasp it. Because I'd not understood when the priest tried to prepare me, it took me a while to make the words mean anything. The priest tried to say a few more words, but I more or less pushed him out of the cell.

Exactly what happened to my father's body on the way back to Ireland is still a mystery. British Airways, the only airline which flew direct to Belfast, refused outright to carry his coffin. So it had to go by Aer Lingus to Dublin and then on by road. But in transit it went missing, and for two or three days it could not be found. Frantic with worry my mother was trying to find it and was given a number to ring in Hereford. She was told a post-mortem had been done. No one could explain why it was Hereford, why there had been a post-mortem, who had ordered it, what its conclusions had been. Then she was told the coffin was at the RAF base at Brize Norton in Oxfordshire. It finally got to Aer Lingus and came to rest where it belonged, home in Belfast. My mother received the bill of almost a thousand pounds, which she had to pay before the body was released. I was refused permission to travel over for the burial.

Two days before his funeral we had a Requiem in the prison chapel, and very unusually they let my uncle Hughie come in, the only outsider who was present. There were a lot of the Irish prisoners, a few of my father's other friends and one screw, Jim McNulty, a PO who had got to know my father well. Hughie said something to him and McNulty, who was visibly upset, said, 'I thought he was innocent.'

So did everyone else in the chapel, but it was good to hear it from a screw.

The day after Joe Conlon died my mother received a letter from the Home Office. It said that, taking into account the many representations which had been made to the Home Secretary regarding my father's state of health, Mr Whitelaw had now decided to arrange for his speedy release into her custody. The decision was made purely on compassionate grounds. It was signed by an official.

25

Parkhurst and Long Lartin

I was trying to hold myself together, wanting very much not to break down in front of the screws. I'd asked for a telephone call to my mother, but they'd turned it down: IRA prisoners couldn't have phone calls. I was very withdrawn, I wouldn't exercise or go to work. I just wanted to lie in my cell and stare at the ceiling. Prisoners, all kinds of prisoners who had known my father, all ages, would be coming in trying as best they could to find words of comfort.

'Gutted I am, about what happened to your dad.'

'Anything I can do, anything. You know where I am, Gerry.'

'He was a lovely man, a good man, so he was.'

I wished they wouldn't. I appreciated the thoughts they were trying to express, but I would have preferred to be left alone.

I certainly wished the chief screw, a man called Malcolm, had left me alone. He called me into his office to tell me, 'Your father's been dead ten days Conlon. We're giving you another four to get over it then it's back to work, back to normal.'

I nearly attacked him. I had been angry and frustrated during my father's last days and had tried to attack the doctor.

I was taken to a cell in the hospital and injected with paraldehyde, which was injected straight into my hip. This left me immobilized. I thought my back had broke. I could only lie on my stomach – I couldn't lie on my back. The pain was excruciating – I never thought I'd walk again. Every move I made sent pain shooting through my back and hips. The effects of this drug lasted for four days, and even then I couldn't move properly. It took weeks to get over it. This was how the prison authorities contained me during my father's final days.

Normality was never going to return. Normality had gone out the window six years earlier, and now my father was dead. I had long periods of depression in prison, lasting weeks. At the end of it I wouldn't sleep for two nights, and then I'd drop off for ten minutes and wake up feeling refreshed.

I was moved to Parkhurst and the change of scene did me good. I slowly began to heal, but one day I was in the governor's office, called down there, and the governor had my file in front of him. And I could see there was something different about it. I had seen this file so often over the years, with the big A stamped on it, and my name and number there. But now there was another stamp, a large red F inside a red circle. I'd never seen this before, so when I came out I asked around, and a prisoner told me it meant I was a suicide risk.

I got a terrible shock. At first I was angry that they should presume such a thing without talking to me, then I was a wee bit scared. There had been questions in the House by now, laid down by Gerry Fitt and Sir John Biggs Davidson, who both took an interest in my father's case. I knew that if the lid came off our case, the Guildford Four and the Maguire Seven, it would cause an almighty scandal. So with F stamped on my file I felt vulnerable. I had a real fear that an 'accident' might occur to me which could then be put down to suicide.

I have my sister Ann to thank for the removal of that stamp from my file. She is a very forthright woman, who doesn't mind what she says to anyone, and when she came over to see me in Parkhurst with my other sister Bridie I told the two of them about this new stamp on my file, and I said, 'Ask if you can see the governor about it, get it taken off.'

She demanded to see him. The deputy governor it was who was on duty at the time, a man called Morrison. So he came down and Ann said to him, 'My brother says there's a red circle with an "F" in red stamped on it, and that this means he is considered suicidal.'

'Well I can assure you that's not on your brother's file. He's mistaken.'

I jumped up.

'You're lying. I seen it.'

'I'm sorry Conlon, but it isn't.'

We argued back and forth like this for a while, and Ann cuts all the crap by saying, 'OK, if it's not on the file, let's have a look. Get the file in here and show it us.'

'Well, it's not the usual procedure to show a prisoner's file –'

'I don't want to read the papers in the file, Mr Morrison. I just want to see the cover where my brother says he saw this stamp.'

So off he went and came back with the file in his hand. In the left-hand corner, in black, had been stamped a big circle with an 'A' in the middle. In the right-hand corner, where I saw the 'F' was a large Elastoplast sticking-plaster.

'There you are,' he said. 'There's only the "A" stamp on the cover. There's no "F" mark.'

'So what's under the sticking-plaster?' I said.

'There's nothing under the sticking plaster.'

So Ann just reached out and ripped the sticking-plaster off the file as he held it in his hand. And there was the red category 'F' stamp. He was taken by surprise. He mumbled something or other and beat a hasty retreat. Afterwards Ann rang up everyone she knew with any interest in the case and told them about this, and how I certainly wasn't suicidal and I wanted the category removed. Two days later I was called down and told that the 'F' was being removed from my file.

Parkhurst, on the Isle of Wight, has a reputation as a very violent prison, going back to the riot there in 1969. The conditions there are very dirty, it has bad sanitation, bad food, and it's difficult to visit. So prisoners are very angry, and they take it out on each other. Everybody carries knives in Parkhurst.

I hated it but it took me out of myself. Now I was in a new prison, new circumstances, and now there was no prospect, if I got into a hole, of my father coming to pull me out of it. I was on my own.

First I had the problem of establishing the trust of the Irish, because the Wandsworth conversations were still hanging around me like a bad smell, and I couldn't automatically carry the goodwill and understanding I had found in the Scrubs with me. Eventually I sorted that out and became on reasonable terms with the Irish prisoners again.

But there were a lot of crazies in that prison, and for eighteen months I was all the time living on my wits. I became, in many ways, a 'successful' prisoner. I was capable of wheeling and dealing with the best of them, I was able to win enough at gambling to keep the wolf from the door, I made friends easily. But as I have already said, prison is like a minefield and Parkhurst was one of the most treacherous.

I was moved to Long Lartin in Worcestershire in November 1981, and was to stay there until 1988, my longest stay in any prison. If a prison can be said to be good, this one was – humane, allowing you your dignity, well-equipped. But even here I was falling into periods of depression, and I was taking it out not just on screws, but on other prisoners, taking advantage of their kindness, insulting them, being utterly obnoxious at times, being too absorbed in my own problems, not thinking they might have theirs, too.

I had a very venomous tongue on me. A lot of the time I took it out on the English, because I had become very bitter. So when the Falklands War came, I was shouting for the Argentinians, when the World Cup came I was shouting for anyone but England, in the cricket – which I became interested in because I had many West Indian friends in prison – I'd be crowing when England were 'black-washed' in a Test series. But it was way, way over the top. At times I was convinced I was going insane.

There was a period when for four months in Long Lartin I was savage. The things I said to good people who tried to help me were unforgivable. People would cook for me and I'd slag off the meals, or criticize them for one thing or another; I couldn't let go, I was always picking away at the scabs. In the end something – or someone – had to give, and more than anyone I have Noel Boyd to thank that it was me.

Noel Boyd was an Ulster Volunteer Force prisoner, a Protestant who had taken part in an attempt to blow up an Irish pub in London. He looked like the little corporal in *MASH*, Radar, a small fellow with granny glasses and a wee beard. He was a tremendous friend of mine, and of all the other Irish, because everybody liked him. He used to come into my cell and sit with me during these periods of black depression, and whatever I said to him he'd come back again, trying to joke me out of it. Then one day he came into my cell.

'You're not going to like what I've got to say to you.'

'Oh? What's that?'

'You're acting like an absolute cunt. All these people have been good to you, all your friends, and you're giving them nothing but a hard time.'

I didn't want to listen, but he kept on. He told me I'd lose my friends in the end, because no one could take the sort of verbal abuse I was handing out for very long. I was going to be eaten away by bitterness and I'd end up in an asylum, buried alive.

'What good is that to anyone? To you mother? To your sisters? To your father's memory?'

And he picked up a mirror and held it up to me.

'Look in the mirror, Gerry. Look at yourself. Your face is changing. Your expression is changing. You're starting to look fucking manic.'

I looked at myself, and I could see he was right. I saw someone who looked haunted. I had wide staring eyes, my cheeks were hollow.

'You'll never clear your father's name looking like that, Gerry, no one'll believe a mad bastard. And what about your mother?'

Noel just went on like this, it was his personal campaign, he'd be talking to me ten, fifteen times a day, like a bad conscience, always there to remind me of what I was becoming.

'Get out of my cell,' I'd say. 'Get the fuck out of here.'

'What's the matter, don't you like the truth? You don't mind being sarcastic and cutting with everybody else. Can't you take a bit of your own medicine?'

I was so angry with him, I'd want to strangle him, but he wouldn't give up.

'Go on, hit me. Will it help? Will it make you feel good?'

I knew he was right, of course. Every night alone in the cell, I'd rip myself to bits for the right bastard I was being for the ingratitude I was showing to these people. But it took the persistence of a Noel Boyd to make me admit it openly and eat humble pie.

'I've got a release date,' he'd say. 'I'm going home next year. But you'll still be in here. When I go home, I want to know you're going to be all right. So what you do is, get up tomorrow morning and go round and make everyone concerned a cup of tea and apologize for being such an arsehole.'

And he made me do it. It switched me back in the right direction again, put me on an even keel. I didn't become a saint overnight. But the threat of madness, of tumbling into a hole I'd dug for myself and never getting out, went away. Noel Boyd, Johnny Joyce and a lot of other patient, understanding men pulled me out of it, and I'll always be grateful they were there.

One of the funniest things that happened to me in prison also happened in Long Lartin. This was when I was taken hostage by a guy I'll call Martin from Birmingham.

He was a wild character who had a long prison record. I'd met him before in Wakefield. He decided to serve his time in Long Lartin on the punishment block as he didn't feel he could adequately deal with the mainstream prison population. The governor had – for months – been trying to persuade him to go on the wings. One night I got talking to him through the windows and he was asking what the prison was like compared to Wakefield, or Parkhurst. I was telling him that, in comparison, this prison wasn't too bad and he should give the wings a try. So, next day, he got permission from the governor, who was delighted at the idea of getting him off the block. So were the screws, as he gave them a bad time.

He had a good day on the wings, seeing old friends he had been on remand with and getting a wee bit drunk on prison hooch. So he put in his application to be transferred to the wings. The governor readily agreed, but unfortunately he went on holiday the next day and – in view of Martin's prison record – none of his juniors wanted to take the responsibility for processing the transfer. Martin was understandably wound up and the next time we spoke about it through the windows I jokingly said to him, 'Well, why don't you take a hostage? Make your point that way.' So he said, 'Well, who would I take hostage?' For a laugh, I was just joking around, I said, 'Well, take me if you want.' Never thinking that he would.

When we slopped out that night, Martin said to me, 'I've got it, I've got the blade to take you hostage with.' I looked at him, amazed, and obviously a bit frightened. But he told me not to worry. What he'd done was to remove the metal handle of a mop bucket and filed it down on the concrete window sill to make a blade. He'd also ripped up a sheet and wrapped it round to use as a handle.

This all gave me a fit of the giggles, so I went along with it all. He said to me that he'd tell the screws that he was going to my cell to get some matches, then he would take out this blade and say he'd taken me hostage. So just before we were supposed to be banged up, he came into my cell. I had my back to the screw, still giggling at the thought of all this. Martin tried to pull out the mop handle, but it had caught in his jeans so there he was tugging away, nearly doing himself an injury. The screw looked amazed as I slammed the door shut in his face and me and Martin fell about in uncontrollable giggles. He eventually managed to get out this 'weapon' and the next thing we knew all the screws were at the door and the farce began.

I even had to tell him to go and smear some antiseptic cream I had in my cell on the spyhole window so the screws couldn't see what we were doing. The screws were asking what was going on, and I had to explain I was being taken hostage and for what reason. Martin seemed incapable of speech. I asked to see the deputy governor. The screw replied, 'Conlon, you don't sound like you're being held hostage, or if you are, you are a very willing hostage.'

Anyway, about ninety minutes later, the deputy governor asked if he could come in. All the screws, he assured us, were downstairs and he wanted to know what all this was about. So we said, 'Sure you can open the door. Come on in.'

Martin was standing by the window waving this mop-bucket handle about. I was sitting on the bed. The governor came in and the only place available for him to sit was on the loo, which we both found very, very funny. Martin still couldn't find his tongue, so it fell upon me to do it. The deputy governor was very understanding and explained to Martin that he'd be on normal location by Monday. We even got an ounce of snout between us. The deputy governor was only too relieved that Martin would go on the wing.

26

Enter the Media

Apart from pulling me back from the brink of madness, Noel Boyd's siege tactics had reawakened my interest in the campaign of letter-writing that I'd started with the help of Shane Docherty at the Scrubs and had worked hard at in Parkhurst. I tried to write five or six letters a week, some to people who had never heard of me or my case. In 1988 I even wrote to Mikhail Gorbachev. I sent these out like a castaway putting letters in bottles, in the hope that sooner or later one or two would be picked up and read. But I was also getting involved in regular correspondence, keeping people in touch with anything that was happening in Ireland, England and America.

There was already a Guildford Four Campaign Group, started by Errol and Theresa Smalley, Paul Hill's uncle and aunt. They had Tom Barron acting as the Secretary, and their philosophy was, make as much noise as possible and if in doubt, hold a press conference. My sister Ann and her husband Joe were trying to do the same over in Ireland. They went down to Dublin with my mother shortly after my father's death to see the Foreign Minister.

I have to say that the government of the Republic of Ireland was a great disappointment to us. Right up until our release they pussy-footed. The Irish Constitution states that anyone born anywhere in Ireland, North or South, is a citizen and has a right to be represented by the Dublin government. So when we specifically asked the Irish government to help us, to make representations to London, to campaign for our release or transfer to Northern Ireland, we had every expectation that they would do their best. Instead they did nothing.

The first contact I had with the Irish Embassy in London was in 1983. They sent a man whose attitude was to do my time and stop writing to the Irish Embassy because they hadn't got time for people like me. I almost hit him.

Even a brilliant letter-writing campaign can run out of steam if it goes stale. There are so many causes, so many innocent people festering in gaol that you have to compete hard for attention. I remembered the George Davis is Innocent OK campaign, which was very imaginative and daring, which was why it caught the attention of the media. I wanted us to do the same.

I got a first chance to pull a bold stroke for myself one day in Long Lartin in 1987, a Tuesday morning. I was the cleaner on the wing, and I had the place almost to myself because most of the men were at work. But I started talking to Danny Thomas, a black guy from Birmingham doing seven years for armed robbery. Danny was always strumming at this guitar of his, and I interrupted his strumming with, 'Danny, why are you not working down here today? What have you done? Have you slipped out of it?'

'No, man,' he said. 'There's a BBC Radio crew coming to do these interviews, six of us.'

'What's the programme about then?'

'Crime and punishment, what else?'

'What time?' I said, all innocent.

'Ten o'clock onwards.'

I could spot an opportunity when I saw one. Obviously someone like me, a Category A man with terrorist convictions, would never be *chosen* to do something like this, so I'd have to get myself in there by pulling a stroke. I was determined to get in on that programme – I knew more about crime and punishment than these others. I discovered where they were doing the interviews, the AG's office, and posted myself with my mop and bucket outside the room. Soon Danny came out with his guitar slung round his neck.

'Hey, Gerry.'

'Danny, how's it going with the BBC?'

'I just came out to tune my guitar – they asked me to sing for them after they talked to the AG.'

So now I knew that Assistant Governor Bill Pike was inside. I would have to go in now, if only to correct the things Pike would be telling them.

'Who are they, Danny?' I asked in case I knew them – prisoners listen to a lot of radio.

'The girl's the producer, Jenny Lo. The man's Hugh Prycer-Jones.'

Danny went back and was in there half an hour. When he came out, the next one on the list to be seen, a rapist from a very respectable background, was going up to the door. I stopped him and pointed out there was no way he was going in before me. When Pike saw me his mouth dropped open, but he didn't speak. I went up to the BBC woman and said, 'My name is Gerry Conlon, I am one of the Guildford Four. I don't know if you've heard about our case?'

She said she had heard of it.

'Well, you should be interviewing me. No one here knows more about this subject than me.'

Jenny Lo turned to Pike and asked him if they could interview me. Very reluctantly he agreed, he even agreed to withdraw. He must have been afraid they would get up and leave if he refused, and then Long Lartin would not have been in the programme at all.

So I spent about an hour with them, shook their hands and left, with them promising they'd use some of what I'd given them. The next day, at dinner time, I was called up to the governor's office.

'You have really fucked me up this time, Conlon.'

'What are you talking about?'

'You gatecrashed the Radio 4 programme.'

'I know I did, didn't Pike tell you?'

The governor clenched his fist and hammered the desk.

'Yes, Pike told me. But more to the point I've just had the Home Secretary on the phone to me, asking me how I could let you, you of all people, get near these reporters. This is the last time you ever, *ever* speak to a woman in this prison who's not authorized to meet you. Now get out of here.'

The programme went out on Radio 4 FM, but since prisoners are not allowed FM radios – in case they pick up police messages – I never heard it. But, true to the producers' word, the programme made it clear who I was and that I was asserting my innocence. On it I said, among other things:

It's an awful burden to be Irish and on a terrorist-type offence in this country. You get really abused by the staff, you know, and it's taken me thirteen years to convince these people that I haven't hurt anyone, that I shouldn't be here. If I was guilty I would be here as punishment for something I'd done. I wouldn't be here to be further punished, further abused ... They try to strip you of your dignity. You've got very little going for you except your pride and your dignity in prison, and they try to steal that from you as well. And unfortunately a lot of prisoners succumb to it. But I don't regard myself as a prisoner. I regard myself as a hostage.

In the whole of my imprisonment, this was the first and only chance I got to speak for myself publicly outside a court of law. I think it was a very courageous act by Jenny Lo and Hugh Prycer-Jones to hold out against pressure, whether it came from inside or outside the BBC, which tried to persuade them to drop my interview in the bin.

But a small section of a radio programme heard by a few thousand people doesn't have the effect of a television documentary seen by millions. It's the kind of publicity you dream about. There were three *First Tuesday* programmes broadcast by Yorkshire TV about either the Maguires or the Guildford Four. The first, *Aunt Annie's Bomb Factory* in 1984, came out of the blue as far as I was concerned. Then, two years later, came *The Guildford Time Bomb*, which I contributed to at first without knowing it. It happened like this.

Some time at the end of 1984, Alastair Logan came to see me full of mystery and said I could help him.

'Certain people are getting interested in the case. They're becoming convinced at last that there's been a miscarriage of justice.'

For all these years, Alastair had stuck by his client Paddy Armstrong and for the case to be opened. So he came back over the next fifteen months, asking me questions, especially of my time in England in 1974. What he was doing, as I eventually found out, was working with the makers of *The Guildford Time Bomb*, which was finally broadcast in summer 1986.

I remember the terror and anxiety I felt when I saw in the newspaper that morning that it was due to be shown. First, there was nothing I could do, or could have done, to influence it. I didn't even know how my written and verbal contributions would be used. Second, I didn't know who else would come on, and whether there were any unpleasant surprises in store. People appearing on the screen and making out I was guilty, saying completely unforeseen things about me. Lastly, I would be watching it with forty or fifty other men who all knew me and would all have something to say afterwards.

In the end it was a significant programme, but I still wrote to Grant McKee to say he'd let off the police too lightly. *World In Action* had done a much more graphic documentary on the Birmingham Six, which left viewers in no doubt about what the police had done to extract the confessions. *First Tuesday* had treated the police, I thought, with kid gloves. I later wrote to Grant to apologize, but the programme had a big effect on me. It was the biggest publicity we'd had to date, and I felt it was important that they told the whole story.

A year later they did a follow-up, *A Case That Won't Go Away*. It didn't add much that was new about Guildford, though it produced a new alibi witness for Paul Hill over the Woolwich bombing. But it did have Cardinal Hume in it, saying that it was a case that wouldn't go away, and that the courts must be ready to admit a mistake when one was made. His obvious sincerity and goodness must have persuaded a lot of people.

But the Cardinal was also working on our behalf in his own way, which was quiet, serious and enormously influential. I was impressed by this, because I always believed that to win we had somehow to find our own members of the Establishment to fight our corner against the majority that would be automatically against us. I knew that there would be people with the right background and connections who had the capacity to think for themselves, and it is just a matter of finding them. The final list of the Great and Good who stuck their necks out for us included Lord Fitt, two former Home Secretaries Lord Jenkins and Merlyn Rees, the late Sir John Biggs Davidson the Tory MP, two Law Lords, Scarman and Devlin, and more than two hundred other MPs, Euro-MPs, American Senators, churchmen.

But I am running too fast. At this stage I hadn't even got myself a solicitor, and there was an awful lot of legwork still to do.

27

Fresh Evidence

The *First Tuesday* programmes had done a lot to push our case into the public eye. On top of that, Robert Kee had published his book *Trial and Error*, which told in much more detail the story outlined in the television programmes. So now I was getting letters from Sister Sarah Clarke and my mother saying I had to be looking for a solicitor, because there could be an inquiry or another appeal. Such was the pressure on the Home Secretary to refer both our case, and the Birmingham Six, to the Court of Appeal.

But the Six's success was our setback. On 20 January 1987, my mother's birthday, Douglas Hurd announced he was sending the Birmingham Six back for an appeal, but not the Guildford Four or the Maguires. It was a hard and confusing time. I was happy for my friends Johnny Walker, Gerry Hunter, Billy Power and Dick McIlkenny, and at the same time terribly sad and deflated for myself. At times I swung down to a level almost as low as when I first came to Long Lartin from Parkhurst.

But there have always been saving graces, and now it was almost a carnival atmosphere on the wing at Long Lartin, which everyone who was there felt – an electric excitement from the gathering of all of the Birmingham Six together as they prepared their appeal. The most dynamic new element was the arrival of Paddy Joe Hill with Hughie Callaghan, the two of the Six I'd not met before. But no, it's tame to say Paddy *arrived* on the wing. Paddy exploded on to it.

I was up in my cell when I thought I heard my name. It was yelled out amid an unholy commotion that had suddenly swept into the wing, a bellowing Irish voice that I'd never heard before.

'Conlon, you gobshite. Get your arse down here.'

I thought I must have misheard, so I didn't move. The third time I couldn't mistake my own name being roared out.

'CONLON! Get fucking down here, now.'

I went out, wondering if it was some new arrival with a grudge against me, wanting to give me a slap. It wasn't. It was Paddy Hill. We'd never come across each other, he wanted to meet me, and this was his normal method of operating.

I saw this small, solid and incredibly animated figure, leaning against the railing at the bottom of the stairs, giving out to all these people around him. His dentures had been damaged when he was beaten at Winson Green prison, so you hardly ever see the man with teeth. His mouth is like one of the puppets on *Rainbow*, the one with the zipper over his lips. But I'd like to see someone brave enough to try to zipper Paddy's mouth.

He looked up, recognized me at once and stuck his hand through the railing.

'What took you so long, you bollocks? Paddy Joe Hill, good to meet you, son.'

Then he pushed his face into mine, spattering me with saliva.

'D'you have any money? D'you have any tobacco?'

'Er, yes.'

'Right, well give 'em me, and we'll talk.'

So up we went to my cell and came back down, and he said straight out, 'I hope you're not feeling depressed and sorry for yourself.'

I was, but I wouldn't admit it.

'Course not, why?'

'Because we're going back, and you're not, like.'

'No.'

He could tell I was only half telling the truth. He turned and again planted his face an inch from mine.

'Well, if I get out of this, you're coming out too. Because I'll be going everywhere, doing whatever I can for you. OK?'

And this was a man I'd never met until five minutes before. We became friends instantly and it seemed as if we had always been friends. We played bridge together, the most feared pair on the wing, mainly because Paddy Joe's dynamism intimidates the opposition to bits. He zooms around like some battery-operated toy, up and down corridors, in and out of cells, badgering people all the way round, never backing off, never letting up.

Paddy Joe Hill is completely outrageous, and he doesn't mind what he says to anyone. One time he went on a visit with a bishop. The bishop said, 'We'll say a little prayer, Paddy, before the visit starts.'

But Paddy had other ideas.

'Never mind the prayers, what about a few quid?'

The bishop looked shaken, because nobody had ever spoken to him like this before. He began to pull out his cheque-book.

'Oh, yes, how much would you –?'

'Well, for a start,' said Paddy, 'I don't take cheques. I want cash.'

That is Paddy Joe Hill.

And with him came Hughie Callaghan, shy, gentle and melancholy, like a country squire. He couldn't have been more of a contrast.

But the door to the Guildford Four's freedom had been wedged shut again, and there was nothing to do but keep on pushing. The Great and the Good were still working away, and behind them the army of ordinary people: Lily Hill, my mother and sisters, the Smalleys, Sister Sarah, Diana St James, who was writing to me from the States, Father McInley, Ros Franey from Yorkshire Television and many, many more. Cardinal Hume led a delegation of Lord Scarman, Lord Devlin, Lord Jenkins and Merlyn Rees in to see Douglas Hurd. They pressed hard for the case to be reopened, listing many matters which our 1975 jury had never heard of, but which might – if they had – have made them see us as innocent. There was a lot of different talk in the air, of a judicial inquiry, an independent tribunal, an internal police investigation, a retrial. The new alibi witness for Paul Hill shown in the second *First Tuesday* programme, had prompted a police enquiry to investigate its potential as new evidence. It was then I decided I must have a solicitor. The legal ramifications were beginning to look never-ending.

The Birmingham Six had a woman solicitor named Gareth Peirce who they thought the world of. So I thought I'd see if she'd represent me. She came up to Long Lartin and I was tremendously impressed by how intently she listened when I spoke about my case. I told her a lot of things about my father, and how I wanted to clear my name and then his name, as he had wished. And she just looked at me and said in a very calm, matter-of-fact voice, 'Well we'll just have to get you out.'

And I knew she was going to do the business. In prison you get used to making snap judgements, and then abiding by them. I made the decision to go with Gareth, and I have never regretted it.

Gareth is like Joan of Arc. She's a fighter and she won't hear of defeatism. She decided from the first that we had to strip my case back to its basics and look hard at all the things that went wrong with my defence at the 1975 trial. Why, first and foremost, hadn't I been able to produce an alibi witness?

'Easy,' I said. 'That bastard Paddy Carey never turned up.'

'But you had another witness, Paul the Greengrocer. Where is he?'

'He disappeared, left Quex Road.'

'Then we'll have to find him.'

So Gareth did what none of my solicitors had ever done, she went to Quex Road and asked to look at their records. She didn't find them at her first visit, because during the 1974 police investigations they'd taken them away and never returned them. Gareth asked the hostel to apply to the police for the return of the records, and meanwhile would they mind telling her what had happened back in '74, from their angle?

She found a lot of things that amazed her. In 1974 everyone connected with republican politics around Kilburn knew that the hostel had been under police surveillance for months. Special Branch men had been in and out of the place, some of them openly displaying their guns. If the court at our trial had known this, would the jury have believed that an IRA active-service unit would be deliberately told, by those who were planning its strategy, to go and live in such a place?

She also found that the priest in charge of the hostel at that time, Father Carolan, had gone to Guildford for questioning. His description of the process supported a great deal of what I had been saying.

Then at last the police produced the hostel records, and suddenly there was Paul the Greengrocer – except he wasn't named Paul.

'Paul the Greengrocer', with his wee trilby hat and passion for green outfits, was really called Charles Burke. It says on the hostel admission card he worked in a greengrocer's shop and that he had been put in St Louis, the room Paul Hill and I had shared with Paddy Carey. If we could only find Charles Burke there was a good chance he might remember October the 5th more clearly than other days around the same time, because that was the night he left the hostel to live somewhere else.

Gareth got on the phone to a string of people called Burke in Limerick, and eventually tracked down a parish priest and then a sister of his. But then came the body blow – the sister hadn't heard from her brother for ten years. She didn't know where he was.

But meanwhile Gareth had done so many other things. She'd taken a statement from my Uncle Hughie who saw me being ill-treated in Guildford, but had never been asked to give evidence at my trial. Even better, she took a statement from my Aunt Kate, who heard me crying out 'Mammy! Mammy!' in Godalming. She talked to Danny Wilson, who got pissed with me at lunch-time on the day of the bombing. She talked to my Aunt Bridget about the telephone conversation I had with her that night at the Engineers' Club. She tracked down in Galway a man called Michael Kennedy who remembered me being in the television room of the Quex Road hostel that night, and he gave her a statement to that effect. None of my previous lawyers had done these things, yet all confirmed details of the account I gave the court of how I'd spent that day.

So she was disappointed in not finding Charles Burke, the one man who could definitely say I didn't do the bombing because I was talking to him at Quex Road hostel at the time. But Gareth felt she was getting somewhere in showing how much evidence there was that could have been called in my defence. Donaldson would not then have been able to tell the court in his summing-up that I had nothing to back up my alibi.

She was also making progress in showing how the police had mistreated me. She got copies of the doctor's report made when I was at Springfield Road. These showed that Dr McAvinney diagnosed an infection and prescribed treatment. The Surrey police did not appear to have followed this up, got me a doctor or any treatment. But Gareth had got hold of David Walsh's notes, taken during our short meeting at Guildford police station. In these he clearly said that I was complaining at the time he met me of pains in the kidney area. As Gareth explained to me, this pain could have been because I was hit, or it could have been infected kidneys. If I was hit, they haven't explained how come. If it was my kidney infection, then it looks as if they denied me medical treatment.

The appointment of the Avon and Somerset police in 1987 to investigate the fresh evidence was – unbeknownst to us – resulting in a whole warehouse full of papers about the case taken from the Guildford files, and waiting there among those papers, hidden by the enormous bulk of the material, were wee scraps of evidence, any one of which would have been enough to send the Guildford Four home and free.

Meanwhile, unaware of this and understanding that the Avon and Somerset police had reported to the Home Secretary that they recommended that he not re-open the case, Gareth felt that the Home Secretary ought to see my new evidence. The police enquiry was extended and we were later to find that two police officers also said they had heard what my aunt Kate said she had heard – namely, me shouting out 'Mammy, Mammy' at Godalming police station in December 1974. New evidence had also come to light for Carole to show that she had been injected with pethidin while in police custody.

By now, on the wing, we were all waiting for the Six's appeal. It happened in November and they went off so buoyantly full of hope, but the massive IRA Remembrance Day bomb had happened shortly after the appeal began, and any sympathetic atmosphere that had built around the Six over the years was destroyed in a few seconds at Enniskillen. Sure enough, appeal was refused. As the Six were all dispersed to three different prisons gloom again descended on the wing. The place now seemed like a ghost town without the booming voice of Paddy Joe Hill.

Cardinal Hume and his delegation kept up the pressure. Archbishop Runcie came in and applied a bit more and, in January 1989, Hurd agreed to refer the case back. Now Gareth went to work with a will. We were going to have a second appeal and we were going to win! But on what she had so far she couldn't be sure of that. What she did know was that all the Somerset and Avon material, gathered in Bristol, would now be available to the defence. She started making trips down there to start the massive task of sifting through it. Sometimes Paddy O'Connor, who was later to represent me at court, would accompany her.

Gareth almost wore out their photocopier with documents helpful to our case, documents tending to show the Surrey police knew little about the IRA, or were saying contradictory things, or had not followed up particular leads. She'd be coming back to me, telling me what she was finding, making me promise to keep them to myself. It was frustrating and exciting at the same time.

But she still wasn't sure the things she was finding amounted to the quashing of the 1975 verdicts. Then amongst bundles of statements emerging from Avon and Somerset was a statement. It read: *Name of witness: Charles Burke. Date of statement: January 1975.* It was a statement about the evening of 5 October 1974.

As soon as she saw it she knew that we had them.

When I heard that Charles Burke had been found and interviewed by the police in 1975, I had simply wanted to know, what did he say? Had he supported my alibi? Well, he had; and I thought good, another brick in the wall. Burke said he *had* seen me at the hostel that evening, and talked to me in my room. But, for Gareth, that was not the clincher. The really important thing was a legal point: the prosecution had withheld evidence from the defence. They had found Charles Burke, they had got his statement *before* my trial, and it was their duty then to tell us. They hadn't done so. End of story. Conviction quashed. Conlon walks. The Guildford Four walk.

Gareth had sworn me to secrecy because she didn't want word getting out of what had happened at Bristol. When the visits ended I would be elated, coming out with a soppy grin on my face and feeling more confident than ever that I would get out of gaol. I started imagining the World Cup, Ireland playing Italy, travelling to New York and things like that. I had tremendous faith in Gareth. She was always optimistic, she always had good news.

Prisoners would ask me what had happened. I would say she told me nothing. They'd say: 'You've got good news – look at your face – tell us what it is.' They felt as if they were on appeal as well, because they knew the brutal injustice we had suffered and up until our case no one charged with terrorist offences had been released on appeal. I would be coming back and they'd all be chatting after work in the corridor and they'd all see I was excited and here I was sworn to secrecy by Gareth. I was dying to tell them but I couldn't. They would badger me – everyone was very excited.

The failure of the appeal of the Birmingham Six resulted in a gloomy period for the prisoners. The boring routine of prison life, the drudgery of what it is all about was worse than usual. Everyone had prayed that the Birmingham Six would be proved innocent. We also felt very sorry for Jimmy Robinson and Michael and Vincent Hickey when the Carl Bridgewater appeal failed. And now everybody was looking to us, the Four.

I wouldn't sleep for days. I would be pacing up and down and looking out the window and knowing what was beyond the wall – freedom – and believing I was soon going to be there.

Meanwhile, Gareth had made another interesting discovery. She turned up a bundle of papers tied up with a label that read 'Not to be disclosed to the defence'. She pulled the package open and began looking through. She was disappointed. Anything with such a label ought to be of really dramatic use to the defence, but instead she was finding things of no great significance. Then she turned over a paper and got such a surprise that it nearly fluttered from her fingers: *another* copy of Charles Burke's statement. This was clearly no accident.

Unaware that Avon and Somerset had already uncovered the material that was going to lead to our release, Gareth went on digging into the mountain of paper in that room down in Bristol and at one point she found some very interesting papers. They looked like verbals, the notes taken by the police to record what was said in interrogation. At our trial, we had a wee gee when Jermey told the court he had written down these notes many hours after finishing the session, but insisted they were absolutely accurate because he had such a good memory. But he hadn't then been able to remember Wigoder's first question to him, put just a few minutes earlier. Gareth found pages of typewritten verbals, with a lot of interesting margin notes and alterations to them.

But we were keeping our mouths shut, not revealing what we had found to anyone, not making public our grounds for appeal until the last minute. We didn't want the press getting wind of what sensational stuff we'd uncovered.

28

The Last Prison

By March 1988 my relationship with Joe Whitty, the new governor at Long Lartin who arrived in 1987 and changed a lot of the routines, had deteriorated so much that it was inevitable he would move me. I was finding him giving open visits to a lot of Category A prisoners, people I felt were one way and another about a thousand times more dangerous than me. But my family had to put up with these horrible visits being outnumbered by screws, and having everything written down that was said. The final straw was when Whitty told my mother that it wasn't in his power to give open visits to Category A prisoners, which I call a lie. Long Lartin had changed from an easy, relaxed prison. I wrote a letter to the Irish Embassy, a very angry letter slagging off Whitty, and asking them to get on to the Home Office about getting me open visits and I put it into the posting box in the morning of March the 28th. That letter never arrived and by five o'clock I was on my way out of the prison, ending up in Full Sutton in Yorkshire. I hated that place. It was a modern prison, all laid out for the convenience of the screws, and the governor was a hard man. I had this arrogance now, of the innocent man who was going to be vindicated. So I was very disruptive. When I went in to see the governor and I hit him over the head with the rule book they sent me on lie-down to Durham – twenty-eight days of ten seventy-four.

The block at Durham was a very hard place because the cells were very small, like stalls, not wide enough to stretch out and about ten or twelve inches between the bed and the wall. It was also infested –

cockroaches, mice, rats – and exercise was inside a thing like a zoo cage. But I was lucky in that I had a friend already in there when I arrived, Tommy Mulvey, and Tommy had a supply line from the remand wing organized.

Lines were made out of strips of bed-linen knotted together, and late at night the remands would hang their line out and a prisoner named Jiffy, whose cell on the block was nearest the remand wing, would throw his line with a hook on the end, and eventually catch the line put out by the remands. Sometimes he'd get it in a couple of throws, sometimes it'd take him an hour. But in the end, Jiffy would always secure the line and then whatever it was would be slid down from remand to us, and then swung along the block from cell to cell: food, orange juice, porno magazines, snout. What we were doing with those lines out the window was ridiculous.

So I survived Durham and then found myself in Gartree. On the first day I arrived I met Joe O'Connell standing in the corridor talking to all the Irish prisoners. A very strange moment. This was the guy who'd led the Balcombe Street unit who'd bombed Guildford and Woolwich for which we were serving sentences. I spoke first and I said to him, 'I'd like to thank you for all you've done to help us and telling the truth.' Joe said to me, 'We told the police the truth. We told the truth in the appeal court. But you know yourself, Gerry, this is just an example of British justice in relation to Irish people. But if there's anything I can do to help in any way, I'll do it.'

I'd just like to say that I know a lot of people would find this strange, but I found Joe O'Connell to be a nice guy. At times I could see that Joe was suffering, knowing myself, Paddy, Carole and Paul were serving life sentences for something we didn't do and he had done. Joe tried to help our solicitors as much as he possibly could by giving them details of what he and the other Balcombe Street people had done instead of us. Also there on the wing I was delighted to find none other than Paddy Hill. Me and Paddy Hill embarked on an intense letter campaign to raise awareness of our cases abroad. We worked together and it bore fruit as we had got a lot of interest in the USA and the Catholic Church abroad. We got letters published in the US press. Senators interested themselves in our case and a San Francisco group which had been set up to clear our names ran an advertisement in the *New York Times* on St Patrick's Day in 1989.

So I found it very difficult not to tell Paddy the crucial points of what was going on in my case.

Gartree was my last long-term prison. By now I could manage day to day in any prison in the system. I didn't enjoy it, but I could cope. I'd seen a lot of changes, ranging from the introduction of screwesses to allowing the Irish to take part in education. Before 1984, Irish prisoners never had the slightest consideration, and we were still fighting a lot of issues: harassment of families, closed visits, temporary and permanent transfers to Northern Ireland. Before, eighty-four Irish prisoners were denied educational facilities. So there had been something like a rethink in the mid-eighties which made life marginally better, but of course it had had to be fought for.

The other side of it was the worry about what was being done to my mind. I still had depressions; I found it very hard to sleep, I'd suddenly see myself as buried alive in the prison system. Sometimes I felt almost like one of those earthquake victims in a pocket of air beneath a collapsed block of flats. And that used to induce little panic attacks, the sudden feeling that I might suffocate, I might be crushed, and there was nothing I could do about it.

Then there were the lapses of time. I'd go into my cell at maybe eight o'clock at night, read twenty pages of my library book, put the book down and lay my head back against the wall. Then I'd sit with my arms folded, picking a spot on the wall opposite and just trying to concentrate on it. I'd do that for a while and then I'd look down at my watch, thinking ten or fifteen minutes had gone by, and it was six hours later. Nothing had happened, that I'd heard, for six hours nothing had registered in my mind. When that first happened to me I was sure I was going mad, but I've since discovered it's common among long-term prisoners. I confessed it to Johnny Walker, who's like a family doctor is supposed to be, very wise and trustworthy, and he just said, 'Gerry it happens to me all the time.'

When I first got to Gartree I was on punishment, but Duncan the governor suspended it half-way through and I went on the wing. I was carrying groceries back from the canteen to my cell, and I passed a thin, shaggy-looking character who stopped and stamped his foot a couple of times to get my attention.

'Gerry! Gerry!'

And he turned to me and I didn't at first realize it was Paddy.

'It's me, it's me, it's Paddy.'

I squinted at him.

'Paddy Armstrong?'

'Yes, yes, it's me!'

I was shocked at the sight of him. He looked like prison life had eroded him, day by day a little more. Once he'd been plump, almost burly. Now he was gaunt, and he had a sick prison pallor that some men get, as if they'd been locked away from the light all these years.

I hadn't seen him since our first appeal was turned down, eleven years ago, and all that time he'd been in Gartree. He worked for years in the prison garden, but they took him off the job after Sid Draper and another man escaped by helicopter from the playing-fields – one of their mates took flying lessons and on the third lesson he hijacked the chopper into Gartree, landed and took off again with two Category A prisoners. Paddy saw the whole thing, his garden was next to the football pitch. So after that he was denied the one job that he found suited him.

The 17th of October 1989 was a Tuesday. I was sitting with Paddy Joe Hill, listening to a bizarre story about his life in Birmingham, when in comes a screw, 'Conlon, wanted in the office.'

I wanted to hear the end of Paddy's yarn, so I said, 'OK, boss, I'll be over in a minute.'

But it was a long story, becoming more elaborate and fantastic all the time, and half a minute later I hadn't moved and this screw came dancing back, all agitated and looking pale, almost shocked.

'Come on Conlon, office, now!'

Paddy flicked out his elbow, saying, 'Well go and see what he wants.'

Having seen the screw's face I thought a disaster had happened, my mother had fallen ill or there'd been some accident.

'You're being moved. Go to your cell and get your things.'

Automatically I said, 'Where to?'

I didn't expect an answer, but unbelievably I got one.

'London. Now go and get your things.'

'London? What for?'

'For your appeal. Now move.'

The screw was in a great hurry to get me out of there, and I couldn't understand why.

'Bollocks, that's not for three months, January the 15th. You're sending me on a lie-down.'

'No, it's London and your mate's going with you. I can't tell you any more.'

I went back down to the prison workshop and I said goodbye to all the friends I'd made, played football with, played backgammon with and had the crack with. I said goodbye to the Londoners, the blacks, the Brummies, and they all wished me well. 'You're going to get a result.' 'Don't forget to hammer them and tell them what they done to you.' 'Don't forget to tell them what prison's like.' The West Indians were giving me hand slaps and I was being clapped on the back. While I was saying goodbye to everyone, I felt very bewildered, not knowing what it meant, but knowing I might not see Gartree again, or not for a long time. So Paddy Hill came back to the wing with me and helped me pack my things, and I went round and gave most of the stuff in my cell away, everyone was saying, 'You're going home, Gerry.'

All the Irish prisoners in the gaol had come round to see. It was very emotional, they were hugging me. We all had tears in our eyes. And Paddy, whose own appeal had been lost nine months earlier, just put his arms around me and hugged me tight and said, 'Be lucky, Gerry.'

Then I walked off the wing.

The reception screw in a prison is a human barometer of how the prison is going to treat you. At Gartree I'd had fights with this Geordie screw over this and that, and it was him I saw on reception when I reported for loading on to the A van. Now, instead of snarling at me as usual, he came over, 'Hello there, lad. Want a cigarette?'

Something wrong here, I thought. This man usually looks at the Irish prisoners like he wants to rip off their ears.

Paddy Armstrong was standing there all in nerves, waiting to be pushed into the A van, saying, 'Something's wrong, Gerry. I don't want to leave Gartree. The appeal's not for months. Where are they taking us?'

'The screw told me it was London.'

'Yeah but they never tell us where we're going.'

'I know. It's got to be something to do with the appeal.'

All I could think was that this was some kind of preliminary hearing, for submissions or something. Gareth had never told me this might happen, but I couldn't think what else it could be – unless it was some kind of stroke the prison authorities were pulling.

We took the M1 and the closer we got to London the more nervous Paddy became. He's never been in Wandsworth, but he'd heard of its reputation.

'It's never Wandsworth they're taking us to, is it Gerry? Jesus, I hope it's not Wandsworth.'

Well, there are four prisons in London, of which we could have gone to three: Brixton, the Scrubs or Wandsworth. Pentonville's got no Category A facilities. As we left the motorway there were still no clues as to which we would end up in.

Suddenly we looked out the window and we realized where we were.

'Hey, Paddy,' I said. 'Look. We're going down Kilburn.'

Edgware Road, Cricklewood Broadway, Shoot-up Hill, Kilburn High Road. It was memory lane. Our old stamping-ground.

Paddy was up at the window.

'There's Rondu Road. Hey, look what they done to that pub. That didn't look like that.'

And I saw MacDonald's right in the middle of Kilburn, something I'd never even heard of in 1974. And Paddy's getting excited, shouting out, 'That other pub's on the other side, the betting shop's next to it.'

'The Memphis Belle? The Cock, Biddy Mulligans?'

'No, no, they're further down. Kilburn State picture-house is first. Now, *there's* the Memphis Belle, they changed the name. What's it called now, Gerry?'

'Looks like the Bridge Tavern.'

'I wonder why they changed the name. Look, the Cock, the Olde Bell.'

'There's Quex Road.'

The suddenly we were in Maida Vale and going under Westway and I remember looking up towards Paddington Station where Hughie and Kate lived and thinking of 1974 and how we used to go to the Club for a game of snooker and few pints.

By now we knew it wasn't the Scrubs, and Paddy was saying as we crossed the Thames, 'It's Wandsworth, oh Jesus.'

'It can't be Wandsworth if it's for the appeal. They haven't got the facilities for meeting the lawyers there.'

By this time neither of us knew for sure where we were exactly, somewhere in south London. Paddy was shaking at the thought of Wandsworth, clasping his hands in the prayer position to keep them still. And then I spotted the sign: *HM Prison, Brixton*.

We were brought out of the A van and the handcuffs came off. Immediately the Gartree screws were asking for the screws' club, dying for a pint, so they dumped Paddy and me in reception and disappeared, leaving us just waiting there, looking around. There was something definitely not quite right. Usually when they brought me into a new place reception had a minimum of five screws in the welcoming party, plus dogs. Here there was only the desk screw, and at one point even he went off for a piss or something, leaving us there alone. I said, 'I don't get this, Paddy. We could probably make a move to get out of here. Where is everybody?'

About five minutes later, with us feeling all naked and self-conscious without our usual quota of screws, the reception screw was back.

'Have you two had anything to eat?'

'No.'

'What do you want? I'll get the guys in the kitchen to rustle you up something.'

Paddy and I looked at each other. Something was definitely wrong. Tea was at four in Brixton, only an hour away, and here was this screw offering us a special meal.

Then he says, as if he'd just thought of it, 'Better get you to the cells. I'm putting you in together.'

This was a flagrant breach of the Category A rules. We should have been locked up separately. So Paddy had a cup of tea and me a glass of water – I never drank prison tea except once, and they'd pissed in it. We sit there sipping, we roll a smoke. Then suddenly the flap on the door comes down and there's a screw looking in at us.

'All right, lads? Big day coming up.'

Then the hatch went up and he'd gone. Ten minutes later, another screw.

'Hi guys. Big day on Thursday.'

'Look, what's happening Thursday?'

The screw started laughing. 'Don't take the piss. Don't make out you don't know.'

Then I was taken out into reception to have my belongings

processed, and I saw a whole phalanx of screws there, and I thought, 'Here we go, this is where I get it.'

But instead one of them held out a packet of Rothmans.

'Want a cigarette, mate?'

The screw processing me just told me basically I could have anything I wanted in the cell.

'How long am I staying?'

He just laughs.

'Oh you won't be here long, will you?'

So I take my bedding and my gear, and I had too much to carry, so the screw going up with me said, 'Here, let me help you with this.'

All those eyes were on me as we walked up D Wing, into a cell on the bottom. The PO's got a big smile on his face.

'We put you in here. We don't want you struggling up those stairs with all that gear, do we?'

The normal routine was they'd pick a cell in the most remote, high corner they could find, just to make you climb the stairs.

'Well that's never stopped you in the past, has it?'

'Come on! Now it's different.'

'Is it?'

'So, what do you want, son? Want some canteen?'

'Can I have some exercise?'

'Sorry, they're all coming in now, it's the one thing I can't do. Anything else you want, son, it's yours.' I can't describe how weird this all felt.

Then all the prisoners started coming in from exercise for their tea, and I spotted Freddie Foreman. He'd just been extradited from Spain, but I'd got to know him years before in 1975 in Brixton on remand. And he stopped when he saw me, doing a double-take, not quite remembering who I was.

'Gerry?'

'That's right, Freddie.'

'Guildford?'

I smiled.

'Yeah, except I –'

'I know, I know. You didn't do it!'

And he ran over to me and just lifted me up and shook me.

'Great news, Gerry. Home on Thursday. Great news.'

'What news? What do you mean, going home Thursday? I've got appeal coming up. What you talking about?'

So he stood back from me.

'You haven't heard?'

'No. I know fuck-all. I've been treated really weird by the screws all day. What's going on?'

'It's been on the news since dinner time. You're going to be released. You'll get one court appearance and you're going to be released.'

He could see I thought he was winding me up, so he checked his watch and started dragging me to his cell.

'Come on, in here. I'll put on the news, four o'clock.'

He put on Capital Radio, a commercial break just before the news. Then Paddy came up looking for me. He stopped in the doorway, just as the news was about to start. I said, 'Listen to this, Paddy. He says we're getting out on Thursday.'

Paddy looked at me wildly, bug-eyed, as the radio said,

In a surprise move this morning the Director of Public Prosecutions has announced that the Guildford Four are to be released on Thursday.

I couldn't hear anything else around me, as if there was a sudden silence fallen everywhere except for the radio.

At an emergency session of the Court of Appeal, set for Thursday morning, the court will be told that the Crown will no longer sustain the convictions of the Four, who were convicted in 1975 of terrorist offences . . .

I remember getting up, I remember that. Then Paddy and I looking at each other's faces, watching the incomprehension changing to knowledge that it was over. It was over. He more or less fell into my arms, and we just stood there hugging each other.

29

Verdict Quashed

We must have got out of Gartree just in time, or maybe they timed the announcement to coincide with the midday bang-up. If we'd still been there and the news broke during association we'd never have got to London that day. Ronnie McCartney told me later that he had been in his cell doing some studying when he heard a banging, a cell door getting a hammering. Then another, and another, until fifty doors were being kicked, battered with chairs and tables, prisoners were screaming and yelling, letting out whoops of excitement. Ronnie upped and hammered on the wall.

'What the fuck's going on?' he yelled to the kid next door. 'What's the banging about?'

'Put on the radio. Listen to the news.'

'What *is* the news?'

'The Guildford Four are going home Thursday. It was on Radio One.'

And Ronnie said he just picked up his chair and started thumping the door with it, along with the entire prison, the whole place was vibrating. People were breaking open buckets of prison hooch and swinging the stuff from cell to cell, people who hadn't spoken to each other for years were having a drink together – sharing everything together – and so it went on all afternoon. After the cells were opened up again, people were walking around openly drinking hooch. It was a hell of a party and the next day the entire place had a hell of hangover.

I had seen Paul Hill just a few times. We had been in Parkhurst together for less than a year, most of the time not on the same wing, and for a short time during the Birmingham Six appeal at Long Lartin – he came up from the Scrubs to release Category A cells for the Six while their appeal was being heard. Paul was thinner and older, but he'd not changed nearly as much as Paddy.

We had all spent a long night at Brixton – I'd not been able to sleep at all – and now we faced a long day, our last one as prisoners. It might seem unnatural that, while everyone knew what was going to happen next day, for the duration of this day we were still under all the artificial restrictions of the Category A code: dog, two screws, handcuffs, A van, close visits, book. But I didn't feel it was unnatural. After fifteen years the Category A restrictions were part of my clothing, or even part of me. Take a hunchback's hump away, and how does he feel? I'd have felt naked if they hadn't enforced them.

So when I suddenly had a visit from my mother and sisters – a complete surprise to me because they'd been flown over by ITN – it was still the same old visit, with the screws behind, the dog outside, the tennis umpire writing down the words. But it wasn't the usual strained and unnatural visit because my mother had the most natural and most beautiful smile I'd seen for a decade and a half.

Everyone was smiling. Gareth came in with a big smile.

I gave her a big hug. I thanked her as best I could, but how could I thank her properly for what she'd done?

But I still didn't know what had happened. Why hadn't the appeal gone ahead? We were kept in the dark until the end – seemingly in the warehouse there were *still* things that we weren't allowed to see.

'So what happens now?'

'It's quite simple. The prosecution makes a speech explaining it no longer wishes to sustain the prosecution, and the judge quashes the verdict.'

That night, in the quietness of my cell, I thought about Sir Michael Havers and Lord Donaldson, and how cheated I felt that tomorrow they would not be in the places they occupied in 1975. I would have loved to hear Havers admit, from his own mouth, that the Crown's case against us was based on a load of rubbish. And I felt thwarted that I could not hear Donaldson say the word *quashed*. Because the word was a magic word to me, but how bitterly it would have tasted in his mouth.

I knew the case was one of the most scandalous miscarriages of justice this century, I knew it was already spewing all over the press and media and would keep them busy for some days yet. It was not a matter of pride to me, but not one of shame either. I simply wanted to tell everyone what happened to me, and why. I wanted to damage the system that had damaged me and then somebody would have to put it right. It must not happen again and again and again.

I thought about freedom, another golden word. But it was too big for me. So I stored up the little things it would bring to me, football matches, travel, having money in my pocket, clothes of my own choice. It meant I could cross the road, walk in the rain, cuddle my nieces and nephew not under the curling lip of a screw, eat melons and potato bread and an Irish pie and be with the family.

The authorities were true to form. I was strip-searched when I was opened up that morning and seen by the prison doctor and again in reception when we changed into our own clothes. We stripped off our prison clothes and it was like shedding a dirty skin. I picked my shirt and jeans out of the prison box and began putting them on, clothes our Bridie had been out and bought for me the day before. No one had been shopping for Paddy Armstrong. He still had the same clothes he'd had in 1975, a pair of outrageous flares and some stacked three-inch platform shoes. Paul and I burst out laughing when we saw them.

'Jesus Christ, Paddy, you can't go into court wearing those shoes. Where did you get them from, Elton John?'

I found another pair of shoes for Paddy in my own box, but he had to wear the flares.

With us handcuffed inside, the A van approached the gates of Brixton from within. As they swung slowly towards us, I suddenly saw the world outside in a different way. It was as if we'd been in a dark room looking for the door, and had found it at last and swung it open letting the light pour over us. I radiated. I was smiling from ear to ear as I saw the outside world in this new way. Then we went to court, where I was searched again.

When I first knew her, Carole had been young enough to be still at school. Now she was a woman of thirty-three. But when she came to meet us down below the Bailey, her eyes were shining and her grin was as broad as any young child's. We all hugged her and I felt the occasion gave us a strong feeling of unity, of being the *Four*. Then the screws came and said, 'Put the cigarettes out, you're going up.'

Our family and supporters were all in court this time, and that was great. We held carnations, the symbols of innocence which Paddy O'Connor, my junior barrister, had given us. Counsel for the Crown was Roy Amlot, QC, and he got up to explain that among the files at Guildford police station records of interrogation supposedly part of the interrogation of Paddy Armstrong and Paul Hill, had been discovered by the Somerset and Avon police. Instead of being written as had always been claimed at the trial as a contemporaneous note of their interviews, these records appeared to have been typed in draft and then transcribed later in handwriting.

Amlot explained the conclusion. The verdicts were unsafe, and the Crown no longer wished to seek to sustain them.

Briefly our QCs spoke, Tony Scrivener saying for me that it was a mercy that capital punishment was no longer in force because, as Lord Donaldson had pointed out from the bench in his trial summing-up, this verdict would otherwise have resulted in the executions of Paul, Paddy and myself. The case provided a terrible warning against ever bringing it back. He went on to say that on the basis of withheld evidence, our convictions should have been quashed in any event.

Then the Lord Chief Justice pronounced his judgement. He looked like he was eating a scalded cat and was barely getting the words out. I don't remember much of the detail, but I was hanging on his every word, because there was one I was waiting for. He came towards his conclusion, telling the court that for all these reasons their Lordships no longer felt the verdicts were safe, and it was therefore his duty to pronounce them –

In this very moment I jumped up and tossed my carnation high into the well of the court, and it was followed by the flowers of the others.

And then he said it – *QUASHED*.

We were in the Old Bailey's Court Number Two. In 1975 the

verdicts of guilt over the Guildford Four had been pronounced here. In 1977 the appeal of the Guildford Four had been lost here. In 1989 it was third time lucky. Justice had finally been done.

30
Reborn!

ITN had arranged a reception party at the Holiday Inn near Swiss Cottage. I gave them their exclusive interview – which they well deserved, just for getting my ma and sisters over from Belfast so they could be there for the greatest day of my life.

The reception didn't go well for me. I was beginning to feel deflated as my high wore off. I'd not slept properly for two nights and the flow of adrenalin that had kept me going was beginning to pack up. When I was offered champagne I just wanted a glass of lager. The food that was there, very expensive though I'm sure it was, looked like crap. People were coming up to me wanting to shake my hand, asking me the same questions over and over again. I tried to be polite, but I could feel the strain.

Soon I began to notice there were two big men hanging around me. They always seemed to be somewhere near by. When I went to the toilet, one of them, a big Scotsman, followed me inside. In the lift, I had the two of them with me.

'Hey, who are youse?'

'We're just here to make sure nobody bothers you, don't take no notice.'

I was shown to my room. The two big men walked along the corridor just behind us and positioned themselves outside the doors of the room. They were security guards, hired by ITN. Whoever had the bright idea of getting them in can't have had much imagination, can't have thought how I would see it. To my mind the only difference between these two and a couple of screws were the clothes.

*

I couldn't get comfortable in the hotel room. I'd spent the evening talking to my family but it wasn't late when I got ready for bed. I knew I was tired, but sleep would not come. As I lay in the dark I thought first about the other innocent people I'd left behind: Paddy Joe Hill, Gerry Hunter, Johnny Walker, Dicky McIlkenny, Hughie Callaghan, Billy Power. I thought about the scores of other prisoners, Irish political prisoners, English prisoners, Palestinian and black, cockneys, con-men and fraudsters, men from every kind of background who'd given me their friendship over the years. I thought of how we made food-boats and tea-boats on the wing, cooked and played cards, shared hooch and tobacco, argued and joked. I remembered ones who'd held me together when I was pissed-off, and others who gave me a laugh and a joke when things improved.

Suddenly I felt utterly lonely. I wanted to go to the window and call out to the next room for some contact. But this wasn't D Wing at the Scrubs. It was the Holiday Inn, and I didn't even know the people in the next rooms. It had been my greatest fear, ever since I knew I would be coming out. After fifteen years inside, would I be able to communicate with the outside?

It was five in the morning when I went along to my mother's room and sat on her bed. I tried to tell her how I felt, how miserable I was in this place. I started to cry, saying it was no better than a prison, and these media people had me held hostage. All I wanted to do was get out. All this time I kept thinking about my father and how he must be feeling. How he knew that this day would come. His prophesy that his death would result in us clearing his name, because without a doubt his death triggered off people's consciences, setting off a whole chain reaction.

I talked about all this with my mother and Aunt Bridget. All the emotions I held in check for years came bursting out. All the things I'd never been able to say to them while I was in prison. We were all in tears, a cloud burst – it was the first real conversation we'd had since 1974. I remember my Aunt Bridget saying, 'Guiseppe up in heaven will be smiling today, 'cos he knows its through him that all this has come about. Now we've got to get his name cleared.'

My head was spinning with all this – thoughts of my father, suddenly being out of prison, suddenly being a free man again. There were only two places I didn't want to be – back in prison or at the Holiday Inn. I just had to get away, to find myself. I knew I would have to readjust, and I didn't feel this was the way to start off. I just needed common sense and people who knew me, who could reassure and help me. My family were readjusting to me as I was to them. So I just rang Gareth Peirce and said, 'Come and get me out of here. They're treating me like a prisoner.'

And Gareth came within fifteen minutes and took me away to her house.

Most long-term prisoners who have a known release date set about preparing for it, and the authorities help them. There are special courses, shopping trips, exercises in handling money again. I had none of this. I was just reborn into the world.

The most frightening thing about this new life – which was also the most exciting thing about it – is choice. When I walked out of the Holiday Inn I had exercised choice. But now I faced an incredible range of strange choices: the choice of clothes, of entertainment, of music, of drinks in the pub. I had a big problem with menus. I'd never seen menus before and didn't know how to cope with them. I didn't know what half the things on them *were*. They all seemed to be in French or Italian and I hadn't a clue what I was supposed to be ordering. So I used to ask for chips.

My eyes almost popped out when I saw the electronic goods shops in Tottenham Court Road – CDs, videos, personal stereos, portable phones, computers, things which the rest of the world took for granted, but which didn't exist in 1974. I thought back to Haslett's in Belfast, as I'd known it. I'd thought then it was like an Aladdin's cave, but this was space age. I'd jumped ahead a decade and a half in one leap and I couldn't believe what I saw.

This also affected how I handled myself with people. I had gone away as a kid, an absolute menace. I came out more mature, but I still wasn't sure whether I could communicate with people in a meaningful way. I needed time to work out where I was in this new world, and how a man like me should talk to it. I had to deal with people in shops, with officials, with bus conductors. I had to learn to cross the road. I had to begin to make relationships with friends and family that were fifteen years older than when I last saw them. I had the enormous worry of sorting out how I was going to relate to women in this new world.

Being a 'celebrity' has made it harder of course. My face was all over the news and the papers in that first week or so, and I had to cope with complete strangers coming up to me and wanting to talk. Prison is a world of no strangers. You know and are known by everybody.

When I was home in Belfast I went for a drink with a friend of mine and I was telling him how I was finding being recognized in the street a bit daunting. He said to me, 'It shouldn't piss you off. This is where you come from. Have a look around you, where you were born, born into abject poverty. You own the keys to one half of the city, the reason being the nationalist people and ordinary Catholic people in the North have known nothing but being attacked by the police in 1969, internment, the dirty protests, the hunger strikes, kids being killed by plastic bullets. People in the North have known nothing but heartache until the release of the Guildford Four. You have no ideals, are not a member of any political organization, or the IRA, but you represent an enormous victory to all these people.'

Now, seven months after my release, I am still buttonholed in the streets. I have realized in this way that my case really is the cause for concern that I imagined and hoped it would be. I feel honoured by that.

My greatest honour has been an invitation to Washington, where I gave evidence at the invitation of Senator Joe Kennedy to the Congressional Hearing on Human Rights. The subject was the Birmingham Six and the rights of Irish prisoners in British prisons, one of the only times the Commission has addressed an issue about a western democratic country. This came about as a result of my meeting with Tom Lantos and Joe Kennedy in November, shortly after I was released from prison. Cardinal O'Connor has been very helpful as well in raising awareness about the Birmingham Six in the USA.

In the immediate future is the judicial inquiry into the cases of the Guildford Four and the Maguires, where at last I believe the British legal system will acknowledge the innocence of my father and the Maguires. There is also another piece of unfinished business, the exoneration of the Birmingham Six. They are all my friends, they are still incarcerated and anyone who has read this book will have no doubt what that has meant and goes on meaning for them. Yet the Birmingham Six are as innocent as I am. Until they come out I myself won't feel I have been entirely released.

People ask me what I will do with the rest of my life. What a question! I say I will travel, get to know the world which I've spent all my adult life excluded from. Beyond that, the future awaits. But I am certain of one thing, I don't want to spend the rest of my life being known only as one of the Guildford Four.

READ MORE IN PENGUIN

In every corner of the world, on every subject under the sun, Penguin represents quality and variety – the very best in publishing today.

For complete information about books available from Penguin – including Puffins, Penguin Classics and Arkana – and how to order them, write to us at the appropriate address below. Please note that for copyright reasons the selection of books varies from country to country.

In the United Kingdom: Please write to *Dept. JC, Penguin Books Ltd, FREEPOST, West Drayton, Middlesex UB7 0BR.*

If you have any difficulty in obtaining a title, please send your order with the correct money, plus ten per cent for postage and packaging, to *PO Box No. 11, West Drayton, Middlesex UB7 0BR*

In the United States: Please write to *Consumer Sales, Penguin USA, P.O. Box 999, Dept. 17109, Bergenfield, New Jersey 07621-0120.* VISA and MasterCard holders call 1-800-253-6476 to order all Penguin titles

In Canada: Please write to *Penguin Books Canada Ltd, 10 Alcorn Avenue, Suite 300, Toronto, Ontario M4V 3B2*

In Australia: Please write to *Penguin Books Australia Ltd, P.O. Box 257, Ringwood, Victoria 3134*

In New Zealand: Please write to *Penguin Books (NZ) Ltd, Private Bag 102902, North Shore Mail Centre, Auckland 10*

In India: Please write to *Penguin Books India Pvt Ltd, 706 Eros Apartments, 56 Nehru Place, New Delhi 110 019*

In the Netherlands: Please write to *Penguin Books Netherlands bv, Postbus 3507, NL-1001 AH Amsterdam*

In Germany: Please write to *Penguin Books Deutschland GmbH, Metzlerstrasse 26, 60594 Frankfurt am Main*

In Spain: Please write to *Penguin Books S. A., Bravo Murillo 19, 1° B, 28015 Madrid*

In Italy: Please write to *Penguin Italia s.r.l., Via Felice Casati 20, I–20124 Milano*

In France: Please write to *Penguin France S. A., 17 rue Lejeune, F–31000 Toulouse*

In Japan: Please write to *Penguin Books Japan, Ishikiribashi Building, 2–5–4, Suido, Bunkyo-ku, Tokyo 112*

In Greece: Please write to *Penguin Hellas Ltd, Dimocritou 3, GR–106 71 Athens*

In South Africa: Please write to *Longman Penguin Southern Africa (Pty) Ltd, Private Bag X08, Bertsham 2013*

READ MORE IN PENGUIN

A SELECTION OF FICTION AND NON-FICTION

Brightside   G. H. Morris

Stuffed with magic, coal grit and wayward, Rabelaisian humour, this wonderful trilogy chronicles the lives of three generations of the Brightsides – a family with an appetite for the extraordinary. 'We've just mined a seam of home-produced – and Northern – magic realism' – *Observer*

Chasing the Monsoon   Alexander Frater

In 1987 Alexander Frater decided to pursue the astonishing phenomenon of the Indian summer monsoon and this fascinating account of his journey reveals the exotic, often startling discoveries of an ambitious and irresistibly romantic adventure.

Love in the Time of Cholera   Gabriel García Márquez

'For fifty years a breath-taking beauty, now old and just widowed, has recoiled in pride and guilt from her secret lover. His desolate obsession has led him into an enigmatic existence in spite of his renown in business. One Pentecost, love found a new tongue with which to speak. Unique Márquez magic of the sadness and funniness of humanity' – *The Times*

The Invisible Woman   Claire Tomalin

'Made visible is Nelly Ternan, and in the process, Tomalin gives us the world of a nineteenth-century actress and most importantly, the real world of Charles Dickens, whose passion for her ... changed his life, his career and his work' – Melvyn Bragg in the *Independent*

Shots from the Hip   Charles Shaar Murray

His classic encapsulation of the moment when rock stars turned junkies as the sixties died; his dissection of rock 'n' roll violence as citizens assaulted the Sex Pistols; his superstar encounters, from the decline of Paul McCartney to Mick Jagger's request that the author should leave – Charles Shaar Murray's *Shots from the Hip* is also rock history in the making.

READ MORE IN PENGUIN

A SELECTION OF FICTION AND NON-FICTION

Yours Etc. Graham Greene

'An entertaining celebration of Graham Greene's lesser-known career as a prolific author of letters to newspapers; you will find unarguable proof of his total addiction to everything about his time, from the greatest issues of the day to the humblest subjects imaginable' – Salman Rushdie in the *Observer*

Just Looking John Updike

'Mr Updike can be a very good art critic, and some of these essays are marvellous examples of critical explanation … A deep understanding of the art emerges' – *The New York Times Book Review*

As I Walked Out One Midsummer Morning Laurie Lee

As I Walked Out One Midsummer Morning tells of a young man's search for adventure as he leaves his Cotswolds home for London and Spain. 'A beautiful piece of writing' – *Observer*

The Secret Lemonade Drinker Guy Bellamy

Before Bobby met and married Caroline he believed in sex, drink and a good time. He still does… 'Sparkling … It cracks open a thousand jokes, some old, some new and some blue. As hideously addictive as drink' – *Sunday Times*

A Thief in the Night John Cornwell

A veil of suspicion and secrecy surrounds the final hours of John Paul I, who died of a reported heart attack in September 1978. Award-winning crime-writer John Cornwell was invited by the Vatican to conduct a full investigation and his extraordinary findings are revealed here.

For Good or Evil Clive Sinclair

'The stories are not only very finely poised but genuinely contemporary, stylistically serious… a striking collection' – *The Times Literary Supplement*

READ MORE IN PENGUIN

A SELECTION OF FICTION AND NON-FICTION

Money for Nothing P. G. Wodehouse

Lester Carmody of Rudge Hall is not altogether a good egg. Rather the reverse, in fact. For his intention is to inherit a large sum from the family silver by arranging its theft… 'His whimsical, hilarious stories aimed to do nothing more than amuse' – *Sunday Express*

Lucky Jim Kingsley Amis

'Dixon makes little dents in the smug fabric of hypocritical, humbugging, classbound British society … Amis caught the mood of post-war restiveness in a book which, though socially significant, was, and still is, extremely funny' – Anthony Burgess

The Day Gone By Richard Adams

'He is the best adventure-story-writer alive … Answers to the literary and personal puzzles of the Mr Adams phenomenon lie buried like truffles in his admirable autobiography' – A. N. Wilson in the *Daily Telegraph*

Romancing Vietnam Justin Wintle

'Justin Wintle's journal is a memorable, often amusing, always interesting diary of a tour of duty in a land where sharp-end history pokes round every corner' – *Yorkshire Post*. 'Compelling reading' – *Sunday Telegraph*

Travelling the World Paul Theroux

Now, for the first time, Paul Theroux has authorized a book of his favourite travel writing, containing photographs taken by those who have followed in his footsteps. The exquisite pictures here brilliantly complement and illuminate the provocative, wry, witty commentaries of one of the world's greatest travellers.